An

E24.99

WALLS OF SILENCE

WALLS OF SILENCE

CATHERINE McCARTNEY

Gill & Macmillan

Gill & Macmillan Ltd
Hume Avenue, Park West, Dublin 12
with associated companies throughout the world
www.gillmacmillan.ie

© Catherine McCartney 2007
978 07171 4249 1

AN
364.1

Index compiled by Cover to Cover
Typography design by Make Communication
Print origination by O'K Graphic Design, Dublin
Printed and bound in Great Britain by MPG Books Ltd,
Bodmin, Cornwall

This book is typeset in 12/14.5 pt Minion.

The paper used in this book comes from the wood pulp
of managed forests. For every tree felled, at least one
tree is planted, thereby renewing natural resources.

A CIP catalogue record for this book is available from
the British Library.

5 4 3 2 1

CONTENTS

On some positions, Cowardice asks the question, 'Is it safe?' Expediency asks the question, 'Is it politic?' And Vanity comes along and asks the question, 'Is it popular?' But Conscience asks the question, 'Is it right?' And there comes a time when one must take a position that is neither safe, nor politic, nor popular, but he must do it because Conscience tells him it is right.

MARTIN LUTHER KING

Chapter 1 ~

‘IRA BUSINESS’

I

Very few of the seventy people in the bar were aware of the horrific attack the IRA man was referring to when he declared to the packed public house, 'This is IRA business. Nobody saw anything.' Many thought he was referring to the fight that had taken place between Jock Davison and Brendan Devine minutes before. Others, amongst them Robert's life-long friends, knew what he was talking about, yet they complied with the IRA instruction: none rang the family to break the news that Robert had been seriously hurt, just as no one rang an ambulance. This was left to the police who found Robert and Brendan dying in the street.

Paula was the first to receive the news and she rushed up to the hospital, praying that she would hear the words, 'Robert is recovering.' The full story could wait. She was met by a doctor and nurse whose sombre and grave look signalled that the news was bad. They directed her to the relatives' room and told her in a professional but compassionate tone that Robert's injuries were life threatening, that they were doing their best, but that it would be best to gather the family together. Paula sat transfixed in the chair while the doctor went on to explain the nature of the injury and the attempts of the medical team to save our brother's life. They left her to the task of ringing round the family. In shock, shaking and crying, she dialled my number. No answer. She kept trying. The news was broken to the others. One by one, each of our lives was shattered in a phone call. Bridgeen arrived home to the news after a night out, expecting Robert to be in bed, only to be told that he was dying in hospital.

Members of the family gathered in the hospital, some sitting in the relatives' room, others standing outside in the corridor. Waiting and waiting through the early hours of the morning for news from the medical team, whispering amongst themselves about where Robert had been and with whom, possibilities were discussed: had he been mugged? Or attacked by loyalists? They couldn't contemplate his death and prayed inwardly that the doctors could save his life. The chaplain arrived, compounding the fear and anguish and dispelling any lingering hope. How could it be that only a few hours ago everyone was doing the most normal things, some in bed, others watching TV and others getting school uniforms ready for the next morning? The only thing on their minds was preparation for the routine of the next day. Now here they were in the hospital waiting for their brother to take his last breath. Gemma, Paula, Donna and Claire sat in the hospital, talking little, and in hushed tones.

The heavy atmosphere was broken by the arrival of Ed Gowdy who burst through the doors in a very agitated and dishevelled state. 'Jock had nothing to with it, Jock didn't do anything,' he said in a distressed voice, before asking about Robert's condition.

'Had nothing to do with what? What did Jock do? What happened to Robert, Ed?' Paula asked in an equally distressed tone.

Ed rambled confusedly about having been in Magennis's when a fight broke out, Devine had his throat cut and then Robert and Devine left. The next thing he heard, he claimed, was that Robert had been stabbed and was in hospital. His arms flailed in the air as he tried to explain the events of the night. His cardigan had blood on the sleeve and he pulled the zip down and thumped his bare chest: 'They put a gun to my chest,' he said. He also pointed to a mark on his face, saying, 'Fitzy hit me with gun.' Ed talked incessantly about what had happened earlier in the evening. He said that when he had left Robert and Brendan, they were all right and were walking out of Market Street. 'They must have got into another fight,' he reasoned. He named quite a few of the people who were involved in the attack and, when he was informed that Robert was not going to pull through but that Devine would survive, he asked, 'What is he going to say when he wakes up?'

Ed's version of events that night was sketchy but he gave enough details and names for the family to be able to put together a picture of what had happened and to be in no doubt that the IRA was involved.

When I arrived at the hospital the next morning at half past eight, Donna was able to tell me that 'the IRA did it'.

More people arrived at the hospital: friends and family members who had been wakened with the news. In disbelief, they stood around, praying forlornly that Robert would pull through. By half past six, the surgeons had done all they could, and they informed the family that Robert would survive for an hour or so. They were unable to stop the flow of blood, as it wouldn't clot, Robert's high level of fitness ironically contributing to this. If by some miracle he survived, the family was told, he would suffer permanent brain damage as a result of the injuries. The news of Robert's impending death descended upon the family.

The feelings that engulf a person on being told that their loved one is passing away and has only one hour to live are impossible to describe. The sense of despair and helplessness is so intense that it is difficult to breathe. You feel suffocated by your emotions. Your mind skips from one image to another: the last time you saw him and what he was doing, what you said to him; him as a little boy, playing on bikes, Steve Austin T-shirt, 'hanchee choma' — a silly phrase he said for months on end during a period of his childhood. All these images flash through your mind and you then find yourself back where you are now, in the intensive care unit of the Royal Victoria Hospital, waiting for him to take his last breath.

Robert passed away at 8.10 a.m. on Monday, 31 January 2005. Most of his family were at his bedside, apart from my mother and me. My mother had gone to Spain on the Friday before, for a week's break with her sisters, so the news had to be broken to her over the phone. The anguish and despair she felt are unimaginable: it is said that there is no pain that equals the loss of a child. This was my mother's second loss, and the brutality and horrific circumstances of Robert's death could only have compounded the pain. She arrived home to a broken and grief-stricken family. Unable to cope with what had happened to Robert, she was sedated and today still relies on tablets to dull the pain.

I had been living in Castlewellan, having moved out of the Short Strand in April 2004. The phone rang three times during the night but each time I reached for it, it rang off. We assumed that they were prank calls and disconnected it. The phone rang the second it was reconnected the following morning and the news was broken to me by my aunt Emily who could hardly speak for crying. I was told that Robert would be dead within an hour.

The journey to Belfast that Monday morning was torturous. I urgently needed to be there, but at the same time, part of me didn't want to arrive at our destination, essentially for the death of my brother. When I entered the intensive care unit of the Royal Victoria Hospital, I was met by numerous members of my family, some standing in groups whispering and crying, others standing alone, struggling with the news of Robert's passing. I went over to my sister Claire and asked, 'How is he?' I had convinced myself on the journey up that things could not have been as bad as Emily had said: people got stabbed all the time and pulled through; the doctors could work miracles. But most of all it was impossible for me to fathom life without Robert.

'He's gone,' came the reply and it was at this point that my world fell apart.

Donna came up to ask me if I wanted to go through and see him.

'No, I don't,' I said. 'Have you been?'

'Yes, I think you should come through.'

As she took my arm, she said, 'The IRA did it.'

I didn't respond to this. At that point I didn't care who had done it; the only thing that mattered was that he was dead. Gone.

We walked together into the intensive care unit and towards a cubicle from which I could hear sobbing. We pulled back the curtains and there he lay on a table, naked from the waist up and still with tubes attached to his mouth. The tubes contorted his features and a white patch covered his right eye. I was in a dreamlike state; I could see Bridgeen sitting on a chair beside the bed but could make little communication with her. I touched Robert's arm. It was still warm and I could feel the strength of his body. How could it be possible that he was dead? He had been young, strong and full of life the last time I had seen him; now he lay lifeless.

The finality of death is so overpowering that the mind can't focus for too long on the reality of it, and confusion and incomprehension take hold. People talk but you can't hear what they are saying and you can't respond in any coherent way: to do so would mean that rationality applied to the situation and there was none in these circumstances. We stayed at the hospital until after ten o'clock and then made our way back to Paula's house in the Short Strand.

II

Paula's house became the focal point for family and friends over the next week. The news of Robert's murder had spread like wildfire through the small community, and people began to arrive, each with their own little piece of information gathered from talk on the street. The names of those involved were passing people's lips by mid-morning. By noon of that day, the house was buzzing with people, some just calling to offer sympathy, others to offer practical help, and family and friends seeking comfort in the company of others who understood their loss and feelings of pain. Others, we were to learn later, came for more sinister reasons; we were told that, in what could only be described as structured briefings, some women 'close to the family' had been reporting back to the Provisional IRA (Provos) what was being discussed in the house. At this time, we were oblivious to the lengths to which the Provos would go in order to undermine us, and the co-operation they would receive from long-standing and trusted friends of ours.

Finding out exactly what happened that night in Magennis's bar was to consume us and we retraced Robert's steps. Our brother had spent the morning at home with Bridgeen and his two sons, Conlaed and Brandon. He left for the gym, kissing Conlaed and Brandon before he went and assuring them that he would see them later. He told Bridgeen that he would be going for a drink and that if he didn't see her at home later that day, he would meet up with her at the christening of a friend's baby that evening in the Chester, a bar/restaurant on the Antrim Road. Bridgeen left soon after him, taking the boys shopping.

When Robert returned from the gym, he left his bag at home and headed to Ed Gowdy's house. Ed wasn't at home, having left for Magennis's earlier, and Robert decided to walk the short distance to the bar to meet up with him.

Magennis's is situated behind the Law Courts in Belfast City Centre and is on the edge of the Markets area. It was a reputable public house, frequented by office workers, lawyers and barristers during the day; at night its clientele was drawn mainly from the surrounding Markets and Short Strand. It had also become a drinking den for the Provos of these areas, in particular members of the Third Battalion of the IRA, known to locals as the 'Hallion Battalion'. Months after Robert's murder,

Magennis's closed down for a while when its daytime clientele stopped going there. It has since re-opened but has never won back its daytime customers. Rumour has it that the Provos have also begun drinking there again.

Robert joined Ed and some other friends in what is called the Whiskey Café of Magennis's. Looking at the bar from the outside, you would assume that the Whiskey Café is separated from Magennis's but it is not. When you enter Magennis's, booths present themselves along the left wall and there is a small space between the booths and the bar. The toilets, which up to half the witnesses claim to have been in at the time Devine's throat was being cut, are through a door adjacent to the booths. The bar stands in a semicircle in the centre, encompassing both the main bar and the Whiskey Café. Standing at the bar in the Whiskey Café you can talk directly across the way to someone standing in Magennis's.

Robert sat at the back wall of the Whiskey Café at a long table next to the fireplace. This seating gave him and his friends a clear view of the television positioned on the wall in the corner beside the front windows. Below the television sat up to four women, amongst them the wife of the man currently charged with Robert's murder, Terry Davison.

After a while, Brendan Devine entered Magennis's and joined Robert's company. Out on bail and due to be returned to prison the following Wednesday, Devine had rung Robert earlier in the evening and invited himself to join him for a drink in Magennis's, a call we wish he hadn't made. In addition to Robert and Devine, Ed Gowdy, Terry McKay and a couple of others also sat around the table. They were boisterous with the drink and were behaving as men often behave when drinking and talking about football. There was no shortage of strong language and rude gestures.

Known IRA and Sinn Féin members entered the bar at various times during the evening. Many of them had returned from Derry where they had marched in commemoration with the families of the Bloody Sunday victims. Robert knew most of the Provos present and he also knew that avoiding a confrontation with them was always the wisest course of action. The Third Battalion's reputation for 'beatings' and bullying was well known, and, on a previous occasion, Robert had warned a friend who was intent on confronting one of these people,

'Don't go down that road with them. They come at you in tens and twelves, never one on one; they're not worth it.' Devine was given the same advice that evening, by a member of the Third Battalion, in what was apparently a genuine attempt to stave off any trouble. More 'brawn than brain', Devine unfortunately was not the sort of person to take such advice on board.

Bobby Fitzsimmons joined Robert's company for a while. He had been brought up across the road from us and we knew his family well. Many of its members paid their respects to Robert during the days of his wake. His sister Betty actually cried and hugged me before Robert's burial. This sympathy was to turn to outright hostility and threats, as we became outspoken about his murder and wanted those who were involved brought to account, including her brother.

Everyone was enjoying the evening and having good 'craic'; there was no sense of animosity or hostility in the atmosphere and the presence of Bobby Fitzsimmons and other Provos at Robert's table, joining in on the 'craic', is proof of this. Robert exchanged pleasantries and banter with other acquaintances amongst the company of the Provos. However, it was when Jock Davison and Jim McCormick entered Magennis's that things turned sour and the atmosphere turned from merriment to danger, and eventually murder.

The presence of Devine in the bar would have aroused Davison's and McCormick's curiosity if not suspicions; his presence has never been fully explained. It was rumoured that Devine had a history with the IRA because of money owed, drugs, and so on. One thing is certain: he was due to meet with the IRA the following day, before he was returned to jail. Why he had arranged to meet Robert at Magennis's despite the dangers is still unclear to this day. When Davison and McCormick entered Magennis's, Robert's friends once again advised Devine not to draw attention to himself, emphasising Jock's status within the IRA and McCormick's reputation for 'brutality'. Devine was advised by all to remain inconspicuous.

Robert's attention was on the football match being screened and he rudely gesticulated at one of the teams. Catriona Murdoch, seated directly below the television, took offence at the gestures and complained to her husband, Terry Davison, Jock's uncle. Terry approached Robert and, after a brief conversation, both men shook hands. Robert apologised for the confusion, more embarrassed than anything else that women had thought he was making rude gestures at them. At this point, however, Devine's presence attracted the attention of the Provos surrounding Jock, and they began to catcall, 'drug dealer', 'tout', and so on. According to Devine, he intervened in an argument between Jock and Robert, claiming that Jock approached Robert for an apology which he refused to give. Devine informed us that he told Jock to 'leave him alone'. At this point, Jock asked him, 'Do you know who I am?' to which Devine says he retorted, 'No, and I don't give a fuck who you are.' Devine also told us that he didn't know who Jock was — despite having been told by those at the table to avoid trouble with him because of who he was!

In any case, the verbal exchange between Devine and Jock turned violent and, at its climax, Brendan's head was yanked back and a bottle shoved into his throat. Jock had sustained an arm injury during the fight, and the blood was flowing from it as profusely as it was from Devine's throat. Panic and mayhem broke out in the small bar, and Robert's table was surrounded by up to fifteen of Jock's henchmen, all contributing their own poison to the already dangerous atmosphere. Jock's injury was quickly seen to and towels and a plastic bag were wrapped around his arm. However, his injury seems to have acted as a catalyst for the order he was to give.

Robert, Gowdy and McKay managed to guide Devine out of the bar amidst the screaming and shouting of women and the smashing of glasses and bottles. A small crowd gathered outside. One woman whom Robert had joked with hours earlier advised him to get home quickly. Robert informed her that he had left his coat inside. 'Don't worry,' she said. 'I'll get your coat for you.'

Robert, Ed Gowdy, Terry McKay and Brendan Devine started to make their way down Market Street just a few yards from the bar. They called a taxi and Ed took his T-shirt off and gave it to Brendan, as it was decided that the taxi man was unlikely to let him in covered in blood. Why they never thought to call an ambulance we still don't know.

For many inside the bar, this was the end of the attack; however, for the Provos, it had just begun. A phone call was made to request a gun, and up to nine of the Provos slithered out of the bar and followed Robert and the others up the street. Two women reported seeing up to nine men enter Market Street with weapons, amongst them sewer rods and a knife. Robert, Brendan, Terry McKay and Ed were making their escape when they were set upon by the gang. McKay quickly got off side and denied that he had been in the street. He claims not to have left the bar, a claim refuted by Ed Gowdy and Brendan Devine and the IRA. According to Gowdy, Joe Fitzpatrick hit him across the face with an iron bar, but before he could be hit again, Bobby Fitzsimmons jumped to his defence, saying, 'He's not to be touched', which would imply a pre-planned attack.

Ed insists that at this point he left the scene or, more accurately, was taken from the scene and assured by the Provos that Robert and Brendan would be fine. He says that he was told by one of the Provos, 'Devine will be seen in the morning. Bert will be all right.' The last he saw of Robert, he was turning the corner into Cromac Street, heading home, being pursued by no one. The IRA was to tell a different version from Ed's account and placed him at the scene minutes before Robert was stabbed.

Only those who were down Market Street that night know exactly what took place next. But what we do know is that Jock Davison was at the top of Market Street and he and Devine were still exchanging angry words, with Devine shouting, 'Come on, I'll still take you on.' Robert was telling Devine to shut up and just walk, but Jock and his gang had other plans. Devine was to tell Paula in the hospital five days later that Jock had given the order that he was to be killed; this order, according to Devine, was made by a finger being drawn across his throat. According to other sources, Jock's order to his murderous gang was, 'Do what yous want.' They did.

A knife was taken from the bar's kitchen and passed on to McCormick, the most dangerous of all those involved. The nine-strong gang pursued Robert and Brendan down the street. Robert stood back, trying to negotiate with these men to give Devine a chance to escape. At 10.20 p.m. a friend phoned Robert's mobile and he heard him say, 'Nobody deserves this' and 'I never hit anyone.'

Devine recalls Robert being surrounded by five men and then falling to his knees. They continued to kick and punch him, stamping on his head. At this point, Devine himself had been stabbed twice and was falling in and out of consciousness. After the frenzied and bloody attack, Robert and Brendan staggered out of Market Street and made their way towards Cromac Street. One Provo, who was not content with the beating he and his associates had inflicted, was still thirsty for blood. He pursued Robert who, by this time, was exhausted and weakened by the previous attack. In cold blood and with no provocation and for no reason, he stabbed Robert and then ran to a waiting car, containing Jock Davison. Together they went up to the Royal Hospital to have Jock's arm attended to.

Robert lay dying in Cromac Street, being comforted by a friend who had come on the scene; Devine was in a conscious state and also crying for help. He was later to tell the family that he came round and the last person he saw standing over Robert was Davison. He says he cried out, 'Not you.' Two policemen came on the scene and an ambulance was called. This was approximately 11.00 p.m.

Meanwhile, the bar doors had been shut when the nine-man gang left, and the customers had been told, 'This is IRA business. No one saw anything.' While Robert and Brendan were being beaten and stabbed down the side street, people, including those whom Robert knew well and with whom he had joked earlier, set about forensically cleaning the bar. Reinforcements were sent for. Ashtrays were disposed of, CCTV tapes taken away and even the outside of the bar was washed down with disinfectant and bleach. Bar staff and management were later to claim that this was a routine clean-up and that they were clearing up the glass from the altercation between Jock and Brendan. The nature of the clean-up operation says otherwise: it was identical to other IRA clean-ups of crime scenes. Items such as ashtrays, bottles and beer mats were all taken off the premises in black bags, at eleven o'clock on a Sunday night. Senior IRA men had been sent for and arrived to oversee and help in the clean-up.

Many Sinn Féin party members were present in the bar that evening, including Cora Groogan, Deirdre Hargey and Sean Hayes, and also Dee Brennan. They all claimed that they had seen nothing. These people were all in the same company that night; they were in the company of those involved in the attack. Yet they claimed to have seen nothing and heard nothing, not even a glass breaking. Sickeningly, women took part in the clean-up. One woman who had joked with Robert earlier was a particularly keen participant and was to become one of our most hostile foes.

The two doormen also claimed to be oblivious of any attack. Tommy Black, a resident of the Short Strand, allegedly suffered an angina attack and went home at, coincidentally, 10.45 p.m. It is alleged that people's names and addresses were taken to instil fear. For some this was unnecessary as many in the bar were sympathisers of those who murdered Robert. Up to fifty people were told that if any information were passed on to the police, they would be treated as informers.

A fleet of taxis had been ordered from a local firm whose drivers they believed could be trusted to keep their mouths shut. For one Sinn Féin member, this belief was to prove mistaken.

As the police arrived, some IRA and Sinn Féin women members including Cora Groogan were leaving the bar. As Groogan got into a taxi a policeman approached her and said, 'You're leaving the scene of a crime.'

'So fuck,' she replied and got hurriedly into her taxi. As the taxi drove off, she commented to her companion, 'That peeler is only after sayin' I'm leaving the scene of a crime, ay right! So fuck, black bastard!'

A man had been stabbed and beaten to death just yards from where she stood and this was her response: 'so fuck'. What Groogan knew of the attack outside the bar is unclear but she was present in the bar when the IRA carried out its forensic clean-up. Is it possible that she witnessed none of this either?

Unfortunately for Cora, the taxi driver happened to be Robert's brother-in-law and very good friend. He knew nothing about the attack on Robert and, as he sat outside Magennis's, he didn't know that his friend lay dying around the corner. This has haunted him ever since.

The inhumanity and lack of empathy with other human beings which was displayed by Groogan's remarks is frightening. These are the people who lord it over the Short Strand and dictate to the people how and when justice will be served, and dress it up as Irish republicanism.

III

By Monday morning, the names of the IRA and Sinn Féin people involved in the events of the night before were known to nearly everyone in the Short Strand, Markets and Ormeau Road. No one appeared surprised at the people involved and some commented that something like this was bound to happen as this gang had been out of control for years. When the police arrived at Paula's for our first meeting, we genuinely believed that it would just be a case of picking these people up. We assumed, as did many others, that they would be safer in the hands of the police because if the IRA got hold of them they would kill them for what they had done. Murdering an innocent member of your own community was tantamount to betraying the IRA and, more importantly, the people, or so we thought at the time. It was beyond comprehension that the Provos would try to protect these people. So naive were we at this time that we believed that by the end of the week all involved would have been charged and our main focus would be on our family and the loss of Robert.

The arrest of Jock Davison at 10.30 that morning, at the Dundonald Hospital, appeared to be a sign that we were right. The first to be arrested in connection with Robert's murder, he had arrived at the hospital without any of his henchmen, an uncommon occurrence for top paramilitary personnel. Two plainclothes police officers with English accents carried out the arrest. Others involved had fled to Killough, a small village in Co. Down. Two of them — Dee and Paul Brennan — were arrested there. Their father informed Paula months later that they had been 'ordered to Killough'. Local people informed the police of their whereabouts, something that would never have happened in the past. The community's disgust was tangible. The Brennans were arrested and we waited in Paula's for word of charges. How long could they keep them?

Within forty-eight hours, the men were released without charge. All had exercised their right to silence. No forensics, no witness statements of any value, suspects refusing to co-operate with the police, and the intimidation of witnesses — all would ensure impunity. This realisation was like an electric shock for us: what do you do when you are up against this? The people who murdered your brother live down the street, people whom we considered friends had information that could lead to arrests but were staying quiet, and we were expected to accept that the perpetrators would never be brought to account for what they had done. It began to dawn on us that these people were acting with the support of the Provisional leadership. They were not in hiding from the IRA but, on the contrary, were taking their lead from them.

We were in shock at this news. We couldn't believe that we were expected to accept Robert's death placidly. Maybe the IRA thought that we would confront Jock and his cohorts angrily but once the grief set in, we would be unable to do much about it. The matter would be contained within the Short Strand and the murderers would just have to brazen it out until local anger subsided. The presence of Bobby Storey in the Short Strand, walking brazenly with Jock, would send the message to the community: be angry but don't act on it. Further news from local people confirmed that the IRA and Sinn Féin were trying to keep the lid on it locally, questioning witnesses and telling people not to talk about it. Our instinct was to go and confront them but we also knew that it would do no good, and it would give them what they wanted.

They must be living in cloud cuckoo land, we thought; we didn't understand their thinking as they obviously didn't understand ours. If they thought that we would quietly grieve but accept that because it was the IRA we couldn't say anything, then they were very wrong. That 'the wrong man died' was true, but not in the sense meant by Jock Davison when he uttered the words to a friend the next day; the wrong man died because he was Robert McCartney, our brother whom we loved as much as our own children, and if they thought for one second that they could just walk away from it, they were grossly mistaken.

Over the next few days, the police were to disclose further disturbing facts about the cover-up: clothes had been washed and burned by local residents, the knife was missing, the CCTV tape in the bar had been removed by one IRA man who had threatened the barman, and the bar had been washed down in an attempt to destroy all forensic evidence. The cover-up by the IRA was difficult enough to swallow but when we heard the comments of Alex Maskey and Joe O'Donnell in the aftermath of the murder we exploded with anger. These comments, combined with what the police had told us, made it blatantly obvious what the Provisionals were trying to do. Alex Maskey, commenting on Robert's murder, coolly assessed, 'Unfortunately this sort of incident involving knives has become all the more common in recent times with tragic results like we witnessed last night.' We waited for him to make a reference to the involvement of his election workers and staff members, but none came. After what the police had told us we needed no further proof that the murderers were not acting on their own.

Alex Maskey's words were to be the impetus for our campaign. Did he speak to the media without any knowledge whatsoever of the circumstances of Robert's murder? Highly unlikely, given the involvement of many of his election workers. Jim McCormick held the post of Treasurer for Alex Maskey's Sinn Féin constituency. The Montgomerys, Davisons, Brennans and Bobby Fitzsimmons were all election workers for Maskey. Deirdre Hargey, due to stand in the council elections alongside Maskey in the upcoming Westminster and local government elections that May, Cora Groogan, Maskey's PA and a former candidate for MLA in Mid-Ulster, and Sean Hayes, another council candidate, had all been in the bar the previous evening.

Alex Maskey would later claim that he didn't know the exact circumstances of Robert's murder, a claim we do not accept. Even if we did, the least we might expect from a responsible public representative is that he would speak to the family of the victim before jumping to the defence of the suspects. Maskey's and O'Donnell's reactions convinced us that Sinn Féin was implicated in the cover-up. It was important to impress on the public an image of a bar brawl that had got out of hand and to portray the use of knives as an unfortunate but common occurrence. Maskey condemned the police for using heavy-handed tactics during house searches for evidence and using Robert's murder as a pretext for harassing republicans. A Sinn Féin press release on 2 February 2005 provides insight into the strategy adopted by the Provos. In it, Alex Maskey slams other politicians for turning the stabbing of a man outside a bar into a political point-scoring exercise, and he describes this as shameful and despicable. He goes on to say, unashamedly:

> The killing of Robert McCartney after a fight in a Belfast bar at the weekend was wrong and an absolute tragedy particularly for his family. There is a growing violent knife culture in our society, which must be condemned, and this incident is an extension of that. However what has also been disturbing has been the shameful attempts of politicians with no interest or stake in the communities affected most by this death to try and score political points. Allegations have been made by Reg Empey, Sammy Wilson, Alasdair McDonnell and now also Mark Durkan. This includes an outrageous claim that republicans are in some way covering up the events of Sunday night and orchestrating the recent trouble on the streets of the Markets. These allegations are clearly untrue and without foundation. There is no cover-up and no orchestration of

street violence. That is why none of these individuals have been able to produce one scrap of evidence to back up their claims. None of these individuals have set foot in either the Markets or the Short Strand in recent days unlike republicans who have been on the streets trying to maintain calm. Their interventions have not been motivated by any desire to help or assist the McCartney family or the local community but have instead been entirely motivated by a despicable desire to try and politick around the tragic death of a young father of two.

Maskey didn't have the courtesy to visit the family at this time. The republicans working in the community were the very republicans involved in the murder, and the political motivations of those politicians wanting to assist us was in contrast to Sinn Féin's political motivations to suppress the truth. A bar-room brawl, a man stabbed, no evidence: not difficult to fathom in today's world how, for the Provisionals' plan to work, all they needed was for Robert's family to be quiet. It is probable that they didn't even contemplate the possibility that we would not be quiet, considering that they had killed thirty-eight people since the 1994 ceasefire — what difference would one more make? They arrogantly assumed that because we were from the Short Strand we would be easily managed and revert to form as they thought; the contempt in which they hold the nationalist people is breathtaking. How I didn't see it before is beyond me; I was obviously living in the comfort of my own cocoon — family, work, an interest in politics generally but not monitoring the activities and spin of political players enough to realise that their talk of equality, human rights and justice was just that: talk. Maskey's condemnation of the police searches of republicans' homes was so transparent, claims of the harassment and unjustifiable actions by the PSNI so predictable and disgusting. Maskey went so far as to contact the Private Secretary of the then Secretary of State, Paul Murphy, to complain about the police searches. A source told the family that he was particularly vexed at the police search of Terry Davison's house. Davison was the man later charged with Robert's murder.

We were furious and upset at Maskey's remarks. Robert lay dead in a morgue and the only thing that Maskey was concerned about was that a few republican homes were being searched for evidence. This was the first indication we got of a political cover-up. Maskey adopted the usual stance of Sinn Féin: when culpable, play the 'blame game'. We interpreted Maskey's and O'Donnell's remarks as nothing more than a disgusting attempt to save Provos' necks to the extent of devaluing the worth of a local man's life. Alex Maskey, along with his colleague Joe O'Donnell from the Short Strand (Deputy Mayor of Belfast in 2005), knew exactly who was involved in Robert's murder; their diatribe over the next two days was nothing but an attempt to sweep Robert's murder, like so many others, under the carpet. Sinn Féin has consistently refused to answer questions relating to this. As the arrests and releases continued over the next few days, we were becoming more and more despondent. Family and friends who had gathered in Paula's home in the Short Strand waited anxiously for news of charges, but none came. Instead the news came that all had been released after exercising their right to silence. We were absolutely distraught and couldn't believe that this was happening. Everyone knew that they were involved, the police knew — how in the name of God could they not be charged? Again came back the same response we were to hear over and over again to the present day: 'No evidence, a forensic clean-up took place and none of the witnesses are coming forward with information of evidential value.'

The police bore the brunt of our frustrations at this news: 'So it's easy to murder people?' 'No wonder they murdered him; they knew they would get away with it; yous are useless', and so on. In the days leading up to his funeral, we were consumed by questions surrounding Robert's murder. We couldn't understand why Robert had become a target of this gang. He was well known by many of them. They knew that he had done nothing to them and that they had no gripe with him whatsoever. In fact, some of them would have sat in his company from time to time, as Bobby Fitzsimmons had on that very night. What drove them to kill Robert in such a brutal way? That they were following orders is something of which we are in no doubt. Whether or not that order was to kill Robert, we are not certain, but we are certain that Jock Davison is responsible for the turn of events that evening and that he could have put an end to the attack at any time. He chose not to. He set his hyenas upon Robert. We know that Robert would have fought back; he would have handled those in this gang with little trouble on a one-on-one or even two-to-one basis. Their use of weapons and numbers points to their cowardliness.

We can only imagine what was going through his mind at the time. He would certainly have been confused at the violence and viciousness being let loose upon him by those in the gang. In our search for answers, we spoke to Gowdy, McKay and Devine but their stories didn't add up and, as time went on, we were to realise that they, like so many others, had been masquerading as friends.

For eight days, people milled in and out of Paula's house, the main topic of conversation obviously the night in Magennis's. People reported what they were hearing on the streets and in bars; the murderers still walked the streets, claiming innocence to anyone who would listen. There were many sycophants willing to placate Jock and his men.

Rumours circulated by the Provos about Robert added to our distress and anger. IRA murders were usually justified by demonisation of the victim, and the latter's 'crime' would be quickly circulated: 'he was a drug dealer', 'he was an informer' and so on. With no evidence whatsoever these reasons would be accepted and members of the community would content themselves that the victim was deserving of his punishment: 'He didn't get it for nothing.' Few stopped to ask themselves about the process of so-called justice employed by the Provos or questioned the right to violate the human rights of these individuals. We were to discover that the same process of demonisation was being used against Robert. Friends brought news of talk that Robert was a 'dissident' or a 'drug dealer'. On one occasion, a friend who had lost her son two weeks after Robert told me that, during his wake, a Sinn Féin member had told her that Robert was a scumbag. She was able to refute his claims, but how many others accepted this flimsy excuse for murder? It was designed to implant in the community's mind a justification for the murder: people had accepted the Provos' lies before; why not now?

The acceptance of the Provos' violence against members of the community is an illustration of how sick we had become as a community. The right of the Provos to violate human rights, deny justice and practise elitism within the heart of the communities they depended upon had become so embedded that people had come to accept it as normal. There was, however, an unwritten code of conduct and understanding between the people and the IRA — a contract of mutual benefit — but nowhere in that contract did it state that the IRA would be able to kill any member of the community it chose to with impunity. Nor did it say: *An IRA man will have the authority to sentence any person or persons with whom he has an altercation to severe physical punishment or death. This authority expands into his private life also.* On the contrary, the IRA's own rules laid down that if an IRA volunteer did the above, he/she would suffer the consequences imposed by the Army Council:

> …any volunteer who carries out an unofficial operation must be suspended immediately pending an investigation. A volunteer found guilty of such an unofficial act will be dismissed from Óglaigh Na hÉireann and is liable to immediate repudiation.

According to Republican sources, this repudiation takes various forms. One form is being isolated and ostracised from the Republican movement itself, which would include being ordered not to drink in certain pubs or enter certain areas. This is a minimum form of repudiation. In any case, Robert's murder was a clear breach of the IRA code of conduct, so everyone in the Short Strand and Ireland awaited the IRA's response, none more eagerly than ourselves. Nothing was to come for over two weeks.

We didn't respond publicly to Maskey's and O'Donnell's remarks at this time, but we put up posters in the local shops and community centre, appealing for witnesses to come forward to the police. Most displayed these posters; others covered up the police badge at the bottom to appease those who were offended by it. One local crèche worker felt the need to express her difficulty with the police badge on the poster, and arrived at Paula's house to do so while Robert lay in his coffin. Her visit was the first indication of the anger our campaign was to generate amongst a small minority in the community, most of whom emanated from the community centre. The validity of objections over the police badge was undermined by the inaction of the same objectors when it came to the murder of Robert. We doubted that these people wanted the murderers brought to justice at all. They endorsed the right of the local IRA to lord it over the community. Despite the upset caused by this small minority of sick-minded people, the majority of visitors to Paula's and Robert's homes came to pay their respect and offer support.

IV

For over a week, Paula's and Robert's homes were full of people coming to offer condolences. People expressed their horror at what had happened and left us in no doubt about their thoughts on the perpetrators. Many also stayed away; those who had been in the bar that night and who had spoken to Robert never came near the wake — either guilt for staying quiet or fear of incriminating their murderous friends in the attack keeping them away. It was only in the early morning that quietness descended on the house and I had the opportunity to sit with my brother on my own. He had been dressed in a black shirt and trousers, his hands crossed in the traditional way with Rosary beads intertwined. He didn't look peaceful, unlike Gerard who had died four years previously and who had been laid out in the same spot. A sense of calm and peace had surrounded Gerard; the struggle to survive was still evident in Robert's face, the bruises and swelling testifying that he had not gone willingly or peacefully. He lay in the house we had grown up in. Memories of better times flitted through my mind, but trying to grasp and hold on to these memories was difficult.

The sound of the mixture of our voices floated in the air, people coming and going, all of us at different stages of our lives. Getting ready to go to school, the music playing upstairs as we got ready to go out, all seated on the sofa on a Friday night watching *Monkey*, a favourite of Robert's and mine, and other memories of life in a bustling house of seven children. Now it was empty of all those lives. Sometimes a swirl of emotion would engulf me: despair, anger and then nothing. No feelings of any kind, a numbness people call it, a mechanism designed by the brain to cope with emotional trauma. Another mourner who had come to pay their respects would break the quietness and stillness of the house. Local politicians came in a private capacity to offer their condolences, a stark contrast to Sinn Féin representatives: Joe O'Donnell lived in the area but stayed away.

Robert was buried on 8 February from St Matthew's Church. I travelled up from Castlewellan, deliberately arriving after they had closed his coffin and taken him from the house. I couldn't face looking upon him for the last time. The church was packed and we had arranged the funeral service as best we could. None of us could speak at the funeral and we asked Robert's friends to say a few words. In an

article in *The Blanket*, entitled 'Oderint dum Metuant', Anthony
McIntyre wrote:

> Watching news coverage of the funeral later in the day, the
> comments of the officiating priest may have passed me by as
> eulogising words sincerely offered as a balm to his family, were it
> not for the observation of my wife. She said that the sentiment
> 'greater love hath no man than this, that a man lay down his life for
> his friends' showed that Bert had more in common with Bobby
> Sands than those who murdered him. (9 February 2005)

Our mother couldn't attend the funeral, as it was too much for her. I
could understand this, as part of me didn't want to attend either,
wanted to deny that it was happening. Over twelve hundred people
were there. At the time, I didn't think the hugeness of the crowd was
unusual. It was only afterwards I realised that those who wanted to
display solidarity with the family and also show their disgust at his
murder swelled the crowd. It was, in a way, a protest. The community
had displayed its sympathy and support for the family the previous
Friday night by holding a vigil on the Mountpottinger Road. 'PIRA
SCUM OUT' had been painted on the walls of the Short Strand. Never
before had such graffiti been directed at the IRA in this area. This did
not deter members of the Provo murder gang from attending the vigil,
whether out of curiosity, arrogance or an attempt to distance
themselves from the murder. But these individuals were shunned by the
people and did not attend the funeral.

After the funeral, family members and a few very close friends
returned to Paula's house. Many others went to a buffet that had been
arranged to give people the opportunity to get together to remember
Robert. That night when I drove back to Castlewellan, I was in a
complete mess. I cried uncontrollably and screamed in rage. Where did
we go from here? How do you pick up the pieces? The murderers and
their co-conspirators were not a consideration at this time; only the
loss of Robert filled my head. What was to become the campaign
enabled me to channel this anger; ironically it may have prevented me
from crumbling completely.

V

Our first interview was given to a local radio station and was an appeal for witnesses to come forward. This was to be the first of hundreds of interviews we would give over the year. At the time we were completely unaware of this and initially each of us was reluctant to speak on the radio: the usual 'You do it', 'No, you do it', 'Would you not do it?' went on before we finally decided that we would all do it. We appealed for witnesses to come forward and spoke a little about Robert as a person. By nature we are very private people, shying away from rather than seeking out the limelight. We were uncomfortable during the interview and relieved when it was over. Gerry Adams was not in the country at the time and we were still living in hope that when he arrived back, he would see to it that the murderers were handed over. After the radio interview, other journalists got in touch. Anthony McIntyre, Suzanne Breen and Henry MacDonald were the first journalists to speak to us directly about the murder. They had a firm grip on what the issue was and their reporting of the story, along with a letter written by our cousin Gerard Quinn to the *Irish News* on 11 February, stirred media interest in Robert's case. Gerard asked how the murder of an innocent man would 'build an Ireland of Equals' and stated in response to Maskey's comments about police actions that the 'only unjustifiable and unacceptable actions' were those of the murderers on 30 January. This struck a chord within republican and nationalist communities, and John Kelly, a respected republican former Sinn Féin member responded:

> The murder of Robert McCartney had all to do with civil law and had nothing to do with political principle or the political process. It was a crime, and no one had the right to threaten or discourage anyone from the community in which that murder was committed against co-operating in bringing justice to Robert McCartney. For an increasing and questioning voice of concern within the nationalist/republican communities throughout the north of Ireland the questions most frequently being asked are: Have we exchanged a fascist and sectarian orange jackboot for an increasingly fascist and totalitarian green jackboot? Have we exchanged a sectarian RUC Special Branch for the special branch of

a militia that imposes its 'law and order' behind a balaclava, a balaclava that brings fear and death into our communities?

Letters poured into the *Irish News* and other newspapers, in the main castigating Sinn Féin and the IRA, others attempting to absolve them from blame. This question was at the heart of Robert's murder and was one that the republican movement was unwilling to face or challenge. Instead, the movement hid behind political smokescreens, at times playing the victim and at others the aggressor.

By now, all the major newspapers in Ireland and the UK had picked up the story of Robert's murder, and Paula's house was in a constant hum of activity. We answered questions from the media over the phone and in person, and we also made preparations to meet with local representatives. We knew from the beginning that media attention alone would do little to bring enough pressure on Sinn Féin and the IRA to hand over Robert's murderers. They would ride out the press. We needed political pressure and set out to seek it. The lack of commitment and action from the Provo leadership convinced us that we had no other choice but to seek help elsewhere. We didn't make a conscious decision to speak out; no planned strategy or tactic was devised nor repercussions discussed. But we instinctively knew what we had to do. Political as well as public pressure was needed.

We contacted the SDLP and our first meeting with Mark Durkan took place on the second Sunday of February. This was to be the beginning of our political journey. The media were our constant companions during this time, and for the next five months we were caught up in what was a media and political whirlwind. This was to suspend our grief, and, to a degree, our energy for the campaign stemmed from the fact that without it we would have had to face up to the reality that Robert was dead. That is something we haven't yet faced.

Two weeks to the day after Robert was murdered, all hell broke loose. The media descended on Paula's house in what seemed like droves, the phone constantly rang and the traffic of people was never-ending. I was still travelling up daily from Castlewellan and would arrive at around 9.30 a.m. in preparation for talking to journalists and arranging meetings with political figures and others. 'Has Sinn Féin been in touch?' was a question that had been asked every day since Robert's murder. As yet, no one from Sinn Féin had visited the family.

This had not prevented Maskey's castigation of local politicians for not setting foot in the Short Strand. The allegation was untrue: they had, but to offer their personal condolences. Maskey did not afford the family this courtesy. He spoke of republicans working on the ground to keep calm but never mentioned republicans working on the ground to keep people quiet. People were told not to talk about Robert's murder. In the community centre, one woman was told, 'Don't be talking about that in here', when she raised the issue. Republicans were eager to speak to those who knew something and were often seen speaking to key witnesses and others. This was the work to which Maskey was referring.

It wasn't until 14 February that Gerry Kelly, Sinn Féin's spokesman on Policing and Justice, of all things, arrived on the scene. Kelly's demeanour was one of confidence — he was here to take charge. He offered his condolences and some weak excuse for not having arrived earlier, something to the effect that he hadn't wanted to intrude on the family's grief. Why would anyone think they were doing that by simply offering condolences?

Kelly let us do most of the talking. We told him who was involved and what we knew. We questioned him on these people and what Sinn Féin intended to do about them, and we asked Kelly outright why the IRA hadn't done anything about them. Kelly's answers were unsatisfactory and to most questions he responded, 'I Can't Answer That', a nickname he acquired from us over the course of the year. We were well aware, as was Kelly, of the usual sanctions the IRA imposed on people who committed crimes against the community; in fact, these sanctions were to be enacted on us over the coming months. It wasn't that we wanted sanctions to be carried out against these people, but the fact that the IRA was not applying its own standards spoke volumes and confirmed that the movement was protecting them.

His explanation was simply that 'a lot of republican families would be upset', 'these people have families; they don't want to leave the area; they shouldn't be made victims of this.' I pointed out that the IRA was not prone to showing sympathy to the families of those it chose to punish. After an hour-long meeting, Kelly was left in no doubt as to what we wanted. 'Ideally we would like everyone who looked at him wrong that night, but that is not going to happen. We want the fifteen,' he was told.

The meeting clarified one thing for us: the leadership had no intention of taking action against these people, simply because they were IRA volunteers. We asked Kelly about Maskey's and O'Donnell's comments, and condemned them; Kelly insisted that they were unaware of the facts at the time.

That meeting set the template for future meetings, Sinn Féin leaders saying little but giving the impression that they were saying a lot. Going round in circles, refusing to take responsibility, claiming it was difficult but they were doing all they could. Nothing was said to reassure us. Given that Adams was out of the country at the time, we still had hope that when he got back, something would be done.

Eventually Gerry Adams broke his silence on Robert's murder, stating, 'There are allegations that Robert McCartney was killed by republicans, I want to make it absolutely clear that no one involved acted as a republican or on behalf of republicans. I repudiate this brutal killing in the strongest possible terms.' He went on to say, 'People with reservations about assisting the PSNI should give any information they might have either to the family, a solicitor or any other reputable person or body.'

Speaking to the media the next day, Paula welcomed Adams's comment. 'It's obvious they have now seen sense. To be truthful, I don't think Sinn Féin were aware of the facts and, now they know the full facts, no human being could do anything other than support us. I would take what Gerry Adams says as a clear indication there is no threat.' At this time, Paula and other members of the family were pretty confident that Sinn Féin and the IRA would do the right thing, but I wasn't convinced. To attack Adams openly at this point wasn't feasible. We needed the support of the republican community and, unfortunately, for many within that community, when Gerry spoke, the heavens opened. Or to be fair, people trusted that he meant what he said, but I could see from the beginning that Adams had no intention of doing anything other than play mind games with us and the people. On the surface, the statement appeared to support us and clarify the republican position but it was a flimsy statement, the least of what he could have said. His call for people to go to a third party such as the family was a clear message that the PSNI was not an option. For myself, the Adams call was clear evidence that Jock and his team were being protected. I responded to his statement generously given the circumstances:

We fully welcome Mr Adams' belated comments on the brutal murder of our brother Robert. We are in full agreement that those involved did not 'act like republicans or on behalf of republicans'. However, the call for those with information to go to a solicitor, priest or ourselves raises questions such as, what would this achieve? Would this bring Robert's murderers to justice? Would this secure convictions? We call upon Sinn Féin to bring all its influence to bear on those who have the power to ensure that these individuals are left with nowhere to hide. We are aware of Sinn Féin's policy on the police but Sinn Féin, as with other political parties, are capable of not being seen to take a certain course of action. These individuals must face justice if we are ever to move on from Robert's death. The community needs to feel safe and free also from these psychopaths.

Gerry Kelly said that he didn't know what I meant by 'capable of not being seen to take a certain course of action'; I don't know now why I included other political parties. If the Provisional leaders wanted people to bring forward information of evidential value, all they had to do was order their volunteers in or impose the usual sanctions against them, mainly exclusion from the Provo circle. In relation to the IRA we were in a weak position. How could you demand that a paramilitary organisation force its members in? The obvious questions were raised: How? What could the IRA do? Did we expect them to mete out their own form of justice? Was asking the IRA to deliver murderers not asking a violent and paramilitary organisation to violate the human rights of the perpetrators? Were we, like the IRA and Sinn Féin, asking for human rights, due process and justice for ourselves but seeking to violate those of others?

This was the minefield in which we had to tread. But ultimately the IRA had forensically cleaned up, intimidated witnesses and was holding these people in its tight embrace. For us there was plenty the organisation could do to deliver justice without using violence or coercion. The IRA could easily have ordered its men to give a full account either to their solicitor or the police; it considered itself an army, an army that was renowned throughout the world as a highly disciplined guerrilla force, and its volunteers obeyed orders. It could have prevented the intimidation of witnesses, expelled those involved and guaranteed publicly that those willing to give evidence would receive its protection, not its wrath.

Sinn Féin, on the other hand, was a different kettle of fish. It was a democratic party seeking executive power in a local assembly. It was responsible for the actions of its members in relation to co-operating with a murder investigation: to take no action or not to encourage them to come forward put Sinn Féin in a quandary *vis-à-vis* democracy. Given also that many of those involved in Robert's murder were members of both organisations, Sinn Féin could not distance itself.

The nonsense of a third party to take statements and information from witnesses and suspects was not only an insult to the family but an utter disgrace and, at times, infuriating. Adams's suggestion that people should bring the information to the family was incredible. 'How is that supposed to work?' we asked each other. We were a family in shock. Were we supposed to sit down and take statements from people, turn Paula's home into an incident room? Over the coming months, the political argument centred around the use of the police. For us as a family, this wasn't the central issue; if the provisional leadership wanted these people brought to account it would happen.

As I write, Martin McGuinness sits up at Stormont as Deputy First Minister, administering British rule in Northern Ireland alongside his old enemy Dr Ian Paisley, who holds the office of First Minister. Ironically Alex Maskey was promoted to Sinn Féin spokesman on Policing and Justice. This was made possible by the IRA decommissioning all its weapons and Sinn Féin endorsing and supporting the PSNI. The hopes of some in my family that Sinn Féin's endorsement of the PSNI would open doors for witnesses to come forward have not been realised. I never believed that it was about policing. The Provisionals have and always had it within their power to deliver the murderers without conceding or compromising their stance on policing. Non co-operation with the police was a red herring. The opening up of the Ombudsman's office for those supposed republicans who wouldn't co-operate with the police on ideological grounds proved fruitless. It was frustrating for us to listen to the police tell us that this person or that person refused to speak, claiming, 'I don't trust the police.' These same people refused to co-operate with the Ombudsman also. At the time, we had agreed with the opening of the Ombudsman's office to accommodate those republicans who may genuinely have had reservations about dealing with the police. On reflection, this was counter-productive in that it gave many Sinn Féin members a veil of pretence of co-operation.

Ultimately at the heart of the issue was the criminality of the IRA, a hot topic on the political agenda since the Northern Bank robbery. Up until Robert's murder, ordinary members of the nationalist community were unaware of how this criminality could directly affect them; after his murder, everyone was clear. Robert's murder illustrated powerfully that the IRA had the power to kill innocent members of the nationalist community with impunity and, more importantly, it demonstrated the reality that the IRA had degenerated into criminality and the cells, which were the core structure of the IRA, were no more than gangs. This, then, was the issue for our family: did Jock Davison and his Third Battalion have the right to kill people from the Short Strand, Markets and Ormeau Road — were the lives of these people now in his hands and was the right to kill and lording it over your neighbours a reward for your part in the struggle? This was the central question, and by continuing to protect the murderers the Provisional movement's answer was Yes.

Adams's comments were quickly followed by an IRA statement on 16 February. It read:

We wish to extend our sympathy to the McCartney family for the loss of Robert and for the grief that they are suffering. The IRA was not involved in the brutal killing of Robert McCartney. Those who were involved must take responsibility for their own actions that run contrary to republican ideals.

It has been reported that people are being intimidated or prevented from assisting the McCartney family in their search for truth and justice.

We wish to make it absolutely clear that no one should hinder or impede the McCartney family in their search for truth and justice. Anyone who can help the family in this should do so.

P. O'Neill

Statements from the IRA are generally taken as truth within the republican community and, over the years of the Troubles, these statements had built up credibility, as the IRA would accept blame for some of the worst atrocities. P. O'Neill's statement therefore seemed clear enough, but the IRA took no responsibility for what had happened when its members had clearly participated in the murder, a senior member had given the order, other members were debriefed in the weeks following Robert's murder and senior members of the IRA visited witnesses' homes on numerous occasions.

Gerry Kelly's comments the next day illustrated the inconsistency between Sinn Féin's public face and its private one: 'I would like to see the family get justice in this, and the people who were involved in this brutal slaying should be rejected entirely by the community … and brought to justice.' People in nationalist areas were being asked to reject Jock and his cohorts while at the same time Bobby Storey and other prominent republicans were frequently seen in the company of Jock. It was clear what the leadership was doing — one message to the wider public but another to the grassroots. Jock was still in the embrace of the IRA; cross him or attempt to reject him and you would be up against the Provos and we all knew what they were capable of. Strong words in public were nothing more that a damage-limitation stunt; Jock was being assured of this regularly. Others involved remained in their community positions, either as community workers, so called Community Restorative Justice Officers, stewards at times of parades and at any republican event that took place. This attempt to distance itself and put the onus on individuals to take responsibility was play-acting or 'spin'. Sinn Féin also issued a statement on that day, reiterating its position and support of the family but adding:

> Others are wishing to turn this into a political football about Sinn Féin's position on policing. This will not assist the McCartney family. The family know our position on policing.

It seemed to us that Sinn Féin and the IRA were guilty of turning it into a political football. Not once did Sinn Féin speak of the forensic clean-up, not once did its leaders accept that intimidation of witnesses had taken place. Even though the police publicly confirmed that witnesses had been intimidated, Sinn Féin continued to dismiss these allegations. The old mantra of 'securocrats' was sung to undermine the truth. Publicly Sinn Féin questioned the lack of progress in the investigation, implying that the police were deliberately dragging their heels on making arrests. They pushed this line behind closed doors also. At one meeting, during which the failure of the three key witnesses was being discussed, Adams asked us why McKay had not been questioned directly by the police. We explained that he was speaking to them through his solicitor but claiming that he knew nothing. We spoke of our frustrations at the legal constraints on the police but he dismissed these as excuses and suggested that 'throwing people into the backs of jeeps' was usually a much more effective method of extracting information from unwilling individuals. It struck us as ironic that privately Adams advocated police methods he publicly denounced. It was also in stark contrast to Maskey's line on the day of the police searches. It was only a ploy, however; we all knew why the witnesses were not talking. Adams was simply trying to deflect responsibility for failure on to the police and to instil in us doubt about the PSNI. The ploy failed.

The IRA and Sinn Féin were taking a stance of protection for some reason no one seemed to be able to understand. There were three witnesses designated by Sinn Féin as the key to the investigation: Ed Gowdy, Terry McKay and Brendan Devine, Robert's friends and all present during the attack. Sinn Féin put no emphasis on the other key witnesses who were also down Market Street that night. These included Dee Brennan, Paul Brennan, Alec Brady, Terry Davison, Gerard Montgomery, Jim McCormick, Bobby Fitzsimmons, Jock Davison and Joe Fitzpatrick. The placing of the onus on the former three was disingenuous. It was no coincidence that none of the three were members of the IRA or Sinn Féin. Over the first few weeks, senior IRA figures visited all three of these witnesses and, as a result, all three refused to co-operate honestly and fully with the investigation. The betrayal by Robert's closest friends was the hardest thing we had to cope with. We were hurt for Robert. He had trusted these people, treated them with nothing but loyalty and love; he died to protect Devine and yet his life was worth nothing to them — not even the truth. His murderers walked the streets of the Short Strand freely, spitting on his grave with every step.

The IRA's statement was further proof that it was unprepared to take action; all it had to offer was words. We drove ourselves mad going over and over the reasons for the IRA's protection of these people. All sorts of theories were put forward and each dismissed. These included Jock's possible involvement in the Northern Bank robbery and possibly holding the IRA to ransom; republicans don't give up their own; loyalty to Jock; someone higher up in the Sinn Féin echelons may have been in the bar that night; the IRA's hands were tied because of the ceasefire or the IRA's orders were being ignored by its volunteers. None of these theories, however, stood up to scrutiny. Informers were an age-old problem for the IRA; republicans do give up their own or at least hold them to account; the movement was unlikely to take so much flak over one man; even if a higher Sinn Féin official was in the bar that night, this wasn't a crime in itself; the government had been turning a blind eye to its criminal activities for years and the notion that volunteers were now ignoring orders was absurd. We were confused by the Provisional stance and distraught at the thought that there was a very real possibility that these people would get away with murdering Robert. This was the constant topic of conversation between us, the media and everyone else who filed into Paula's home.

VI

Media interest was growing day by day, as was political interest. Ordinary people were also very interested in our story and many of them took the time to write letters of support. The differences in people amazed us. Strangers took the trouble to sit down and share their experiences and thoughts with us, convey their support, tell us of their prayers and plead with us not to give up. Yet people we had grown up with turned their backs on us, some providing the warped excuse, 'I'm a republican so....' Some in the community treated us as if we were the guilty party, and we found ourselves shunned, vilified and demonised, accused of being attention seekers or drama queens. 'You're not the only one this has happened to,' became a familiar mantra. An illogical resentment seeped in. Such people forgot about the sick act of murder, and our campaign came to be the bigger crime. We, not the murderers, were to be blamed by these people. Daily updates on the movements of those involved in Robert's murder, going in and out of the community centre, sitting in local bars, walking about with prominent Provos, always re-focused our minds on what was important. The rejection that Gerry Kelly referred to was not taking place.

The trauma was taking its toll on us physically and emotionally. Every day since Robert's funeral we had been dealing with journalists, politicians and others from morning to night. There was no respite, no daily routine, no meal times or quiet periods. Tensions ran high at times. These tensions were to intensify as the campaign reached its climax. Donna and Gemma felt that the press were being too intrusive and that there was a danger of sensationalising Robert's murder. The rest of us were of the strong opinion that Robert's murder needed to be highlighted at every opportunity as eventually the media would move on to the next story, so we had to capitalise on the interest while we could. We were all deeply traumatised by Robert's murder and, as with any other family at times of great stress, the people you are closest to are usually on the receiving end of your frustration. Dealing with the media and politicians was too much emotionally for Donna and Gemma and they couldn't cope with the constant questions, being asked to repeat over and over what had happened. Many reporters wanted to know how we had found out, how we felt, what Robert was like, and so on. We found it difficult to answer these questions; it was too hard to talk about our loss and who Robert was. We were being forced to come to terms with his death unnaturally. I found it impossible to talk about the personal loss and any time these questions were asked, journalists were redirected to Paula or Claire. This was probably unfair as they also had difficulty coping with this but they always held it together.

Bridgeen, meanwhile, was in pieces. Conlaed and Brandon were crying for their daddy constantly and asking questions that tore the heart out of her: 'Where was he stabbed?' 'Why was he stabbed?' 'Did it hurt Daddy?' 'Did he cry?' Robert had been the centre of these two little boys' lives. From the moment Conlaed was born, he doted on him, and when Brandon came along, he had two sons whom he indulged and loved intensely. It is still hard to look at Conlaed and Brandon without pain; they are constant reminders of the future Robert and his small family were robbed of.

We longed for a phone call from the police informing us that witnesses had come forward and arrests would be made soon. It never came and we continued on with our arrangements to meet with political representatives from the government in Dublin.

We travelled to Dublin on 23 February to meet with Dermot Ahern, the Irish Minister for Foreign Affairs, and with representatives from the other political parties. During our meeting with Mark Durkan, he had offered whatever help his party could give and he stuck to his word. I got contact numbers of all the relevant people in the South and we arranged meetings with whomever we could. Seeking the help of Irish ministers first, rather than British ministers, was deliberate on our part. The only people who could hand over Robert's murderers were the Provo leadership and the only way they would do this was if enough pressure was applied on them. To seek the aid of British ministers would have wrongly weakened our position within the republican/nationalist community. The Provos and their sympathetic press would have used it as a weapon to distort the facts of our campaign and deflect attention away from the real issue. Just as they tried to demonise Robert, they would try to isolate us from our own community by peddling nonsense that we were anti-republican seeking the help of the Brits. This is not to say that this argument was not used against us — it was — but to meet with British ministers would have put bullets in their guns.

Gaining the support not only of the Irish political establishment but of the Irish people was paramount. The voice of the Southern people was very important to Sinn Féin. The party was less, if not at all, concerned with the people in the North as it is guaranteed its mandate up there because democratic politics in the North are warped and twisted; but the people in the South are different. They are used to democracy and all that that entails: accountability, rule of law, proper conduct on the part of political parties. Robert's murder exposed to them a party that was incapable of adhering to the most fundamental principles of justice, and if anyone thought that that was in the past, they were to think again. Getting our message out down South was extremely important to us and we will always be thankful to the Irish people for their support. Just as in the case of Garda Jerry McCabe, it is the people who care about people; to politicians people are political collateral.

On the way down in the taxi, the six of us reflected over the previous few weeks and, in between the tears, we laughed at the idea of Gerry Kelly's consistent answer to all our questions: 'I can't answer that.' Gemma and Donna performed a song in his honour, one rap version and one disco. Tears streamed down our faces at their antics, the hysteria of laughter out of proportion to the funniness of the performance. But it helped to release some of the tension and pressure that had built up over the previous few weeks.

We were due to speak on the *Marian Finucane Show* the following morning. This was our first proper interview on live radio or television and we didn't know what to expect. Not only was it difficult enough having to expose our family to the media and the country, but it was made more difficult by the fact that we were the ones having to do it. It was really uncomfortable for us and especially at a time when we were still very much in shock and traumatised. This state of mind was probably an aid, in that in normal circumstances we would have run a mile.

While we sat in the reception area of Radio Telefís Éireann that morning, we heard Gerry Adams refer to Robert's murder as 'manslaughter'. Mr Adams said that Justice Minister Michael McDowell was 'using this person's killing, this person's murder or manslaughter or whatever it happens to be, in a way against Sinn Féin and also around the whole issue of policing.' We were incensed at this. It was three weeks since Robert's murder and it was inconceivable that the Provisional leadership did not know the exact circumstances of his death. They would have known how Robert was pursued down the street and set upon by the gang. They would also have known that a knife was sent for, as was a gun, and that this pre-planned attack was not a spontaneous bar brawl as they had tried to portray it initially. That Adams was still promoting this image cemented our belief that they were protecting the murderers.

That first radio interview was a difficult one as we had never been in a radio studio in our lives and we were all very nervous. We were asked questions about growing up in the Short Strand and about the IRA; we had to try to explain the relationship between the community and the IRA and how we viewed that organisation. Did we support its campaign of violence? Was its cause just? And so on. We were completely honest. During the Troubles, the IRA was considered as defenders of nationalist communities, and it would be fair to say that we tacitly supported the IRA as did many others in our community. This tacit support was set in a context of conflict. The Short Strand was an area deeply affected by violence. The RUC, loyalists and the British Army were regarded as the real oppressors, and the IRA the defenders. This attitude was prevalent in communities like the Short Strand; it was only during the peace that people could focus their minds on other aspects and causes of the Troubles. This line of questioning revealed a very uncomfortable reality to me: in Northern Ireland, justice was qualified, and unless victims were believed to be 'whiter than white', their right to justice was questioned.

After the programme, we set off for the Dáil and met with Dermot Ahern and colleagues. Adams's comments resolved our determination and at that meeting we spoke passionately about the need for the government to put pressure on Sinn Féin and the IRA. Little distinction was made between the two organisations — it was generally understood that we were talking about one and the same organisation. To pretend that Sinn Féin didn't know what the IRA knew was nonsense and gave Sinn Féin a veil to hide behind. Sitting around a long table in a very elegant room with people who basically have the power to make things happen or not instilled in us a sense of trepidation. There was no doubt that the condolences offered were heartfelt and their offer to help sincere, but we were always aware that these people were politicians who essentially had an agenda and that Robert's murder suited that agenda at this particular time. Changing circumstances could dilute or reinforce commitments, and from the beginning we were aware of this. It was our duty to ensure that we held these people to promises made.

We relayed the story again. The questions were what could they do, what were they willing to do and what did we want them to do. As far as we were concerned, we wanted it on the table at any future talks. We didn't ask for it to be made a precondition but we did argue strongly that Sinn Féin's fitness for government could be assured only if its members were committed to the rule of law. Their conduct in Robert's murder proved that they were unfit to hold any office and, particularly and most importantly, an office dealing with issues of policing and justice. We were pleased with the outcome of this first meeting. Dermot Ahern told the press afterwards that the murder of Robert was at the top of the agenda for future discussions with Sinn Féin and the British government, and said that Robert's case now joined that of Rosemary Nelson and Pat Finucane, as well as the McCabe murder. This seemed to us a positive and genuine commitment but, as it turned out, it was just another act of political theatre.

We met all the political parties and independent TDs in the Dáil that day for an exhausting round of talks, repeating the story over and over.

All conveyed their condolences and support, and all, I believe, were genuine. We returned to Belfast that day, and the following day we were to meet with Gerry Adams for the first time and listen to what he had to say about Robert's murder.

VII

On returning to Belfast, we got a call from Gerry Kelly, saying that Gerry Adams wanted to meet with us the following day, 24 February. The IRA statement had intensified media interest and our first meeting with Gerry Adams opened with Paula's words: 'Thank God you're here, Gerry. This is turning into a media circus.' Now that the man himself had taken over at the helm, Paula and the others believed that the end was in sight. I had my reservations. The fact that it had been allowed to go this far spoke for itself, but I was willing to listen to what he had to say. We made a conscious decision to have that first meeting in Robert's home, an attempt to connect Gerry to our reality. This was our brother's home where he lived with Bridgeen and his two sons; we wanted Gerry to see that Robert was a real person and to gain some feeling for the family's loss.

Exactly what was said at that meeting has long since faded out of memory. Nothing was said to convince us that continuing with the media or seeking help from political representatives was unnecessary. We were planning a rally in the Short Strand at the end of the week and were making plans for America. Nothing Gerry Adams said rendered this course of action unnecessary. On reflection, he said very little to deter us from campaigning, given that Sinn Féin was being put under immense pressure which was to continue for months, and had elections coming up. Given that the party was adamant that it supported us, no one tried very hard to convince us that they were doing all they could. They listened, offered their sympathies and then left. Strange, under the circumstances.

The following day, we received a phone call offering a meeting with the IRA. This would give us the opportunity to confront those responsible for the cover-up. At this time, we had accepted that the IRA leadership did not sanction Robert's murder but the forensic clean-up had required resources that the IRA provided. We didn't expect too much from this meeting from the outset. Ultimately, however, meetings were unnecessary if the IRA intended to do the right thing. We travelled up to the agreed meeting place, went through the open front door and said casually to the person in the front office, 'We are here to meet with the IRA.' We were directed upstairs into a spacious, sparsely furnished room whose décor was reminiscent of a past time. Five chairs were arranged in a semi-circle in the middle of the room, facing the fireplace; another chair was placed further back against the wall, and Gemma took this one. We sat waiting for the arrival of our hosts, not knowing what to expect, talking about the disgraceful position we were in, asking if this would do any good and becoming increasingly annoyed at their lateness. We joked that maybe the room was bugged and they were listening in, trying to suss us out.

Eventually two men came into the room and apologised for being late. They took the two wooden-backed chairs facing us and introduced themselves as Pádraig and Sean and declared that they were representatives of the IRA Army Council and had the full authority of that council. We in turn introduced ourselves. They offered their condolences and explained that they had asked to meet us so that they could give us an account of their internal investigation into Robert's murder. There was nothing distinctive about the two men, one in jeans and a checked shirt (from Dunnes, Paula pointed out afterwards), the other in a pullover and trousers. No balaclavas or guns, as some journalists reported. A week or so before, a journalist had asked, 'Are you not afraid that you have annoyed some very dangerous people?'

'We've annoyed them?' I replied exasperated. 'They'd have a cheek to be annoyed. We've annoyed them? They've annoyed us!'

For many people, the IRA was a ruthless guerrilla army whose secrecy and longevity had shrouded it in mystery. Meetings with ordinary mortals like ourselves were uncommon and could be dangerous; that was the perception. Like many other secret organisations and individuals who build up a mystical reputation, the truth is far removed from the perception. For us it was just another meeting in a long list of meetings. We were not afraid; we had nothing to be afraid of: the IRA men were the defendants, we the accusers. The IRA was trying to make its case; we were trying to get it to take responsibility for its crimes.

We braced ourselves for the details of the brutality of what happened that night in Magennis's. Pádraig reached into his back pocket and pulled out a sheet of paper that looked as if it had seen better days. It was tattered and torn and, from time to time, he scribbled notes on this already-worn paper. He told us nothing new; their findings were an exact account of what we had told Sinn Féin, no fresh information or details. We sat listening curiously but not intently, and interrupted now and again to refute certain claims made.

'Jock and Robert were friends,' Pádraig read out nonchalantly.

'That's a load of rubbish. Robert couldn't stand the man,' I said.

'Well, this is what our investigation has revealed.'

'"Jock and Robert were friends." Jesus Christ, is he trying to be funny? Did he tell you that?'

'He said they were mates and Robert used to live out the back of him; they never had any problem with each other.'

'He's a liar.'

'Why would Robert be a friend of that big-nosed bastard?' said Donna.

'Well, it's obvious he's lying to you. So you are just putting in whatever he says?'

'Do yous want to meet Jock?' Pádraig suggested.

'Why would we want to meet him? We don't want to listen to what he has to say. He's the cause of this. He gave the order. No, we don't want to meet him.'

'He says that you requested a meeting with him.'

'He's a lying bastard. One of his friends approached my uncle and asked if he could talk to him. When he arrived up to the meeting, Jock was there. Why would we want to talk to that bastard?'

'Well, we'll take that out of the statement.'

'You'll have to because it's not true.' We looked at each other incredulously.

Pádraig read on, claiming that Gerard Montgomery knew the person who got the knife, destroyed the knife, threatened the barman, took the CCTV, destroyed clothes and other evidence. The version he wanted us to believe was that Jim McCormick was the man responsible for the stabbing of both Brendan Devine and Robert.

'What did he do with the knife?'

'He ground it down.'

'Bastard.'

He read on, giving a very flimsy account of the events of the night. 'Sean Montgomery arrived on the scene and thought republicans were being attacked.'

'Attacked? Who were republicans being attacked by?' I asked.

'He says he drove up to the bar and saw a crowd and thought republicans were being attacked.'

'So, let's get this clear. Sean Montgomery who lives in the Markets and works in the Strand, drove up to Magennis's bar which is in the Markets and saw a crowd of republicans, every one of whom he would have known, and two men being surrounded by his friends — one of these men he certainly did know — and thought that republicans were being attacked. Who did he think republicans were being attacked by?'

'I don't know. This is what he told the investigation. I am unfamiliar with the area and have no reason to think that he was lying.'

'Well, once Sean discovered that republicans were not being attacked but were doing the attacking, what did Sean do?'

There was no reply to this; we were to find out at a later date what part Sean played in the sordid events of that night.

'Right, we'll take that out.' And he scribbled out the sentence referring to Sean's account, just as he had done with the reference to Robert and Jock being friends.

We sat listening languidly as he read on. The atmosphere was heavy but not intimidating or menacing in any way; neither was the discussion, but there was a quiet anger and dismay bubbling inside each of us. It was ridiculous that we had to press the IRA to stop protecting Robert's murderers.

After Pádraig had finished reading, it was our turn to ask questions. Donna asked, 'What about the gun?'

'What gun? There was no gun.'

'Ed Gowdy told us a gun was put to his chest; we also know that a phone call was made for a gun.'

'There was no gun. No volunteer can get access to a gun; that would be a serious breach of the ceasefire.'

'There was a gun. Ed said there was a gun and I believe the only reason our Robert had his hands in the air and was under their control was because a gun was being pointed at him.'

They insisted that there was no gun. We insisted that there was. I asked them why the Army Council had never taken action against these men despite numerous complaints from the people of the areas that they lorded over.

'We are unaware of any complaints.'

'Was there a breakdown in communication or did Jock and Co. make sure that nothing was sent further up the command chain?'

'We'll be looking into that.'

Paula asked why the IRA had recruited men like Jim McCormick, a well-known disreputable character. Had the vetting procedures failed or was any scum welcome these days? They got vexed at this, offended at the accusations that the IRA recruited scum.

'We don't vet volunteers.'

'It was my understanding that the IRA vetted people.'

'Apparently Jim McCormick joined up in 1996 and some of the others were kids at the first ceasefire. Did nobody tell them that the war was over, or is that not why they joined?'

Their vexation was immaterial to us. I had read an autobiography of an IRA volunteer, Jack McNally; he talked of how, while in prison in the 1950s, he and his republican comrades had refused to eat food prepared by criminals, murderers and rapists. They succeeded in persuading the prison authorities to permit republican prisoners to cook their own food. Now these criminals were being recruited and protected by the IRA. We gave examples of the activities of these men prior to Robert's murder, how attempted rapes had been overlooked, that they were misogynists and child-beaters, who let it be known that they were in the IRA and used the organisation for their own self-interest.

Pádraig said, 'I wouldn't know these people from an Easter egg', but insisted that, as far as he was concerned, an IRA volunteer's duty was to remain anonymous: IRA life and personal life were completely separate; when he went out to socialise, he took his IRA hat off at the door. He claimed that he socialised with people outside the organisation, unlike the Third Battalion who hung about in gangs. Paula then asked if IRA volunteers took a pledge to 'die for Ireland'.

'Yes,' Sean said.

'Well, then, they are not being asked to die for Ireland; they are being asked to tell the truth. Some of them are unlikely to serve more than a few months for their part; why won't they go in?'

'Why are you protecting people like this?'

'We're not protecting them. These people mean nothing to me. I would put a bullet in their heads!' said Pádraig, an expression to illustrate his disgust for these people. Whether this was real or not, we'll never know. Donna said that she would shoot them in the morning herself.

'It's not easy to kill a man,' replied Pádraig.

'I'd find it easy,' said Donna.

'No, you wouldn't,' one of us said, I can't remember who.

'Yes, I would. I'd execute them!' She was angry and frustrated.

Donna then jumped up from her chair, giving Sean and Pádraig a fright. 'Cramp,' she said. She stretched her legs and started to walk about the room, continuing her discussion with Pádraig on execution. Out of us all, Donna is the volatile one. All this talking and having literally to beg for Jock and Co. to be brought to justice was compounding her anger at Robert's death. Throughout the campaign she has had to sit on this anger and vent it in other ways.

Pádraig claimed that ten years ago, they would have shot these people.

'Yeah, and how would you have explained fifteen bodies washing up on a beach?' Donna asked.

Pádraig was visibly surprised by the reference to fifteen; he had been talking about two. This was a hypothetical conversation and the rest of us sat on, waiting for rationality to resume. Conversation focused on what followed next: they denied intimidating witnesses and preventing people from coming forward. They explained that Gerard Montgomery, Jim McCormick and Jock Davison would be expelled from the organisation.

'Can they get back in again? asked Donna.

'It depends on the crime.'

'Well, what about Jock? Can he re-apply?'

'Yeah.'

'When?'

'Maybe six months or so.'

They claimed that Jock had left the scene before Robert and Brendan were attacked and was unaware of his men's intentions. His crime had been to be involved in an argument in a public house. This was a complete whitewash. We knew it and they knew it, but this was their position. *This is a fucking disgrace*, I thought. *What was the point of this meeting?* We all sat completely unimpressed and I was tempted just to walk out. It reminded me of one of those dreams I commonly have, in which someone close to me has been in a serious accident or is dead and I am trying to explain it to other members of the family, but they don't react. They continue on with what they are doing, half-listening to you and saying, 'Ah, I know', in a nonchalant manner, as if it doesn't matter what has happened. In these dreams I usually end up screaming and crying, running frantically from one to another trying to get them to grasp the reality of the situation, and they never do. The intense feelings of frustration and despair are released by screaming. This meeting had a similar feel to it, minus the tears and screaming. These people did not seem to grasp that Jock Davison and his henchmen had beaten and stabbed Robert to death. He was dead. How did they expect us to react to expulsions and, not only that, but possible reinstatements? We were in a parallel world to these people.

I resisted the temptation to walk out but tired of their explanations. We talked of witnesses and they pledged that no witnesses had anything to fear. They spoke of McKay, Devine and Gowdy and, like Sinn Féin, believed that these three could unlock the case. We went round in circles about what could be done to encourage witnesses to come forward. They claimed that Montgomery and McCormick had been ordered to go in but were refusing, and if they forced them in, it could be counter-productive. We discussed the downfalls of ordering people in: they could claim that they had confessed under duress and the trial would collapse. They then left, saying that they had to see someone. We didn't discuss what they had said as it was a pointless exercise. They were going to do nothing. Food arrived in the form of fruit and hobnob biscuits. It had been a long day and we all joked that Pádraig and Sean were probably sitting in a chippy, eating their tea.

They returned in a more hurried fashion than they had left. Something was afoot. They asked if we had discussed what we had been talking about. They said that they had two men under house arrest and that there were helicopters circling. They suspected that the families were getting worried and had phoned the police. At the time, we never thought to point out the irony of this – so-called staunchly republican families asking the PSNI and British Army for help in finding their staunchly republican loved ones being held by the IRA.

'Well, you'll have to let them go,' I said. 'You can hardly hold them forever.'

'They might abscond; we could make it physically impossible for them to do so.'

'Look, if the police gather the evidence against these men, then it won't matter if they abscond. They will be murderers on the run. We don't want anyone harmed; we just want the evidence to be brought forward and for you to stop protecting these people.'

'Can you assure us that safe houses won't be provided for these men if they do run?'

'Yes,' replied Sean.

'Why don't they phone home?' asked Donna.

'There's no phone in the house where we have them.'

'Can they not use a mobile phone?' Donna replied tersely.

'No. The signal might be traced.'

'Why don't you get them to write a note to their mammies telling them they'll be home for tea?'

The absurdity of this was comical and I don't know what all this play-acting was about. They obviously thought we were in awe of the IRA and would accept their dramatics about men under house arrest. Before we left, they tried to reassure us that they were doing all they could to help us to get justice. The statement would call for witnesses to come forward. Were we happy with this? they asked. 'Mmh' was our response.

It was a five-and-a-half-hour-long meeting. It had been a long three and a half weeks. We were traumatised and exhausted and we still hoped that the IRA would do the right thing, but again its actions, not its words, would prove this. We left the meeting on what can be described as cordial terms with the IRA. Donna sarcastically asked, 'How do we get in touch with you again — smoke signals?' As we parted, we shook hands with each of them and Sean finished with, 'Thank you for saying that we did not sanction your brother's murder.'

'That's OK; you didn't,' one of us replied.

On reflection, it would have been wise to prepare for this meeting as there were so many questions we didn't ask. However, we returned home and discussed with other family members and friends what had been said. None were convinced of the IRA's sincerity. Some couldn't figure out why it was in the IRA's interest to protect the murderers and hoped that over the coming days the IRA would act. This small degree of optimism was evident in an email I wrote:

...I think that although we are hopeful that we may be seeing the beginning of the end to this ordeal it is still important to think ahead in the event of failure to bring all involved before the courts or to go to the police … I think the IRA are going to have difficulty with this as they seem content to hand over the two killers but no one else so we may still have a fight on our hands. We have to pressurise the IRA into handing all their members who were involved over and if this happens then there should be the evidence to convict. If there isn't then a cover-up is still in operation.

Apparently there was quite a lot of activity around Jock's house today, with Sinn Féin representatives and some of those IRA who were involved in the events of that night.…

As it turned out, I was wrong in my assertion that they were willing to hand over two of the killers.

The IRA issued its second statement that evening, claiming that it had expelled three members. When I arrived up to Paula's house the following day, the media had already gathered in the small court. I had to write out a hurried response in a house full of people. I persuaded Claire to read it to the waiting media. It reiterated our position and questioned the accuracy of the IRA's account, which refused to admit the number of people involved. For some within the Short Strand, the expulsions should have been the end of the matter. Three local women went on the radio to castigate us for continuing with our campaign despite the IRA's actions. These women didn't give their names but we recognised their voices — two of them had grown up across the street from us. We responded graciously, telling the interviewer that they were entitled to their opinion and if three IRA expulsions were the value they put on their loved ones' lives, that was their decision; it wasn't justice.

For some, the IRA had gone too far, illustrating how distorted and confused people had become about the IRA's role and the ideals of human rights and justice. It was an ugly side of the community we lived in. For others, the IRA did not go far enough: veteran republicans expressed the view that those responsible should have been shot not only for the crime but to restore the IRA's credibility and prevent it from being sullied by such a crime. For these two sections of the community our campaign was to become a source of irritation and anger. Those who wanted the murderers protected resented us from the outset while those who supported our demand for justice were uncomfortable with the pressure being applied on the IRA and Sinn Féin and felt that we were allowing others to use Robert's murder as a stick with which to beat the republican movement. From our point of view, the IRA and Sinn Féin could put a stop to the campaign any time they wanted. Instead of directing witnesses, intimidating witnesses, and protecting Jock and his men, the IRA had only to order its men in or put an end to the intimidation.

Sinn Féin and the IRA did nothing. Senior republicans such as Bobby Storey were regular visitors to the Short Strand. Until proof of the IRA's and Sinn Féin's sincerity translated into action, we were not going to stop.

VIII

The rally was Paula's brainchild and one of which I was wary. Asking people to come on to the streets was a huge risk, not because of the fear of violence but because of a fear of a low turn-out. This would play straight into the Provisional hands; they could argue that we were isolated within the community and that the people believed the movement was doing all it could.

News of the rally was spread mainly through the media. We had no experience of this sort of thing at all and we hurriedly arranged speakers, equipment and posters and wrote a speech. We considered speakers and decided that Eamonn McCann was someone we respected for his outspoken views and tendency to say things as they are. He was a man of conviction, one who had never sought personal power or credit for anything but spoke for the people. His dynamic delivery of speeches was also a consideration. We were delighted when he agreed to speak. Paula was enthusiastic about the rally and was confident that the people of the Short Strand would respond. She had faith in their judgment and believed that Robert's murder had been a crime against the community as well as us. This was the first speech I was to write on Robert's murder, which is clear from reading it over, but it came from the heart and it was sincere in its message.

Everyone gathered in Paula's house before the rally, all in anticipation of what was to come. Worry and nervousness pervaded the air. Paula had been nominated to read the speech and she was terrified. To get up in front of the people of the Short Strand and basically demand that the IRA hand over members of that community was a frightening prospect, but she never wavered. Some family members had gone round to set up the makeshift stage and speakers. When they returned, we asked if there was anyone there.

'A few people have gathered.'

'Oh shit,' someone uttered. 'Only a few?'

Alban Maginness called in to offer his support. 'What constitutes a good crowd?' asked Paula nervously.

'Around 200 would be good,' he replied.

'Well, hopefully we'll be able to manage that,' said Paula, unsure.

This was a risk: if very few turned out, it could damage, although not stop, the campaign. Rumours were circulating around the Short Strand that it was an anti-republican rally, a claim being made by republicans close to Jock, and other sympathisers. It was nothing of the sort. It was a message from the Short Strand to the Provisional leadership that IRA murder of innocent members of that community would not be tolerated. It was the IRA's responsibility to do something.

At two o'clock, we left Paula's house to make our way towards the shops where the rally was to be held. I felt sick, my legs were shaking and I gripped the pole of the placard tightly. The situation was surreal. The placards had a picture of Robert and the words, 'Who's Next? Why?' The children walked in front, all proudly carrying posters of Robert. As we came onto the Mountpottinger Road, we could see that a substantial crowd had gathered and we sighed in relief. As we got closer, the crowd started to cheer, and people shouted, 'Good on yous', 'We've had enough of that scum.' Another exclaimed, 'There'll be no more beating wee boys up.' The sound of clapping and cheering filled us with emotion. This was our community, Robert's community, and it was sending a clear message to the IRA. This was the most memorable and important day in the whole campaign. Veteran republicans stood amongst the crowd, respected members of the republican community within the Short Strand, and their presence was symbolic. The calibre of those people and that of Jock Davison's crowd could not be compared; the latter were a disgrace to the republican movement and their continued protection a further slur.

Jock sympathisers stood a short distance from the crowd, observing, but the presence of these people didn't deter the crowd. In the past, taking note of who was at rallies not supported by the Provisionals was enough to put people off attending, as they didn't want to be marked out. This crowd was not intimidated, however.

Paula took to the stage and read out the speech in a nervous but steady voice. She said later that her legs were shaking so badly, she thought they were going to buckle beneath her. But she did well.

Eamonn McCann then delivered his thoughts on Robert's murder. He spoke of Bloody Sunday and how some of those who had been involved that night had come back from Derry after marching in commemoration and solidarity with the families of the victims of Bloody Sunday. 'How dare they?' he thundered. His speech received a rapturous applause and the rally was a success from our point of view. The people had sent the leadership a message: Robert was a member of their community and they wanted justice.

Unbeknown to us, Alex Maskey and Deirdre Hargey had attended the rally; the audacity of these people was unbelievable. Maskey, we could understand to a degree. Sinn Féin was adopting a dual strategy: showing public support but working hard on the ground to ensure impunity and operating a whispering campaign against the family. Maskey's absence probably would have raised more questions than his presence. But to bring Hargey along with him, Hargey who had been present in the bar that night and was in the company of those involved in Robert's murder and cover-up! She did not go forward to the police, a solicitor or anyone else until the media outed her. Like her Sinn Féin colleagues, she reiterated the party line on television, urging people to come forward, yet she herself had remained silent. When she eventually did provide a statement, it was the same as the majority of the other 150: 'I saw nothing and I heard nothing.' It is unlikely that Maskey was unaware of this. It is unlikely that any Sinn Féin member in that bar did not report it to the party.

That Sinn Féin is a strong, disciplined party is no secret. Very few steer away from the party line; even senior politicians sing from the same hymn sheet on every issue; there is no dissension. Dissent and you're out. It is difficult to believe that these members kept what they knew of the events of the night hidden from their Sinn Féin bosses. Sinn Féin believed that her presence and that of others would remain undetected. Hargey went unpunished for her refusal to comply with the party leadership and was, in fact, being put forward as a council candidate in the upcoming local elections. It was this fact that prompted Paula to say that she would stand for election.

Maskey got more than he bargained for that day. He was speaking to the media, spouting the usual Sinn Féin line about how they supported our campaign, congratulating the IRA on the actions it had taken — three expulsions — and taking the opportunity to indulge in Sinn Féin doublespeak, when my uncle approached him and demanded loudly that he 'hand the other twelve over.' This caused a stir and Maskey had no response to it. No point in trying to tell the people of the Short Strand that they had done all they could; these people had come through thirty-five years of the Troubles — they knew every wheel and turn of the IRA and Sinn Féin. Political manoeuvring wouldn't work here and the wool couldn't be pulled over these people's eyes. Hargey stood at his side, nonplussed. Maskey muttered his protestations and made his exit with Hargey in tow.

We returned to Paula's, elated at the turn-out; it had been a risk but one worth taking. We hoped that the leadership would listen and that it would all end. Back in Paula's house, we discussed the possible effects of the rally. Relatives and friends had noted the presence of Jock and his supporters, standing just a short distance from the main body of people outside the house of a sympathiser, but we were on what could only be described as a 'high': the response of the community had been fantastic and strengthened our resolve. They knew what the issue was at this point; it wasn't blurred by politics. Years of experience had taught them that the IRA could deliver justice if it chose to. The people were demanding it. Anyone who later argued that the people who attended the rally were anti-republican or were trying to force Sinn Féin towards policing were contemptuous of the voice of the people. Veteran republicans who were well respected stood amongst the crowd — men and women who, having been released from prison, worked constructively on the ground to realise the principles they had fought for. One ex-prisoner in particular was a highly respected member of the community and he had stood with us. To ignore this man's demand for justice was to dismiss the contribution he had made to republicanism and to devalue his beliefs.

If the Short Strand was expected to give protection to the IRA, which it had done for years, then it expected protection back. The bullyboy tactics of the local IRA over the past years had instilled a deep sense of fear and resentment towards the Third Battalion. Complaints to the local Sinn Féin office brought no respite or response. A local who worked in the Sinn Féin office on the Ormeau Road before 1998 commented that when he worked there he was inundated with complaints from local people about the brutality of this group, yet nothing was done. The IRA at our first meeting claimed to be unaware of any complaints. Jim McCormick, the man charged with common affray but named to us by the IRA as the knifeman, held the post of Treasurer for this same office right up to April 2005. The Third Battalion of the IRA was very active, not only in the IRA, but in Sinn Féin also, and was considered highly by the latter; its men were used as bodyguards for Adams and McGuinness on a regular basis. According to a republican source, Jock Davison was a confidant of Adams.

The IRA was traditionally a secret organisation and, when I was growing up in the Short Strand, the identity of volunteers became known only when they were either imprisoned or killed. By 1998, a child on the street could have told you who was a member of the local IRA. Secrecy was no longer beneficial to the purpose of this gang; belonging to the IRA provided a status and power required for lording it over the community rather than fighting a colonial war against the British. The effect of this notoriety, however, had impacted on the mystical and romantic image of the organisation; the unsavoury character of its volunteers only brought the organisation into ridicule and disrepute. Veteran republicans who were no longer active were increasingly frustrated by the activities of these post-ceasefire soldiers and there was hostility between them. Unfortunately their influence or lack of protest allowed the Hallion Battalion to vent its brutality on the community to a degree that the British or loyalists never achieved. The peace dividend for the Short Strand was living in a walled ghetto, being controlled by a group of thugs masquerading as community activists and local defenders.

I was perplexed by the complacency of the community in the face of this gang's brutality. They had faced British and loyalist brutality with resilience and lack of fear, yet the growing cancer of the Hallion Battalion went completely unchecked and ultimately reached its climax with the murder of Robert, a local man. But on this day the people had spoken, Robert's murder had jolted them from their complacency. The IRA had a choice to make: it could either listen to the people or continue to protect murderers. It chose the latter.

Chapter 2

GROWING UP IN THE SHORT STRAND

The sound of shouting and screaming drifted through the skylight window into my room at the top of the house. The familiar sound signalled that the area was under attack and drew people from their homes and the bars to investigate. Partly out of curiosity and partly out of concern, I rushed downstairs and out the front door. A familiar sight greeted me. The street was awash with people: men, women and children were running frantically to and fro, their faces bursting with anger and their screams and shouts piercing the warm August night air. My eyes scanned the street and the crowd searching for Robert and Gerard but the swooning of the crowd as it advanced and then retreated just as quickly made it difficult to focus. A Protestant crowd jeered from behind a line of RUC Landrovers, and bandsmen with puffed-out chests goading the Catholics on the other side were clearly the source of the attack.

It was August 1991 and the marching season was coming to an end. A group of bandsmen on their way home from the day's marching and drinking had decided to stop at the Short Strand for some good old-fashioned sectarian harassment of the small Catholic population. The Catholics, as usual, rose to the occasion and defended the area admirably. The passion and conviction of the area's inhabitants more than compensated for their small numbers. Riots and sectarian attacks were experiences common to the Short Strand but the dangers could never be underestimated, and the residents could never be complacent about them. The potential for serious or even fatal injuries was very real. The RUC could open fire with lethal consequences, missiles could cause serious harm and, for anyone captured by the other side, a severe beating was guaranteed and possibly death. The presence of the RUC, or the Protestant cavalry as it was in the minds of many of the residents, inflamed tensions and tempers further as guns were pointed towards the Catholic defenders. The refusal of the 'peelers' to push the Protestant crowd back forcibly, given that it was blatantly clear that they were the aggressors, led to a tirade of abuse.

'Why don't you go up and arrest them, ya black bastards?' 'Look at them pointing their guns at us; it was them that came down here,' people roared.

'It's a fuckin' disgrace. Don't move on. Let them move that crowd; we live here,' others shouted in response to the attempts by the police to disperse the crowds.

There was no doubt in the minds of the people as to what was occurring: the Protestant marchers were being allowed to intimidate and harass their Catholic counterparts whilst the RUC turned its guns on the Catholics to ensure that they didn't overcome their opponents. Local youths attacked the police along with the Protestants and, in turn, the 'peelers' drove Landrovers carelessly on to pavements in pursuit of the teenage boys, confirming what the Catholic residents already knew. As far as the RUC was concerned, we also were the enemy. Some local residents attempted to speak to the RUC but their complaints were brusquely brushed aside.

The whole place was in chaos. People were shouting obscenities at the police and goading the other side. Others residents were trying to calm the situation down by driving people further down the Mountpottinger Road away from the riot, but they were ignored or told to 'fuck off'. I remember one man shouting, 'Get you weemin in!'

'Away an' fuck,' came the angry retort from a woman.

I could feel the adrenaline flowing through the crowd. For the teenagers, these riots were a great source of entertainment, and reasoning with them was impossible. I could see young men clap each other on the back for a 'good throw' or brave chase. Male bravado and impressing peers were as much their priority as defending the area. These riots were far from harmless fun, however, and a person could be killed or seriously injured if they were not contained or controlled. I feared the male aggression that had no reason or constraint and could result in horrendous and senseless violence.

As I scanned the street, I couldn't locate Robert or Gerard. I asked neighbours and friends if they had seen them and was told that Gerard was standing further down the street with some friends, but Robert and a friend had chased some bandsmen in the direction of the Mount — Protestant territory. I panicked. Robert had stupidly left the safety of the Short Strand. The Protestant crowd was getting thicker as the noise attracted more people to the scene. Robert would have to get through that crowd to reach safety. If he got caught up the road, he would be killed; I was sure of it. Tensions were running so high that anyone caught on the wrong side could expect at best a beating. I ran up to the RUC cordon and explained frantically to a woman officer that my brother had gone up the road. He had to be brought back. She told me that she couldn't do anything but tried to assure me that he would be all right.

I was becoming hysterical as my mind conjured up images of Robert being beaten mercilessly. The shouts of the angry Protestant mob left me in no doubt that Robert's life was in danger. I felt helpless. People were running to and fro, screaming and shouting, and the chaos was drowning out my voice. I was in no mood for taking orders. 'Get into the house!' someone shouted and shoved me. It was the same man who had earlier told 'weemin' to get in.

'Fuck off!' I screamed back at him. 'My brother's up there. I'm going nowhere until he's back here.'

The air was thick with profanities: 'Yous black bastards', 'Orange bastards' from one side. The other side responded in kind: 'Fenian bastards!' And on it went. I was later told that before the RUC had arrived on the scene, the battle between the bandsmen and the residents of the Short Strand had been face to face. Every punch carried the weight of the centuries-old hostilities that existed between the two sides. The hatred each side felt for the other beat savagely within them. The Short Strand had witnessed hundreds of riots over the years but it was rare for both sides to get so close. The traditional throwing of bottles and bricks usually prevented direct contact but on this occasion both sides had engaged in good old-fashioned 'fisticuffs'.

From the scene on the Mountpottinger Road it appeared that the bandsmen had come off the worst from the encounter. The local youths and bandsmen had battled it out on the waste ground, and the scene was reminiscent of an eighteenth-century battlefield. Bandsmen, unsteady on their feet, staggered about, whilst others lay wounded on the grass. The wounded bandsmen hobbled back up the road, nursing their wounds, defeated but alive. In the grip of the frenzy, a group of young local men had surrounded the motionless body of a bandsman and continued to kick him mercilessly. A local onlooker intervened to stop the attack, trying to push or pull them away from the body on the ground, but he was roughly fended off. In exasperation, he threw himself on top of the bandsman, shouting at the top of his voice, 'That's enough! What do you want to do — kill him?'

At that, the group stood back and, with the help of another man, the bandsman was carried as far up the Mountpottinger Road as they could go, where his fellow bandsmen retrieved him. This gesture of humanity amidst the sectarian madness and hatred that engulfed the area that night was an expression of the true nature and character of the people from the Short Strand. This was not the first time I had witnessed the people coming to the aid of those under attack from some mindless youths of the area.

In the midst of the chaos, I was still waiting anxiously for a sighting of Robert, and at long last he appeared from the crowd, safe and in a mood of bravado. I was furious with him and let him know it. Chasing bandsmen up the Mount was not only stupid but also extremely dangerous. What did he think would happen if he got caught by a gang of men? My givin' off to him had no effect — in his usual manner, he brushed off the dangers, telling me to 'wise up'. It didn't matter now, though: he was back, and that was all that was important.

Within minutes, another drama unfolded. An ambulance had arrived to take away the injured residents but was being attacked by women and youths who were shaking it frantically. No one seemed to understand why the ambulance was being prevented from moving off. 'Who's in it?' people asked, confused. Was a bandsman in it, a peeler? Who was causing such a violent reaction? Eventually the youths and women were hauled away from the ambulance and it drove off. In fact, the injured in the ambulance were residents of the Short Strand and, unbeknown to me at the time, my mother was one of them.

Later, Paula recounted how my mother had come by her injuries. They had been sitting in the living room watching TV when Robert and a friend had come bursting through the door and run into the kitchen. Grabbing the empty milk bottles from their usual place, they had run out again, without saying a word. My mother and Paula had jumped up quickly and followed them, asking unanswered questions and issuing warnings to be careful and to stay out of trouble, all of which had gone unheard or, more accurately, unnoticed. That the 'orangies were in' was obvious but they hadn't expected them to be as close as they were. Out on the street around thirty bandsmen in full uniform were making their way into the area. Not surprisingly, Paula and my mother began to panic — the sight of thirty angry and violent-looking men heading their direction was frightening. They were naturally fearful for Robert and his friend, the only two men in the street, who stood equipped with only a few milk bottles — hardly likely to stave off the oncoming attack. Undeterred, however, Robert and Meeky advanced and then charged, throwing the milk bottles at the bandsmen who scattered to avoid the oncoming missiles. Some retreated whilst others continued their advance, ducking and weaving to avoid the bottles.

My mother was standing at the bottom of our path, shouting fruitlessly to Robert, when, from out of nowhere, a bandsman appeared and hit her over the head with his drumstick. As quick as he appeared, he disappeared. With blood pouring down her face, she was led back into the house by Paula. Screaming in panic and anger, Paula called an ambulance and, having seen to my mother's wounds as best she could, she went back on to the street.

The primeval shouts of the bandsman had alerted the attention of other residents and a slow dribble quickly developed into a flow of people standing in defence of the area. It was the screaming that had alerted me and, when I arrived, the riot was nearing its end. Contented that Robert and Gerard were safe, I joined neighbours and friends to discuss the night's events and observe the rest of the proceedings. After an hour or so of mainly verbal exchanges across the RUC line, the main bulk of both crowds dispersed. A small crowd of Protestant youths remained at the top of the road, hoping for a fresh kick-off, as did a small group of youths from the Short Strand, but to no avail.

And so another battle in the Strand's long history of sectarian battles had come to an end. Everyone knew that it wouldn't be the last but everyone was agreed that, once again, the people of the area had defended it proudly. There was no sign of IRA presence that evening, as on many others. No shots were fired in defence by the 'ra'. It was the ordinary men and women — people like Robert — who defended the area and did so on most occasions.

My mother was released from hospital after a few hours and we jokingly chided her for rioting. Her injuries proved, however, that sectarianism was indiscriminate, women and children as good a victim as any.

Such incidents left a lasting impression on the young people of the area and shaped their adult attitudes and political perspectives. The Short Strand's identity and solidarity were consolidated by such experiences. The small Catholic enclave situated on the edge of East Belfast had carved out a territorial space for itself amidst a sea of Protestantism. The population of over three thousand zealously guarded its territory and right to exist. A 'them and us' mentality was ingrained in the psyche of the people; to hurt one was to hurt all.

In many ways, the Short Strand is typical of any working class Catholic ghetto in Belfast but its geographical position gives it the edge over others. The survival of this small Catholic enclave, particularly through the worst days of 'the Troubles' when sectarianism was intense, is a great source of pride to the people of the Short Strand. The motto adopted by the 'Unbowed and Unbroken' expresses not only the spirit of the residents but also their experience, resilience and strength. To come from the Strand automatically identifies a person as a republican/nationalist/Catholic. The area and the people have paid dearly for this identification, many with their lives. Robert was to be one of them.

For over thirty years, the area was constantly under sectarian attack, heavily fortified and controlled by a paramilitary force. 'Freedom' is a word that is commonly spoken and sung about in the Strand, but it is a concept not experienced nor indeed fully understood and appreciated. As Robert's murder was to show, the people were responsible for some of the chains they wore, but not all.

As late as 2002, the community experienced one of the most vicious sectarian onslaughts in its history. Named 'The Siege of the Short Strand', it was one of the worst sustained attacks witnessed in living memory. The residents who bore the brunt of the violent attacks suffered horrendously, not only through the material damage that was done but also in terms of the psychological trauma suffered by men, women and children. So intense was the fighting that people had to move from their homes and children had to live away from parents until it was safe to return. Seven years into a 'peace process', the people of the Strand had thought that they had survived the worst of the Troubles. However, the Strand in 2003 resembled the Strand of 1973. Peace seemed to have evaded the area and its people. Previous riots were scuffles compared to the Siege of the Strand, with violent attacks day and night for months on end. Everyone feared for their own and their family's safety and a tangible sense of foreboding pervaded the area during one of its darkest episodes. For the first time in its history, it seemed that the small enclave might not be able to survive the attack. Absorbing the trauma, however, the Strand emerged from the crisis, as the motto said, 'Unbowed and Unbroken'; communal ties strengthened and solidarity entrenched, the people emerged defiant. The Strand had overcome one of the biggest challenges to its survival in recent years and had triumphed.

However, a bigger challenge was to confront the small community within two years. Unfortunately the Strand would not survive this challenge intact. Its communal ties would be fractured and its identity questioned, its moral fibre and integrity put under the spotlight.

There is no doubt that the Strand has left on Irish politics an indelible mark, both negative and positive. In pride of place is 'The Battle of St Matthew's', of June 1970, which is cited as not only a defining moment in the history of the Strand but also as a turning point in the fortunes of the IRA. It is often claimed that the first Provisional shots of the Troubles were fired that night. Billy McKee, with his small unit of IRA volunteers, defended the local church from attack. The battle entered Short Strand and republican folklore because of the shooting dead of three loyalists, along with a local IRA volunteer, Henry McIlhone. Before these shootings, the IRA had been the subject of nationalist mockery and anger at its inaction or inability to defend areas during the burning of Catholic homes by loyalist mobs. Poking fun at the IRA, 'IRA, I Ran Away' was scribbled on walls. Billy McKee and his unit from the Short Strand redeemed the IRA. From that date onwards, it had a strong presence in the Strand. It had earned the people's respect and support through its defence of the area and would continue to have this support for as long as it continued to defend the people.

Robert's murder has also left an indelible mark on the Short Strand's history and its place in republicanism. Unlike the Battle of St Matthew's, however, it will be neither commemorated nor celebrated, but looked on as one of the darkest and most shameful episodes in the Strand's history.

The Short Strand was a good place to grow up in despite the violence, deprivation and poverty. Everyone was in the same boat, and so there was no shame attached to not having the latest commodity or fashion. My generation was born into the conflict, known as 'the Troubles' or, for the more zealous, 'the war'. It was all we knew and, unlike our parents, we had nothing to compare it with. We accepted the hostility or hatred between Catholics and Protestants as the natural order of things, rarely questioning it and, if we did, getting very unsatisfactory and unclear answers.

Territorial confinement, separate schooling and violence reinforced division, segregation and separateness from our Protestant counterparts. We didn't think about the complexities of our situation; we just accepted the way things were. Our development from children into teenagers and then adults was shaped by our experience of life in an area that measured 300 metres by 300 metres. Nuclear and extended families shared this space: mothers and daughters lived in the same street, sisters around the corner, brothers over the way, cousins up the road, and so on. Generation after generation lived their entire lives in the same streets, each broadly following the path the other had taken before them and others would take after them. The word 'insular' always springs to mind when asked to describe the area.

As a community, the Strand can be traced back as far as 1830 when a small Catholic community settled on the edge of the River Lagan. With the building of St Matthew's Church in 1887, it became a *bone fide* Catholic parish. Like most working-class areas of Belfast, it was made up of Victorian streets with rows of terraced houses. Two up, two downs, or 'kitchen houses' as they were more commonly known, housed the area's Catholic inhabitants. These tiny houses had been built to accommodate the industrial workers of East Belfast whose needs did not include luxuries such as privacy, or so the city fathers thought. A typical 'kitchen house' consisted of a small living room, a kitchen or 'scullery', two bedrooms and an outside toilet. They housed families of up to ten or even more and, as late as the 1990s, two families still lived in the last remaining two that stood in Moira Street. A childhood friend of mine once lived in this street. She was one of six children — four boys and two girls — and they all shared a bedroom. As the oldest boy got older, he was relegated (or promoted) to the sofa. The only way to get into the children's bedroom was through the parents' bedroom. The lack of privacy was stark. There was no nook or cranny to escape to in the search for some peace and quiet, as every space was taken. Despite their small size, however, there was always room for one more, and people were always welcomed, and the houses spotless and cosy. Our house on the Mountpottinger Road, by contrast, boasted three bedrooms (four when the attic was converted), an inside bathroom, two living rooms and a front garden. Not luxurious by any stretch of the imagination, it did provide basic facilities denied to many other residents of the small working-class area.

Many people recall the old street with nostalgic romanticism, lamenting the loss of character with the demolition of the old streets and breakdown in community spirit. Some of the old Strand streets survived the redevelopment that began in the 1980s. These included Mountpottinger Road where we grew up, Madrid Street and Harper Street. Unlike the tiny 'kitchen' houses, the houses on these streets could be refurbished and modernised for contemporary living.

As children we were unconcerned with adult worries and sought only the pleasures of life that the Strand had to offer; because of the Troubles, we were confined to the area and such pleasures were few. Although children made up a significant proportion of the Strand's population, there were very few facilities for the young. Derelict houses and run-down playgrounds was all the area had to offer its youthful residents. The dilapidated and dangerous state of the houses did not act as a deterrent and very few adults thought of pointing out the dangers. Health and safety was not a concern and, unlike today, the fear of a lawsuit was non-existent, and so children jumped carefree from one unstable window ledge to another. We climbed walls on the verge of collapse and scaled roofs with skeleton rafters. It was great!

The older teenagers roamed these houses for less recreational purposes, mainly stripping them of any lead or copper that could be sold to scrap merchants for a few pounds. Children played street games for hours on end, stopping only for dinner and then bedtime. Football, handball and other noisy games were played by local youths. The gable walls of houses were used to play ball games and the roads for football, skipping, rounders and many more. The poverty prevalent in the area gave the children a freedom that dwindled as the area prospered. Nowadays children are constantly moved on with the rise in property ownership. People have become less and less tolerant of children playing in the street, fearful of the expense of a broken window or damaged car. It is ironic that my generation had more freedom than my children: we enjoyed the freedom of the streets. The other freedoms denied to us would become apparent to us only with time and experience.

I remember the 'Short Strand pleggie' capturing the imagination of the young in the area for a time; it was rumoured that people carried out Black Magic there. The 'pleggie' was situated on the edge of the River Lagan. I cannot recall its ever having been a playground, and the debris left from its previous occupants didn't suggest that it ever had been a playground, but it was referred to as the 'pleggie'. Tales of animal slaughter on an altar (a slab of concrete) and of men and women dressed in black cloaks chanting satanic verses spread throughout the area and titillated our gory childish imaginations. The 'pleggie' was a place to be feared and we dared each other to go there alone when darkness fell. Very few took up the challenge. The older children ignored such tales and used it as a drinking den, as they did Blair's yard, a disused industrial site whose huge chimney towered over the Strand until its demolition in the 1980s.

Other industries and factories hinted at the Strand's place in the industrial history of Belfast, as well as the sectarianism. The Sirocco Works on the Mountpottinger Road employed mainly Protestant men who walked to and from work through the Strand. The retaliatory shooting by the IRA of a security man at the Sirocco in 1979 put an end to Protestants walking to and from the factory, now that they had been marked by the IRA as 'legitimate' targets. Other industries included a stitch factory in Beechfield Street and a factory in Seaforde Street, from which a stink would exude, equalled only by the stench of the River Lagan in the summer. As children, we believed that the smell was the glue made from the horses that were brought to the factory to be melted down, or so we were told. We readily accepted the colourful 'melted horse' story.

Another disused site that provided us with hours of entertainment was the old tram depot behind the Mountpottinger Road. The grit for the roads was stored here also and we used to swing from a length of black rubber, landing on the huge pile of grit. Playing in the 'salts' (so named because of the taste of the grit) was a popular pastime, as was roaming the eerie interior of the old Picturedrome on the Mountpottinger Road. All ruined remnants of a Strand that had seen better days, before the Troubles. The other building that comes to mind is the Salvation Army church, similar in stature, with blue railings, again situated on the Mountpottinger Road on the corner of Carlton Street. I cannot recall the building being used when I was a child but its presence pointed to a more diverse and dynamic period. We haunted these old buildings and streets that, in turn, provided hours of fun.

The sight of carefree children running the streets of the Strand, however, told only one side of the story. For many, this carefree façade masked the reality of another conflict that was being waged behind closed doors in many homes. The Strand shared a drinking culture with many other working-class areas of Belfast, and at one time the area boasted nine drinking houses. Adults had plenty of choice when they decided to indulge in the most popular of adult pastimes; roughly one in three streets had a drinking house on it. The Brit, Rosebud, St Matthew's, C.E.S.A., Pensioners, Kelly's, Lavery's and Sean Martin's are just some that I can recall. Many men spent their wages in these bars, my father included. Tragically these establishments were also prime targets for sectarian attacks and, in 1975 and 1976, the Strand Bar and Bridge Bar were bombed, claiming the lives of eight people and injuring many more, some seriously.

Of course, bingo, darts and other so-called sporting facilities provided an additional activity to the main one in the bars, namely drinking. And the clubs and bars also attracted young adults eager to taste the supposed delights of the adult world. For many years, the Sunday-night disco in St Matthew's was the highlight of the week for young people. It was here that courtships were played out and the next generation was introduced into the adult pastimes of drinking and clubbing. The St Matthew's disco was for the over 18s, whilst the younger teenagers attended the Thursday-night disco in the McArt centre, a newly built centre in Beechfield Street. It was the closest thing the Strand ever got to a youth centre.

As a young teenager, I attended the disco on a Thursday night and danced away to Bad Manners, The Kinks, Duran Duran and many others. We watched as the boys, dressed in their respective fashion, Mods or Skinheads, eyed each other up and competed for the girls' attention. Together there were probably only about twenty Skinheads and Mods, but their allegiance to a culture outside of the Strand connected us to the outside world and generated an excitement and curiosity that was in stark contrast to the mundane routine of life in the Strand. Their different tastes in music and dress brought colour to the uniformity of every other aspect of life in the Strand. The devotion to a culture, whether of Mods, Skinheads, Punks or other expressions of youth, underlined a desire for normality; the bombs, sectarianism and downright repression of the conflict did not infiltrate the world of Haircut 100, Madness and the other bands and interests of teenagers.

The centre lost its funding not long after its establishment. The rumours about the reasons for this varied. One version was that funds had been misappropriated, another that the cultural activities such as classes in the Irish language upset the authorities, and another that guns had been found on the premises and the IRA's use of the place had caused its downfall. Whatever the truth, it was a shame that such a centre was closed as it provided much-needed respite and fun for teenagers like me. A community centre was built on this site in the 1990s, and it was from here that the campaign of exclusion, isolation and vilification was mounted against us after Robert's murder.

The conflict was the backdrop to our existence and daily lives. There was nothing unusual about a soldier prostrated at the bottom of the garden path, gun pointed at an unidentifiable target. We simply stepped around him and went on our way. Bomb scares were so common that, on occasion, people refused to take army advice and evacuate their homes because they suspected that it was a hoax. Some suggested that the army lied about the bomb scares to inconvenience the locals. More often than not, there was no bomb. The degree to which the violence permeated our young minds was illustrated in the childish songs we sang and how we reacted to the news of another act of mindless violence. I can remember singing a pop song that had been adapted to express our anti-RUC sentiments. It was a particularly popular adaptation and went, 'Last night I saw your momma plantin' a bomb, woke up this morning an' the barracks was gone.'

Singing about the bombing of a local police station was in keeping with our experiences. The news of murders and attacks came through daily. When the news of another shooting or attack filtered through, the first question many people asked was whether the victim was a Catholic or Protestant. There was an unnatural lack of empathy with victims from the other side; it was almost as if the victim had been complicit in their own murder because of their religion. Although few triumphed in the murder of Protestants, there was a sense of relief that it wasn't 'one of ours'. A 'let them grieve theirs and we'll grieve ours' attitude prevailed. My parents shed little light on the causes of the troubled society we lived in. 'Who are the goodies and who are the baddies?' I asked one day. I was only about eight at the time.

'Well, to us we're the goodies and to them we're the baddies,' my mother answered, which explained nothing. This is the only conversation I can recall having with my parents about the conflict. This may sound strange, but we didn't discuss the politics of Northern Ireland at home, not in any depth anyway. We commented on the events of the day but nothing else.

The barracks referred to in the song still sits on the Mountpottinger Road. It is designated for demolition but, for those of us growing up in the Strand during the Troubles, this huge green monstrosity of a building was a physical symbol of the oppression by British forces of the Strand people and our nationalist counterparts. Its high walls surrounded by steel-wire mesh, cameras, blocked-up windows and the lookout post signified the relationship between the people of the Strand and the RUC. Hostility, suspicion, fear and hatred of them were, we believed, reciprocated. The barracks was a target for the local IRA: paint bombs, coffee-jar bombs and protests. The IRA's attacks were completely ineffective against the defended fortress but it kept the IRA's profile up.

We navigated not only the sectarian map of Belfast but also the hazards of living in a republican/nationalist stronghold like the Strand, which was marked by the British as an IRA hotspot. A heavy security presence was prevalent throughout the Troubles. The barracks kept the locals under constant surveillance, and securing intelligence on IRA personnel and operations was the main focus of its interest. The presence of British Army and RUC checkpoints was a constant impediment to the freedom of movement. Because they had the power to 'stop, search and arrest' without reasonable cause, these checkpoints inspired stress and fear in the local populace. Belonging to the Strand guaranteed a stop, if not a search, or worse, an arrest. For men, the latter was common. They could be hauled off to Castlereagh holding centre on very weak grounds and held for days. The right to stop and search was justified by the British because of the IRA campaign; the residents viewed it as nothing more than an excuse to harass and torment them. The RUC, UDR and British Army were seen as merely the bigoted armed wing of the state. Stories of their enjoyment at humiliating locals were rampant and instilled an intense hatred and fear of these patrols. They were the visible and brutal representation of the oppression and injustice suffered by the nationalist people.

Tactics were adopted to avoid contact with the uniformed authorities. Avoiding eye contact was commonly practised in an attempt to deflect attention away from oneself, to avoid the unpleasantness of a 'stop and search'. An RUC man or soldier saying 'hello' or passing the time of day was also a discomfort that avoidance of eye contact staved off. It felt rude not to reply but the latter could be interpreted as evidence of collaboration, or at least acceptance of the enemy. Not a wise thing in an area like the Strand at the height of a bloody sectarian conflict. Going unnoticed was the safest option.

The checkpoints were much more than a harassment tool but were, in effect, a counter-insurgency tactic employed by the authorities to obtain information from the locals on IRA activity. Individuals were often arrested on flimsy grounds and taken to the notorious Castlereagh Barracks where torture was used to extract information and confessions. Anyone stopped by the RUC or army faced the prospect of such a fate and so it was customary for passers-by to stand a little way off and wait until they were released. Bearing witness to the behaviour of the officers was important and, if an arrest were made, the family would immediately be informed by the witness, as most probably would be the local Sinn Féin centre.

Of course, if you were arrested, the ordeal did not end with release. The tiniest piece of information was important to the security forces and so the IRA had also something to fear from the locals being arrested. After the ordeal of being arrested, a further debriefing session took place, this time headed by the IRA. It was completely voluntary of course; just doing your bit for the cause and the community was how it was perceived and justified. The detainee had nothing to fear as long as they didn't tell the security forces anything but told the IRA everything. '£10 touts' were a constant headache for the IRA and at one time there were so many of them that an amnesty was called. Those who had been acting as 'touts' for small sums of money were offered an amnesty by the IRA in exchange for admitting their guilt and debriefing the IRA on their activities. I don't know how word of the amnesty got around but some of those who were named at the time as having come forward are still alive and well today and are still living in the Strand, so it would appear that the IRA kept its word.

For those who were caught 'touting', the fate was less merciful. No sympathy was accorded to those the IRA branded as 'touts'. A bullet in the back of the head and having your body dumped somewhere was considered a just punishment. The claim that the IRA acted in the interests of the community went unchallenged. The families of those branded 'touts' were shunned, humiliated and isolated on the word of an invisible organisation. So much trust did the community put in the claims of the IRA that many accepted its explanations and wafer-thin evidence. The British were the enemy and whatever the IRA did was done in the name of the 'cause'. The IRA was part of the community — the sons and daughters of the community — and, for many, the protectors of it. If the IRA killed anyone within the community, it was because that person had endangered the community. Simple logic dictated complicity in the IRA's right to punish or even kill people of its choice. Punishment beatings were common; kneecapping was the usual punishment of choice. Depending on the crime or, more accurately, the personality of the perpetrator, it could be a flesh wound or could leave the victim with no kneecaps.

On many occasions, the condemned man went voluntarily to receive his punishment. An IRA representative would call to the house and inform him of the arranged time and place. It was made clear to him that if he didn't turn up, the punishment would be a lot more severe. A refusal to take the punishment could mean having to go on the run. I rarely heard anyone express disgust at the IRA's actions, and no one spoke of the total hypocrisy and irony of the practice of 'summary justice'. Men were shot for being informers or drug dealers on the word of the IRA. Bestowed with a power that went unchecked and which it abused on many occasions, it was able to silence its critics easily, if not by the community's acquiescence in its actions, then by fear.

The murder of 'informers' could, to a degree, be seen as part of the IRA's war operation, but the organisation took on other issues that had more of a moral basis to them, and dealt with them in a completely immoral fashion. Yet still no one challenged them. The IRA sought to control areas like the Strand by taking responsibility for all aspects of life in it. By attempting to combat a wide range of societal issues — domestic violence, child abuse, drug dealing and taking, petty crime and any other misdemeanour — they created moral mayhem and caused suffering to many people. Such realities were at best unknown to the majority of the community, or at worst ignored. A much bigger war was being fought during the Troubles.

What is now one of the most uncomfortable aspects of looking back at life in a community ruled by the IRA is how easily we accepted the IRA's excuses and reasons for injuring and putting people to death. No evidence of guilt was required; word would quickly spread that the victim was an 'informer' 'drug dealer' or some other criminal type, a danger to society. When the news of a punishment beating leaked out, people would ask what the victim had been accused of and the answer was quickly given. 'Well then, deserved it, the wee bastard,' was a common retort. The guilt of the perpetrators was assumed because the IRA had said so. Silence enveloped the incident very quickly and there was very little talk about the punishment or, indeed, murder. So accepted was the judicial role of the IRA that the threat, 'I'll get the boys for ya', tumbled from the tongues of little old ladies shooing children away from their doors. When Gerard was eight, he was caught throwing eggs at the school windows, and a nun told my mother that if it happened again, 'the boys' would be 'dealing with it'. Part of this was pure laziness of course: direct and immediate retribution was at times much preferred to the more laborious and tedious process of proper redress and justice, and there was always satisfaction of the natural desire for vengeance. But underlying this was a belief that the IRA was looking after all our interests by removing or punishing people. Acceptance by the community of such excuses was an indication of either how much they trusted the IRA or how much they distrusted the state; it is difficult to say which.

Such considerations, however, did not vex the minds of the people surviving in the Strand. Back then, the IRA played little noticeable part in the day-to-day lives of most members of the community, apart from those families from whom the volunteers were recruited. There was no shame in belonging to an organisation that used brutal violence to achieve its aims; on the contrary, they were considered heroes, and we were constantly reminded of the sacrifices they made in serving the community and Ireland. The Hunger Strikes and the death of ten young men cemented its reputation as a serving, rather than self-serving, body. The lure of adulation and hero-worship drew many young men to join up, many who in the real world couldn't achieve the status accorded to IRA volunteers. Doing time for the movement bestowed on a family an enhanced status similar, but not comparable, to that acquired by families whose son became a priest. The family was considered just a notch above the rest, self-sacrificing and serving a higher cause.

Of course, the character of some undermined this status. There was an element within the membership who used the organisation to bully and threaten others. Unable to survive and thrive on their own merit, they would openly flaunt their connections to achieve their own ends, regardless of how petty. Members of the IRA also used the organisation to settle personal vendettas, a gross abuse of their position that went largely ignored by the leadership. And if a revenge attack went seriously wrong, the victim's name would be blackened to appease the conscience of the community.

It is impossible to tell how many young men and women from the Strand joined the IRA. My only contribution to the struggle consisted in delivering the *Republican News* along with a friend, but I was never interested enough to read it. As far as I know, none of my close friends joined up and neither did my siblings. Robert and Gerard were not interested in politics at all. Everyone knew that the IRA was in the district and, as discussed above, most people sympathised, if not supported it. Given the backdrop of the Troubles, people could more easily identify with those who were claiming to defend their rights rather than those who were stamping all over them. Bombings, shootings and torture were the daily diet of the people of Northern Ireland for over twenty years, and the Short Strand had had its share of tragedy. Those in the frontline of any conflict are the least able or likely to view things in a broad context. The truth is what they see and experience every day on the streets.

Unlike our parents, we had no experience of living in a relatively peaceful and normal society and unfortunately the prospect of doing so was unlikely, and rarely voiced. For my generation, bombs, murders, intense sectarianism and riots formed our world, alongside music, boys, fashion and homework. We had known nothing else. And then the ceasefire was called in 1994, and by 1998 it seemed that we had been the lucky ones: we had survived the Troubles.

By the time of the first IRA ceasefire in 1994, the redevelopment of the Short Strand was near completion and modern housing estates had replaced most of the old streets. The identity of the old Strand was hinted at in the street and court names: Perry Court, Seaforde Court. The row of houses on the Mountpottinger Road where we had been brought up still remains in its original form. My mother and father bought number 92 Mountpottinger Road in 1963 after their marriage and it was here that they raised their seven children: Gemma, Paula, Donna, Catherine, Robert, Gerard and Claire. The first four girls came in quick succession, no more than eighteen months between each one. Robert arrived three years after me, and Gerard a year after him. By the age of thirty-one, my mother had six children, and at the age of thirty-seven, she gave birth to the last family addition, Claire. We were an average-sized family — some families boasted sixteen children or more.

My father's family roots in the Strand can be traced back over 100 years. My grandfather was a small businessman who owned a rag store that operated from Seaforde Street. He and my grandmother had seven children; one, Rosaline, they lost at the tender age of five. She was knocked down and killed by a tram as she crossed the road, ironically at a zebra crossing, while she and an older cousin were on their way to Murray's shop on the Mountpottinger Road, to buy sweets. Her penny dropped and rolled from her hand on to the road, and just as quickly she ran after it. The oncoming tram had no time to stop. The news was quickly carried to my grandfather, who was lying down at the time. He jumped the stairs in one leap and rushed to the scene, followed by my father, who was only ten at the time. The image of his sister's lifeless body has never left him, and he stills find it difficult to talk about that day. By all accounts, Rosaline, or 'Lean' as she was affectionately called, was a lively character and regularly entertained the family with her rendition of 'Annie get your gun'. Her loss was deeply felt by the family.

My father left school at the age of fourteen and embarked on an upholstery and carpet-fitting apprenticeship. His main occupation was carpet-fitting but I remember from time to time my mother sewing material for suites he was covering. Although his wages as a carpet-fitter sustained the family, they left little room for luxuries, and my mother did a variety of jobs over the years to bring in extra money.

My mother had also left school at fourteen, despite having won a scholarship to Rathmore Grammar School that could have offered the opportunity to follow a profession. Instead she chose to go to secretarial school from where she went on to work in McKinney's grocery in the Markets. At the age of eighteen, she met my father whom she married two years later. Within six short years, she had four children and her path as wife and mother was set. She worked outside the home also, and as a child I accompanied her to one of her many cleaning jobs in the evening. I can still recall the stink of the animal-feed factory where she cleaned the offices. Robert was to work in a place like this one day. Cleaning offices paid a pittance but fitted around the family.

As the years went on and we became more independent and less demanding of my mother, her innate potential and dormant ambitions began to surface, and she embarked on various business ventures to improve her family's standard of life. The most embarrassing was the transformation of our front room into a shop. For a teenager, the embarrassment was unbearable and I passed through it trying to pretend it didn't exist. It was done on a whim: years before, the wall between the front room and back parlour had been knocked down to create one spacious living room; now the wall was rebuilt and we were relegated to the small back parlour. When the front room was fitted out as a shop, I couldn't believe it: a shop in the living room practically overnight! Of course the younger ones were delighted with the constant supply of sweets. Paula didn't mind it either and served in it from time to time. But Donna, Gemma and I were less than impressed. Gemma recalls standing outside the door one evening with her new boyfriend (current husband), when a man came walking up the street and shouted to her, 'Is the wee shop open?' Mortified, she shouted back, 'Wee shop? I don't know if the shop is open. Away down an' see,' and pointed down the Mountpottinger Road in the direction of the other shops. The man looked at her confused but, noticing that the lights were out in the house, he walked on. She couldn't hide the truth forever, however. To my immense relief but mother's consternation, the shop had to close because of the objections of other businesses in the area.

Our house was noisy, as one would expect with seven children. As we got older, it got noisier, with music coming out of every room, together with the sound of laughter or arguments. We had very little compared to today's teenagers but we didn't notice. The back attic of 92 Mountpottinger Road buzzed with the excitement and anticipation of three teenage girls getting ready to walk the streets of the Strand, in the not-forlorn hope of spotting the current fancy. The anticipation and excitement multiplied threefold on a disco night. In spite of the area's small size, it was still possible to miss a sighting of the boy you fancied in the Strand, but his presence at the disco could be virtually guaranteed. After all, what else would he be doing? The disco allowed a girl the opportunity at least to gaze longingly at the boy of her dreams, even to be in his company or, the ultimate, to get noticed by him and asked out. It could provide days of conversation and imaginings. In the front attic, Robert and Gerard engaged in less sophisticated activities. Boxing, Atari and absconding via skylights kept them entertained. Gemma, the oldest, shared a room with Claire, the baby. Like the rest of us, she shared in the trials and tribulations of teenage life but she was also to be the cause of many of ours.

Our favourite night of the week was Friday. Not only were chips on the menu, but programmes such as *Monkey* were also served up. It was a particular favourite of Robert's and mine and the music and fight scenes more than made up for the muddled storyline. Our television viewing was limited to after school and Saturday mornings. Most of the rest of the time, viewing was dictated by my mother and father, and the theme music signalling the news would drive us children out on to the street or upstairs, as did the theme tunes of *Coronation Street* or *Emmerdale*, both of which warned of boring adult material.

As a family, we rarely sat down together even at meal times and we were certainly not a family who discussed events in our own lives or in the world outside. General chitchat and petty squabbles were the order of the day — nothing more taxing than the daily grind or eventualities that the coming evening might bring. The outside conflict was certainly never discussed in front of us children, if at all. As with most things, we took our instruction on this matter from the streets. My parents instilled discipline but were not necessarily strict; bad behaviour was always punished and my father was a stickler for coming in on time. But apart from this, rules were not rigid. The most depressing and negative influence in our lives was our father's drinking, but we just had to live with and around that.

We went to St Anthony's Primary School on the mainly Protestant Woodstock Road. We would walk the daily journey, only occasionally getting a welcome lift. St Anthony's location spoke of more tolerant days when the two communities lived side by side in relative harmony. By the time I was in Year 7, though, the ravages of the Troubles had taken their toll on the school, and the sectarian division that had intensified was depicted in the roll call of one pupil in Year 5. Catholics had moved out of the area and were fearful of sending their children to a school in a predominantly Protestant area. The school recovered temporarily during the late 1980s and 1990s, mostly with an influx of children from the Strand and the amalgamation with the boys' school across the road, also called St Anthony's. But inevitably the small numbers caused its doors to close in 2001.

Robert and Gerard attended St Anthony's Boys' School and Claire attended St Anthony's when it was mixed. She shared a classroom with people who one day would play a part in murdering her brother. Even at the height of the Troubles, we made the daily trek up to St Anthony's and, despite having to walk through a Protestant area at a time when murders, bombs and shootings were a daily occurrence and when sectarianism was at its height, we walked hassle-free. On one occasion, I did get my hair pulled by two boys whilst waiting outside a shop, but Donna and her friends admirably chased them down the street. I suffered no injuries apart from hurt pride and a dent in the violin case I was carrying, which had fallen to the ground in the struggle.

Overall, school life was uneventful and at the end of primary school, I followed the three oldest to St Monica's Secondary School on the Ravenhill Road. Robert and Gerard went to St Augustine's, the boys' school also on the Ravenhill Road. Both these schools attracted the bulk of their pupils from the Strand, Markets and Ormeau Road. Claire, the youngest, was the only family member to attend Grammar School. She went to Fortwilliam in the north of the city.

My parents took a passing interest in our education, and my mother made sure we attended school every day. But there was no question of keeping a close eye on educational progress and development; we were left mainly to our own devices. St Monica's didn't exactly instil in its pupils a desire to achieve, either. Domesticity was regarded as the fate of most of the girls at the school and on prize nights past pupils who had become hairdressers or secretaries were paraded on stage as examples of what St Monica's could turn out. The professions were not for St Monica's girls and going to university was not even an option. Nevertheless, time at St Monica's was pressure- and hassle-free and I left at the age of sixteen with five O levels under my belt, which wasn't bad given the lack of study and interest.

Having left school, I went on to complete my A levels at college, and then on to Queen's University where I graduated in 1991 in Politics/ Ancient History. Gemma had gone down the same path a few years previously, studying History at Queen's and graduating three years before me. Paula and Donna chose to go into full-time work after leaving school at sixteen. Paula flirted with study on and off for a few years but didn't return seriously until her mid-thirties. Robert and Gerard left school as soon as they could and began work. Claire continued at school and went on to university where she studied English.

All of us chose our respective career, work or domestic path relatively unconsciously. Gemma would probably take issue with this, however, as she maintains that from an early age she was determined to succeed at something. Displaying tendencies typical of most eldest sisters, she was more house-proud than my mother, and it was she who nagged us about the untidiness of the house. She would also complain about how much food we ate and for years dictated that everyone was allowed no more than two slices of bread at tea-time!

During her teenage years, Gemma was a punk, much to the consternation of Paula whose Sunday-night disco was on more than one occasion ruined by Gemma turning up in some outlandish outfit. One time, the black-bag dress and used-teabag earrings worn by Gemma proved too much for Paula. In stark contrast to the fashion sense of Paula and the other patrons of the disco, the sight of Gemma brought tears to Paula's eyes. We younger children couldn't have cared less about Gemma's dress sense, just as long as she didn't use our stuff to enhance her outfits! Donna's school blazer was once subjected to a night in the rain, Gemma having stashed it under the hedge after a night out, to avoid detection, but not having banked on the weather. A soggy woollen blazer that never regained its original shape or size was the only cost of Gemma's rebellious punk days. Aside from the bossy side of her nature, my eldest sister could also keep us entertained for hours, story-telling and playing games. Her childish sense of humour and inclination for practical jokes acted as a balance to the less agreeable side of her nature.

Far from getting uptight about the untidiness of the house, Paula was more often than not being chastised for not being in it. Her fun-seeking and sociable nature directed her to spend most of her time with friends and, according to my mother and Gemma, she spent most of her life sitting on the Murphys' windowsill in Thompson Street — an accusation hotly disputed by Paula to this day. She started smoking at the age of thirteen, the only rebellious act undertaken by her as a teenager. An easy-going and laid-back person, she rarely worries about what tomorrow will bring, concentrating more on getting there. Paula followed in the footsteps of our mother by marrying at the young age of twenty. She spent most of her twenties and thirties raising her family, and returned to college in her late thirties with the hope of gaining a degree.

The impact of Donna's hot temper is softened by her good nature and generosity. Donna left school at sixteen, and went to work full time in Dunnes Stores. We were constantly reminded of her weekly contribution to the household income; unlike the rest of us, she was the only one earning a full wage. She was also the only one with disposable income, and she spent it mainly on clothes. As she was the most fashionable of the four older sisters, her clothes were always in demand when we were teenagers, and Gemma had a dangerous habit of taking without asking. This usually ended up in very heated arguments or fisticuffs when caught out.

Arguments and fights were commonplace at home. Gemma and Donna were usually the two main combatants, as Paula and I always avoided confrontation if possible. This wasn't always possible, however, and, apart from Donna and myself, all of us had a go at each other at some point. I was the shyest of the four oldest girls and had a quiet nature like Paula, but a more serious disposition. Donna and I shared the back attic and, in an act of compassion, permitted Paula to join us. By rights, she should have shared the back room with Gemma but, understanding that this would have been an unpleasant fate, we agreed that she could share our small attic room! She took up residence under the sloped roof and, apart from a few disagreements, we all got on well. Donna nagged Paula and me about smoking in the room and more often than not we were relegated to the landing. It was in this room that we shared the joys and pains of growing up. Although the youngest of the four, I shared in the chitchat about boys, clothes and friends. Study and school were talked of only for their social value, and the Troubles were not discussed at all.

The age gap between Claire and the rest of us girls was such that she lived in a different era from us. Unlike us, she had no one to share her experiences with at home and it wasn't until she reached her twenties that she joined the rest of us as an equal. Claire's laid-back personality and warm nature contrast sharply with her experience of life. As has been the case for all of us, life has dealt her a hard blow but, unlike us, events in her personal life have compounded the harshness and cruelty of that blow. As a child, Claire grew up with the protective cover of her two big brothers, both now gone.

Robert and Gerard shared the front attic. They grew up in a house full of older sisters who were very protective of them, even though they were more than able to look after themselves. Robert was the first boy born after four daughters. His mop of copper hair (although he always denied he had copper hair, arguing that it was brown!) marked him out from the crowd and, as was to be expected, he got away with very little. 'Hey you, the one with the ginger hair' or 'It was the one with the ginger hair' the identifying cries. He was very quiet natured and, although not talkative, he was mischievous, a leader and popular.

The earliest indication of his mischievous nature was when, at the age of six, he phoned the police and told them that there was a bomb in Comber Street. My mother was mortified when the police arrived at the door to investigate. Robert denied everything, claiming that Claire, who was aged three months, had made the call. Eventually the truth was extracted from him and he got off with a 'talking to' by the policeman, and that was the end of the matter. For Robert anyway. My mother still recalls how embarrassed she was. She was unwell that day, and had been lying on the sofa when the police called. Still undressed at midday and with Robert and Gerard off school, she cursed Robert's mischievousness for making her look neglectful. Every time she recalls this story, she adds, 'God knows what that policeman thought of me.' Fortunately the police refrained from evacuating Comber Street that day, something for which the residents would have been thankful if they had known. I doubt they would have laughed, as we did, at Robert's mischief.

Apart from climbing walls and the usual boy stuff, there was only one more occasion when Robert brought trouble to the door. At the age of ten, he and a few friends smashed the windscreens of four cars. As usual, he was immediately identified and the matter brought to the attention of my mother who was once again mortified. She offered to pay for the damage as well as punishing Robert for the deed. It was initially assumed that the windows had been broken because of stone-throwing, but my mother became suspicious at the number of windows broken. She asked Robert if he had done it deliberately. He unreservedly answered, 'Yes'. My mother was stunned. When she asked him why, he said that the car was 'an old banger'. My mother was furious with this reply and proceeded to lecture him severely on respect for others' property. The 'old banger', as he described it, cost him and Gerard six months' detention at home. We all felt that the punishment meted out to Gerard was unfair, as he hadn't been involved, but my mother always seemed to take them as one. Regardless of our petitions on behalf of Gerard, they both had to do the six months. My mother, on the other hand, had to pay the bill, and she recalls bitterly the underhandedness of the wronged party. Having been informed that they had got the windscreen fixed at the cost of £30, she handed over the money, only to discover a week or so later that the cost of the windscreen had, in fact, been £20. My mother was deeply insulted at this underhandedness and went round to ask the people why they had lied about the price. They replied nonchalantly that the extra £10 was for the inconvenience!

As a younger brother, Robert was a typical pest but amusing with it. He was very witty and was renowned for delivering 'one-liners' which could often embarrass the recipient. He wasn't malicious or vindictive but liked to amuse his peers and colleagues, sometimes at the expense of others. For a few weeks when he was about fourteen, he went through a phase of talking backwards just to irritate the rest of us. We tried to combat this by joining in but didn't have the patience for it. He loved action movies and, from a child, idolised action heroes from Steve Austin to Arnold Schwarzenegger.

Robert grew into a very strong and independent person and was in steady work from the day he left school. He had no interest in politics and his ambition was to be 'the richest and the strongest man' in the world, so he joked. He wouldn't be rich, though, if his generosity had anything to do with it. He would give money to anyone who asked for it and rarely pushed for it to be paid back. He didn't scrimp and save, and spent his money as quickly as he earned it. In his youth and early adulthood, most of his time was taken up with work, training and socialising. He was an uncomplicated character, didn't vex himself over the issues of the day and worked to live. By the age of thirty, he still hadn't settled down and we were beginning to wonder if he ever would, when he met Bridgeen and his life became more focused and purposeful. The proudest days of Robert's life were the births of his two sons. He and Bridgeen moved into 92 Mountpottinger Road and together they planned a future that included marriage, a new home and the fulfilment of other dreams and desires.

Gerard's innocence in regard to the window-smashing incident was unusual. When he and Robert were children, they did most things together, shared the same interests and friends. As teenagers, their lives took separate paths, yet they always looked out for each other. Gerard was the rebel of the family and was to have a troubled life. Unable to settle down in a job, he drifted from one to another. He held a variety of menial jobs but, by the age of twenty-three, he was suffering from chronic depression which saw him withdraw more and more from daily life and people, including us. It was ironic to us that Gerard should be the one to suffer from depression as we had always thought of him as a 'free spirit', doing what he wanted and not bogged down with worries like work and bills. As a young teenager, his activities drove us to distraction, and for a couple of years hunting Gerard down was a common pastime of ours. The oldest three, in particular, were very concerned about his drinking and the trouble he was getting into and would search the Strand and further afield for him. 'Gerard, there's your sisters!' was a common cry amongst his friends and, seeing the approach of two or three stern-faced sisters in hot pursuit of Gerard, his friends would flee as fast as him. On the occasions when his sisters managed to catch up with him, they would march him home, lecturing him all the way. He didn't listen and would be at the same thing again as soon as he was free.

Although mischievous, Gerard was a good-natured and sensitive person; he loved a laugh and his smile lit up his face. His catchphrase was

'Lend iz a fiver', and we used to marvel at how a 'fiver' took Gerard out for the night: it got him a 'barrack buster' (a three-litre bottle of cider, nicknamed 'barrack buster' because of its size) and ten Regal. Robbing Peter to pay Paul was also his speciality. At times, nobody could work out who owed whom because of Gerard's money handling and borrowing. He was a popular character in the Strand and, like Robert, stood up for himself. He was also fervently loyal to his friends and family.

As our lives filled up with children and work commitments, we were less aware of what was happening in Gerard's life and didn't see the gradual breakdown in his mental health. Having had no experience or knowledge of mental health problems, we were totally unaware of the symptoms. His breakdown came as a shock but what it meant still didn't sink in with us. He was only twenty-three and so we expected him to recover from the episode quickly with the help of drugs. However, for the next five years his mental state deteriorated and he was in and out of Knockbracken Health Centre, a place he detested. He was prescribed tablets but they were of little use to him. We were of little use to him either.

For the last couple of years, Gerard stayed in his room. This young man who had been so full of life had become distant and cut off from the world, with no interest in anyone or anything, even his family. Paula recalls how, when Robert brought Conlaed home, Gerard merely looked at him uninterestedly. She knew then that Gerard was very ill, as Gerard loved children and would have been delighted with Robert's two. The lack of interest was his illness, not Gerard.

Gerard was conscious of his illness and the life it had stolen from him. On 27 December 2000, he left 92 Mountpottinger Road at around two o'clock in the morning. He walked the short journey from the Strand and over the Queen's Bridge. Then he calmly jumped over some railings and walked down the stone steps into the River Lagan, where he drowned.

We had been naively hoping that he would get better with time, and his suicide came as a complete shock. His death devastated our family; we blamed ourselves for not being aware of the danger signs and for not doing enough to help him through his illness.

Our roots in the Strand run deep, and more so now than ever. It is the names of the streets and people of the Strand we recite when recalling memories of childhood and adulthood. Now these memories are recalled with a sense of sadness, though, as names of past friends no longer hold the same sense of nostalgia or warmth. Some names cause anger and hurt, whilst others are avoided. Our memories and experiences of the Strand have become distorted and blurred by Robert's murder. For us, the place is contaminated with the blood of our brother and the treachery of many friends. But this alone is enough to guarantee that we will always be connected to the Strand.

On 30 January 2005, Robert kissed Conlaed and Brandon, said goodbye to Bridgeen and left '92' for what should have been a typical Sunday get-together with friends. He walked down Mountpottinger Road, passing the houses of friends and neighbours, as he had done since a child. One family friend recalls seeing him pass her window and saying aloud to no one in particular, 'There's Robert away past.' It was her way of saying 'hello' to him even though he couldn't hear or see her. This was the last time she was to see him alive. It was the last time he was to walk along the street where he had lived his whole life. He walked over the Albert Bridge and into Magennis's bar, joining many people from the community he had just left. He was greeted by many as a friend and joined a table where he was welcomed as one. He sat with men and women from the Strand that day, shared a joke and a drink with them. He was a man amongst his own people and should have been in one of the safest places in Belfast.

Chapter 3

THREATS AND
INTIMIDATION

Just as our campaign brought out the best traits in human nature, it also brought out the worst. For some so-called republicans, the rally we had organised was too much. The following day, the police arrived at Paula's and Bridgeen's to tell them that they had received a bomb threat. These threats greatly upset Bridgeen who feared that she and Conlaed and Brandon would become the targets of this gang's vengeance. We couldn't believe that some people would target Bridgeen and the children, vulnerable targets whose partner and father they had murdered. These were the people who had been celebrated by the IRA in West Belfast at a function for the Third Battalion of Belfast that very same week. Cowards — who followed a man up a street with weapons and stabbed and beat him to death and then terrorised his children — being hailed as great fighters for Irish freedom! The paradox was baffling.

The perverse and sick-minded rose to the surface to lambaste us also with their putrid thoughts. Letters generally addressed to the McCartney Sisters, but on some occasions addressed to one of us personally, contained obscenities and death threats, amongst other things. They arrived within the first few weeks of Robert's murder and were sent by a wide range of people. Religious zealots wrote, declaring that Robert deserved to die because he and Bridgeen were unmarried. According to the writer of that letter, the IRA had done society a favour. Others contained newspaper clippings of Robert and his children smeared with excrement. Claims that we were seeking the limelight and didn't care about Robert appeared on the internet. Other messages accused us of enjoying the media attention and using our grief as an attraction. Anonymous messengers who claimed to know us well declared that we were harlots, thieves and prostitutes and that two of us regularly serviced the soldiers at Palace Barracks. We were criticised for meeting with President Bush because we had attended anti-war demonstrations, whilst others questioned our republican credentials because they had never seen us at a republican rally or protest.

Even though such incoherent, malicious and evil comments could come only from the heads of crackpots, they did hurt a little. It was unbelievable that we had become the target of such hatred because we refused to allow murderers to walk away. These people did not mention the heinous and brutal way in which Robert had been murdered.

It wasn't only strangers who were resentful and angry at our refusal to grieve quietly and unobtrusively. Many within the Short Strand itself were resentful for reasons that didn't make sense. Visitors to Paula's home carried in the general feeling of the people from the area. Mixed with support were those angry at our demands for justice. People argued with each other in the street over the legitimacy of our campaign. One exchange of views between a man who had lost his brother to loyalists and a woman who had lost her brother to the IRA was recited to us. The man had commented to the woman, 'He wasn't the only man to be murdered. What about my brother? He never got justice.'

The woman got angry and replied, 'Your brother wasn't killed by the IRA — my brother was, but what happened to Robert McCartney was wrong.' The IRA had justified the killing of this woman's brother because of his anti-social activities.

All three men were murdered, all three families deserving of justice but they were divided over its pursuit. We shook our heads in anger and disappointment at such remarks. It was absurd to argue that Robert's murderers should walk away because so many others had in the past. We suspected, however, that such reasoning masked the true feelings of those expressing it. Support for the Provos was a more likely cause of such twisted thinking. As hurtful and exasperating as such remarks were, we tried to ignore them and refrain from confronting these people.

The cowardly actions of others, however, were much more difficult to ignore. Neighbours whom we had grown up with turned their heads, pretending not to see us in the street or standing at Robert's door. At first, we thought we were imagining such incidents. Only weeks before, these people had come into Robert's house and cried over his coffin. They had hugged us and couldn't tell us how sorry they were for Robert and us. 'How's your mummy and daddy? God love them, this will kill them,' they had sympathised. We had nodded in agreement, stuck for words in response. Now these same people would quickly divert from our path, avoid eye contact and shuffle into their homes, rather than pass the time of day with us. It was related to us that a life-long acquaintance of the family had said, 'I'm a republican', as an explanation for why she couldn't support our call for justice — because our campaign was criticising Sinn Féin and the IRA. 'Who does she think we *should* be criticising?' we asked, exasperated. It was no wonder they had been able to carry out a murder and cover it up.

Women from the area were to show their support for the IRA in a despicable way a few months later when they picketed Bridgeen's home, demanding her exile. For us, we could only lament the actions of these people. We couldn't understand how friends and neighbours could act in such a shameful and disgraceful way. Not one of them had the courage to articulate their views to us privately or publicly; they hid themselves amongst the crowd and chanted along with the voices of those who advocated impunity for murderers. Such actions and words did nothing to weaken our resolve — not once did we contemplate stopping our campaign, and the hypocrisy of these people spurred us on.

Our isolation from the community began slowly. At first, the support had been overwhelming as the vigil and rally had shown, but this changed when we returned from America. Time had moved on and the Provos still hadn't delivered the murderers. Continued protection of those involved was sending a clear message to those on the ground. Our trip to America was portrayed as a Sinn Féin-bashing exercise, and many thought that taking the issue from the shores of Ireland was a step too far or, more accurately, the Provisionals thought that this was a step too far. Our motives were questioned, as was the importance of one man's murder: did it deserve such international attention?

As far as we were concerned, the wrong questions were being asked and the wrong people being questioned. If those critical of us were genuine in their misinterpretation of our campaign, this did not excuse them for failing to ask questions of Sinn Féin and the IRA. Why did they continue to protect murderers? Although some critics were genuinely confused, others were fully aware of the truth, that the IRA had retrospectively sanctioned Robert's murder by sanctioning the cover-up. P. O'Neill's and Gerry Adams's statements proclaiming that Robert's murder was a crime related to the act, but their consistent omission of the cover-up was tactical. The truth was that many were involved in Robert's murder and the clean-up that night, and so the two could not be separated. The IRA's admission of sanctioning the cover-up would have confirmed that the organisation had degenerated into nothing more than a criminal gang, a 'green jackboot'. Instead, the Provos chose to condemn the murder as a 'crime'. This is what the IRA's grassroots would expect and it consistently drew attention away from the cover-up. This raised more pertinent questions. Unfortunately, many in the press and political circles missed the complexity of this. It was minutiae but, as the old saying goes, 'The devil is in the detail'. I now wonder if Pádraig was mocking us when he remarked when we first met with the IRA, 'Thanks for saying that we did not sanction it'.

Our task was formidable if not impossible. The decision to sanction the cover-up bound the IRA and Sinn Féin to the protection of murderers. They had done it so many times before and it had worked, as it would do in the future, but this time they were not getting such a smooth ride. This greatly upset them and some of their fervent supporters. The latter were not shy in expressing their feelings towards us and, after our trip to America, this irrational hatred reached us by letter. Bridgeen received a particularly nasty one claiming to be from a Sinn Féin and IRA supporter. He claimed that if we didn't stop doing what we were doing, he would stab Robert's children. According to the letter-writer, we were discrediting the republican movement and would pay for it. It was a chilling letter, to say the least, but obviously written by some 'nutcase', a fanatical supporter of Gerry Adams and P. O'Neill. We shrugged it off as best we could but in the back of our minds we were conscious that the 'mad' ones could be pretty dangerous. Bridgeen was particularly concerned. Brandon and Conlaed had been singled out and she could not dismiss the real possibility that this man was capable of carrying out his desires.

With such strong feelings of venom and hatred towards us, these people could attack any one of us at any time of the day or night. There was also a real sense of fear on the ground regarding our safety, and police comments that one of our children might be found in the River Lagan in six months did little to allay fears. Bridgeen walked the floors for nights on end, checking doors and windows. The previous bomb threat and hate mail had also been upsetting, but the evil intentions in this letter jumped from the page. As far as we were concerned, Sinn Féin and the IRA were responsible for these fanatics, even if they had no control over them. The Provisionals had created an environment that encouraged such thinking and their constant claims that they were the victims of Robert's murder fed into the confused state of such minds.

The Provos engaged in a more sophisticated and less direct tactic of destruction. They supported and undermined us simultaneously: publicly, we received the support of every Sinn Féin representative who was questioned on Robert's murder; but at grassroots level, we found ourselves at the receiving end of a well-oiled rumour mill and ostracism exercise. Such tactics had been used against others critical of the Sinn Féin leadership; men and women who had done their time, so to speak, for the cause had been ostracised and demonised by the main republican body, because they were viewed as dissenters or troublemakers. We now found ourselves in this category and the Sinn Féin propaganda machine went into overdrive, ensuring that our message was distorted from one of justice to one of Sinn Féin bashing.

Attempts were also made to blacken Robert's name. We were told that people from outside the area were being fed nonsense about him: they were told that he was a dissident, a drug dealer, and so on. Fortunately, within Belfast anyway, they were unable to make the mud stick, as too many people knew him and the truth, but it didn't stop them from trying. As mentioned earlier one woman told me that during her son's wake in Ardoyne, an IRA man claimed to her that Robert was a scumbag. Whispering in her ear, his arm around her shoulders, he tried to persuade her that the IRA would try to help to find out what had happened to her son. He had been beaten up and left unconscious on the road. He had subsequently been run over by a car and had died of his injuries. His mother was adamant that the IRA knew who was involved. She dismissed his persuasions and rebuked him, 'Just like yous did with Robert McCartney?' Slightly taken aback, the IRA man replied, 'Robert McCartney was a scumbag!' Fortunately this woman was not receptive to his lies and rebuffed him, telling him to take his arm off her shoulder and leave her son's wake.

In another incident, Peter Montgomery approached a German film crew in Market Street in July. A brother of Gerard, the man named by the IRA as the one who had supplied and destroyed the knife amongst other things, he demanded to know what the crew was doing. Having been told that a documentary was being made about Robert's murder, he asked angrily, 'What about his victims?'

The callousness of these people was beyond description. They did not have an ounce of shame, remorse or even compassion. Coming up against such adversity was not frightening but sickening. Rising above such perverseness was difficult at times, and eventually it drove Paula and Bridgeen from the Short Strand.

Others tried to shut us up by taking direct action. A few days before the trip to America, the police arrived at Paula's and Bridgeen's and informed them that a woman had rung through two bomb scares. After a quick search, the threat was declared a hoax but the question remained: What were we doing that was so wrong? Coming on the heels of the hate mail and threats to kill, it was unnerving for Bridgeen, but Paula shrugged it off.

Although the bomb threats and hate mail proved ineffective, our antagonists continued with the use of weightier threats to try and shut us up. After our return from America, a trip that had been very successful and effective in putting Sinn Féin under pressure, we each received a visit from the police, warning us that 'criminal elements' were threatening to take action against us. The source of the threat was obscure, yet the only criminals we had annoyed were those who had murdered Robert, and they belonged to the IRA and Sinn Féin. Were the police being deliberately ambiguous? They insisted that they couldn't confirm that the IRA was behind the threat but handed over a little red pamphlet containing security advice. 'I'd prefer a gun,' I quipped.

The likelihood that the IRA was behind this threat was slim — it simply wouldn't make sense for the organisation to threaten us — but its members were responsible and we knew which members. Either the gang members personally or people close to them were behind the threats. In all probability, they were being made by people whom we had previously regarded as friends or at least acquaintances. Too cowardly to face us, they chose to hide behind phones and pieces of paper.

Our paths were to meet, however. The anger of both sides would eventually spill over into verbal explosions and serious assaults.

In April, we thought it time to mark the spot where Robert had been murdered, to bring flowers there and to pray. We decided that a vigil would be appropriate and set about organising it. Two months previously, the Short Strand community had come out in strength and demonstrated disgust at Robert's murder. This vigil would be an opportunity to do so once again. We knew that the IRA and Sinn Féin had succeeded in muddying the waters so much that the people were now confused and frightened, but the vigil was a religious occasion, a time for reflection and prayers, not a protest or rally, although a dignified message would be sent to the IRA and Sinn Féin. We believed that calling on the people was important, even if they failed to turn out.

A few days beforehand, Paula, Donna, Claire, Gemma and Bridgeen set out to deliver leaflets, detailing the time and date of the vigil. A serious attack of sciatica had left me incapacitated and awaiting their return. The first leg of the delivery went smoothly. They returned halfway through for more leaflets, and Donna told me how she had posted a slip through Bobby Fitzsimmons's door. As she was walking up his path, she had seen him through the window, eating his dinner whilst watching TV. She went up to the window and waved the slip of paper at him and then shoved it through his letterbox. She told me that he had got flustered, shifting his plate on his knee and unsure of whether to flee or not. We may have dismissed Bobby's discomfort at the time but others didn't, as we were to learn later.

This incident was minor in comparison to what my sisters reported on their return from the second leg of the journey. Most people had received them with smiles and welcoming words, taking the leaflets and offering quiet words of support. However, as they reached the housing estate where Jock lived, they noticed that a crowd of women had gathered whose unfriendly expressions warned of danger. Unafraid and undeterred but prepared, they split up to deliver the leaflets. Most people took a leaflet and offered words of support. However, trouble was minutes away. Claire approached one woman standing at her door.

'I don't want one of those,' the woman snapped, without even looking at it or asking what it was.

'Fine,' said Claire and walked off.

Paula, meanwhile, noticing the hostile glances coming from one woman, shouted over to Gemma, 'Don't go to that door.' Gemma moved off and went to another.

Connie Davison, Jock's wife, then approached Donna, and, clutching her cardigan across her chest, she called out, 'Donna, can I have a wee word with ya?'

'What is it, Connie?' Donna asked curtly.

'Jock had nothing to with it,' Connie said in a meek voice.

'We'll see him in court, Connie,' replied Donna tersely.

Connie's mask fell away. 'Oh, you'll not see Jock in court,' she said nastily.

'We'll see,' said Donna and walked off.

The crowd of women who had been observing this exchange began to make disparaging remarks about the leaflet drop and our campaign. Tempers flared, and Gemma, leaning over a gate, shouted at one woman that her brother had been murdered. Another woman then chirped up, 'He was nothing but a bully and a child-beater!'

Paula, who had been telling the others to stay calm and not to rise to it, swung round. The source of the accusation infuriated her as much as the accusation itself. 'No,' she said firmly. 'That was your brother.' She pointed at the woman and, in a calm and measured tone, repeated, 'That was your brother and don't you forget it!' The woman's jaw snapped shut and she took a step back.

Years previously, this woman's brother had been put out of the area for allegedly abusing a child; the details of the abuse were disturbing. Now this man's sister was disgustingly trying to blacken Robert's name, accusing him and using children to do so. She voiced no more accusations once her memory was refreshed. The verbal exchange continued, all the time being filmed by one of Jock Davison's friends, while Jock himself hovered in the background.

Bridgeen had become emotional because of the things the women were saying. One of the women shouted to her, 'What are you cryin' for? He's dead; get over it!'

'Yeah, real men killed him!' another joined in.

'Go back to where you came from!' shouted someone else. 'People in this area need houses.' Bridgeen is from the Falls Road. She is not known for being easily upset but she was shocked at the cruelty of the words.

We didn't expect sympathy from these women and could take whatever filth they wanted to hurl at us, but to vilify Robert was unforgivable. We were in no doubt that the ambush had been orchestrated, that the crowd had been told to provoke us into a confrontation that would be caught on camera. However, despite immense provocation, the five had kept their nerve.

Journalists who had sources on the ground confirmed our suspicions. We were told that news of the leaflet drop had reached the Provos and a meeting had been hurriedly convened to discuss what action was to be taken. The source had told the journalist that a local Sinn Féin representative had chaired the meeting at which the master plan of catching us fighting on camera was hatched. The most frustrating thing about all of it, though, was the lack of proof. People would tell us what the Provos were up to but no one would stand over it in public. It was always 'off the record' or 'can't tell you who told me'. Although the information was useful, not being able to use it was frustrating.

The leaflet drop had been completed and, after a long day, everyone returned home, thinking that the drama was over for the day. That night, Paula and Bridgeen sat chatting about the events of the day. As Bridgeen wasn't from the area, Paula was filling her in on the history of the women who had confronted them. Through the window she noticed a woman approach and, as she looked closer, she recognised Betty Fitzsimmons, Bobby's sister. Her red face and marching demeanour warned that it wasn't a social visit. Paula rose from her seat before Betty reached the door and ordered Bridgeen to 'get ready for Betty'. Bridgeen didn't know who Betty was or what she wanted but Paula's tone indicated danger. Paula and Betty, on the other hand, knew each other well. The Fitzsimmonses had lived across the street from us for many years and we had crossed swords with them on a few occasions as children.

Betty slammed open the gate and marched up the path. Paula already had the door open, waiting for her. There was no exchange of pleasantries. Betty embarked on an onslaught of abuse, accusing Paula and the rest of us of intimidating the IRA and of harassing her brother Bobby.

'Why, what's Bobby afraid of, Betty?' Paula asked through clenched teeth.

'Our Bobby's not afraid of anything. Our Bobby didn't do anything.'

'Ay, you keep tellin' yerself that. Now, go away, Betty.' But she refused to move.

Paula left the doorway and began to shoo Betty down the path, waving her arms and repeating over and over, 'Go away, Betty; just go away, Betty.' But to no avail.

Bridgeen was looking on and asking from time to time, 'What does she want?'

Betty, her face flushed, continued on with a diatribe of accusations and Paula eventually snapped. 'Murderers,' she shouted at the top of her voice. 'Scumbags.'

'Our Bobby had nothing to do with it,' Betty screamed back, still threatening Paula and Bridgeen with exile.

Eventually Paula's repetitive shouts of 'murderers' and 'scumbags' drove Betty off, and Paula and Bridgeen went back inside, Paula shaking in anger and Bridgeen in shock.

The audacity of such people was beyond comprehension. Betty's audacity did not end here, however, because the next day the police arrived at Paula's and informed her that Betty had lodged a harassment complaint against her. The complaint was a complete farce that Paula could refute if she chose, but Betty was not a priority or even a consideration and we had no time to waste in following up on such nonsense.

Paula wasn't the only one to receive solicitors' letters warning that the police would be called in if she continued to harass certain individuals. Jock Davison and Bobby Fitzsimmons's solicitors issued Donna and Gemma with similar letters a few weeks later. Walking in Castle Street one day, Gemma and Donna had noticed Davison and Bobby walking in front of them, and Gemma had shouted, 'Hey Bobby, murder anyone today?' The two cowards had quickened their pace and, with their heads down, marched quickly on, disappearing into the solicitors' office. A few days later, the two letters arrived, warning once again that the police would be asked to prosecute if the 'harassment' happened again. 'Would that be the same police that the Provos don't co-operate with?' we asked.

The Provos' net of intimidation was flung wide and no one was exempt. When we went in search of a priest to say prayers at the vigil, we found that no one was available. The local priest excused himself, explaining that he wouldn't be there that day and couldn't rearrange his diary. We then approached another Belfast priest. Initially the response was positive but the day before the vigil, I received a phone call from him in which he apologised but said that he couldn't lead the prayers: he had been visited by residents who had advised him that there was going to be a counter-demonstration. 'You mean a counter-vigil, Father,' I responded. 'Because we are not having a demonstration.' The priest thought it best to concede to the residents' advice to stay away from the vigil. This response from the local priests was disappointing, to say the least. We suspected intimidation and, although we tried to understand the priests' fear, we couldn't forgive their lack of courage and leadership. The Catholic Church's benign attitude and failure to support us publicly was disheartening.

Paula phoned the Bishop and advised him of the situation. 'It will not look good if there is no Catholic representation at this vigil,' she advised. The Bishop agreed and a Jesuit priest was kind enough to step in and lead the prayers that day. There was no counter-demonstration.

The vigil outside Magennis's was the most difficult of all and brought home vividly the events of Sunday, 30 January. We walked the street that Robert had walked and imagined how he felt being pursued by a gang of up to fifteen men with sewer rods and other weapons. The shouting and screaming, frantic hand movements as weapons were swung in all directions and Robert pleaded for his life and then fell to his knees. And when he was on the ground, the continued kicking and beating, and stamping on his head. Was he conscious at this time? Did he know what was happening to him? For over two months, we had been so busy with press and meetings that we had been able to switch this image off, but here in Market Street we could not escape from it. The horror of the attack was tangible; I could feel the heavy presence of the terrible act in that street. I was emotionally drained on this day; I couldn't speak to anyone and I found it difficult to focus on what was happening around me. The only thoughts that swirled in my mind were of Robert's journey from the bar to the street.

Around 350 people turned out for the vigil despite the day being cold, windy and wet. Amongst them were Alex Maskey and Gerry Kelly. Sharing an umbrella, they stood motionless with stone-set faces.

Whatever their reasons for attendance, it was an insult to Robert and they should have had the integrity to stay away from such an occasion.

We returned once more to Paula's home in the Short Strand, relieved that the visit to Market Street was over. It was an upsetting day, but also an enlightening one. As we had expected, the turnout at the vigil was lower than at the rally, an indication that our support in the Short Strand had waned either out of fear or conviction, but we were surprised at the absence of friends who had given no hint of their fear or conviction.

One friend's absence was specifically noticed. For twenty-five years, a day had rarely gone by without our seeing or speaking to each other. Initially a childhood friend of mine, she had become very close to Paula and spent a lot of time with her on a daily basis. She was regarded as a family friend and we often joked that she was the sixth sister. She was privy to everything that happened in our lives — all the joys and sorrows — and when Gerard died, she had been a tower of strength and support. She was godmother to two of my children and I to her daughter. She was also godmother to Paula's daughter, and if anyone could have been relied on to fight to the death for us, we would have expected it to have been this friend. There are very few memories that we recall in which she doesn't play a part. Sadly those memories are now soiled and these days, when we speak of the past, we ignore her part in it.

All of my family, including Robert, had a high regard for this loyal and trusted friend of twenty-five years' standing. We had shared with her the trials and tribulations of teenage life, music, boys, hair and clothes. She would have been the last we would have cited as capable of turning her back on us and taking the side of Robert's murderers. She had grown up with Robert alongside me and witnessed his transition from a child to a man. And yet in her betrayal she condoned his murder; she may as well have been down Market Street kicking and beating him as the others had done. In addition to the betrayal itself, the other aspect that dumbfounded us was the reason for it: it was and remains a complete mystery to us and we can only guess at the motives behind it.

At first, her uneasiness went unnoticed. We were so busy with everything else, and the house was always packed. When it was first mentioned that she was 'acting weird', Paula's response was, 'No way! Catch yerself on!' It was like accusing one of us of acting suspiciously.

We were so busy that we didn't register her lack of lustre or energy when it came to our campaign. When she didn't turn up at the vigil, however, alarm bells rang. When she arrived in Paula's a few days later with the excuse that she had been in bed with vomiting and diarrhoea, she was unconvincing. She sat pale faced, contributing very little to the conversation but listening to everything. Her work brought her into contact with many people in the Short Strand, but now that we stopped to think about it, any time she was asked, 'Did you hear anything?' she would reply, 'No, nobody mentioned anything.' This was difficult to believe. Everyone else who came into Paula's had some titbit of information that they passed on, regardless of how trivial. Everyday greetings became an indication of where people stood on the issue, and people would tell how someone had either ignored or acknowledged them. However, this close family friend had nothing to tell — and this despite the fact that her sister was living with a top Provo. No opinions or news ever seemed to come her way. She didn't even seem to have an opinion herself. Her behaviour became more disconcerting and suspicious as the weeks went by.

One example was on the night of Robert's month's mind, held on 1 March. A month's mind is a Catholic tradition of holding a religious service to remember the death of a person one month on. A camera crew outside the chapel had been asking passers-by if they had anything to say. Most just hurried past, saying nothing, afraid of something they couldn't or wouldn't articulate. The camera approached this very close family friend, and asked if she had anything to say. Gemma recalls that her face went white with anger and she swung her arm in a defensive gesture at the camera and retorted, 'Fuck off!' At the time, Gemma noted this as an over-reaction. Although our friend was known to be shy, it wasn't shyness that Gemma detected in her retort, but anger. She couldn't understand why such rage had been expressed at the cameraman. Over the coming months, however, it would become sadly clear.

While we grew increasingly suspicious of our friend's behaviour, it took us longer to become convinced of her treachery, and she continued to visit Paula's home until eventually we could no longer ignore her deviousness and betrayal. I have struggled to make sense of her cowardliness, but to this day we still don't know why she turned her back.

The final straw for me was her attempt to claw back information about the part played by some people in the clean-up. We had been told of the involvement of one particular woman in cleaning up after the attack, and had also been told that this woman had spoken to Robert minutes before the attack. However, our close friend tried to convince Paula that the woman had not spoken with Robert at all. Still, Paula remained unsure of her treachery, and to accuse her of such on suspicion alone would have been unforgivable. The air was thick with unsaid accusations as she sat amongst us, and the conversation was strained. Eye contact became impossible, as did conversation. One day when I arrived at Paula's, she was sitting in the living room whilst Paula busied herself upstairs. I went upstairs. A few minutes later, Donna arrived, as did Claire. We sat upstairs to avoid a person who, a few months previously, I would have trusted with my life. Now she could not be trusted to listen to a conversation. She continued to visit over the next few weeks, although less frequently. I never saw her again from the day I went upstairs.

The last time Paula saw her was the day Terry Davison was charged. She was sitting in Paula's house, watching the news. Paula recalls that the conversation between them was strained, with long silences and exchanges of trivia the main content, unnatural given that a man stood in the dock charged with Robert's murder. Our friend's partner came in and, when he was asked if he had seen the news, he said that he wasn't aware that Davison was in court that day. Paula knew right away that something wasn't right. He was a close friend of Frankie Brennan, father of Paul and Dee Brennan, two suspects. He was also friendly with the Provo crowd faithful to Jock. His pretence of disinterest wasn't convincing and masked his support for Davison. As the news reported on Davison's appearance in court, Paula commented that Davison would break like a plate.

'He'll not squeal,' was the smug reply.

'How the fuck do you know what he'll do?' retorted Paula, furious at this blatant show of support for Robert's murderers.

The man left quickly. Our friend sat on for a while and then left, and that was the last time she visited Paula's home. We can only guess at the reasons for her betrayal and none of them justifies it.

Although the most hurtful, hers wasn't the only betrayal. Past and current friends had attended the wake to show their respect and sympathy, friends whom we hadn't bothered with from school and some of whom we hadn't seen in years visited Robert's home. Many of them still lived in the Short Strand and in the first few days they were open about what they had heard on the streets concerning the events in Magennis's. This information enabled us to build up a picture of the evening and we passed every detail on to the police. Those who had been in the bar stayed away. At the time, we thought nothing of this but as time went on and we found out more, we began to realise why they stayed away. The vigil held on the Friday after Robert's murder had been organised by a friend, if not a close one. We regarded her as a genuine person of integrity. For weeks she visited Paula's daily, bringing in newspapers and spreading them out to read from them aloud. She helped Paula with the daily chores and couldn't be of enough help. Then one day she passed Claire in the street.

'She's only after totally blanking me,' Claire told Paula. 'What's wrong with her?'

'I don't know,' said Paula. 'She was in here the other day; nothing was said. Maybe you've imagined it.'

A couple of days later, Claire passed her again and this time there was no mistaking the fact that the woman was ignoring her. We shrugged off her betrayal, though. She was a busybody more than a friend, and we were unconcerned at her loss.

Like most people, we knew many people in the Short Strand but had few friends. In fact, we could count on one hand those whom we had retained as friends throughout the years. Friendships spanning twenty-five years or more were put to the test and proved to be worth nothing. Another lifelong friend of Donna's was also to prove unworthy of friendship. She too had been a regular visitor to Paula's since Robert's murder and she too would say little but listen to all. In this case, however, we were familiar with the less than savoury traits of her character. Untrustworthy, two-faced and a 'Walter Mitty' was how people described her, but she would do things for people that made her useful. We did not welcome her visits and instinctively we wouldn't speak in front of her. 'What does she want?' or 'Is she here again?' were common remarks when she appeared.

Then one day Claire saw her get into a car with Paul Brennan, a suspect in Robert's murder. Claire felt instantly sick: this woman was coming around to Paula's expressing disgust and sorrow and then casually getting into cars with Robert's murderers, laughing and joking. When we were told months later that the Provos had sent women to Robert's wake and then to Paula's to gather information and report back, the reasons for her continued visits became clearer. Initially, however, we thought her behaviour was nothing more than that of a woman who didn't have the strength of character to take a stand. On hearing the news, Donna rang her up and asked her why she was sharing cars with the men who had murdered Robert. She stuttered some excuse, telling Donna that she was only getting a lift. Donna told her bluntly that she couldn't be friends with Robert's murderers and with her — she had to choose.

She arrived in Paula's house a short while later crying, a well-known trait of hers, claiming that we were spying on her and were intimidating her. Why should she be forced to take sides? she cried. Claire and Paula looked at her impassively. 'Take sides' — is that how she understood Robert's murder? They were disgusted and told her that she could do what she liked but that she couldn't expect to be welcomed by us while she cavorted with murderers.

Paula's choice of friends proved to be no better than Donna's or mine. One friend, again one of over twenty-five years' standing, used a petty disagreement between their two daughters to distance herself. What was frustrating about the behaviour of these people was the cunning and disingenuous way they distanced themselves. Not one of them had the courage to talk to us about their fears, if that was the reason for distancing themselves. Some people's motives were self-explanatory and had nothing to do with fear, but the others' actions were less clear. We had been friends with these women for over a quarter of a century. If they had genuine fears for their safety, or even ours, they should have expressed them, not exited in such a cowardly fashion. We didn't expect anyone to put their lives in danger for us, and a phone call would have been enough to show support. Instead, they betrayed us and, as Paula says, harmed our campaign by participating in our isolation from the community.

Never before had the murder of a local man fractured the community. Just as friendships were destroyed and betrayed, so too were family relationships. Sisters and brothers no longer talk. Some relationships will never heal, and close friends and family members will remain strangers. Morality became blurred and people took sides. Taking the side of murderers cannot be easily undone. Paula and Bridgeen had to live in this community, and it was worse for Bridgeen as she had to bring Conlaed and Brandon to school every day. St Matthew's is in the Short Strand and every morning she had to look at the faces of the murderers and their relatives. A picket outside Bridgeen's home in September was the last straw and Paula and Bridgeen decided to the leave the Short Strand.

The anger and frustration that many within the community felt about Robert's murder bubbled throughout the spring and summer. We had received a second threat after our return from Europe where we had secured support from the European Parliament in the form of a contribution towards a civil action. The Provisionals were furious at this, and Mary Ellis, a Derry Sinn Féin representative, asked why we couldn't raise the money ourselves just as other families had to do. Of course, it wasn't the promise of a monetary contribution that enraged Sinn Féin but the principle on which it had been promised. Twenty-five European countries had agreed that Robert's murder was a 'terrorist act', thereby justifying the release of the funds from the Victims of Terrorism funds. It was this premise that infuriated Sinn Féin who had argued that Robert's murder was a common crime, and nothing to with politics, ignoring the fact that the cover-up had been sanctioned by the IRA and therefore fell into the category of political terror. Sinn Féin's duplicity had failed to dupe either the European Parliament or the people from the Short Strand who punished them at the ballot box. Deborah Devenney, who keenly replaced Joe O'Donnell as the Sinn Féin council candidate, failed to retain the seat because of Robert's murder. This, coupled with our success at the European Parliament, prompted Sinn Féin representatives to attempt to undermine and silence us using 'words'.

Faceless Provos reverted to form and threatened to burn our homes and businesses. Once again, we ignored these threats and continued to challenge Sinn Féin loudly. Throughout May and June, we continued with our meetings and attended awards ceremonies. There was no direct intimidation of us, but an incident at the end of June raised the temperature once again. On a June night, Bridgeen's window was broken with a brick. The next day, the media had got hold of the story and contacted Paula, asking who was responsible. Paula guessed that

Bridgeen was under threat from 'republicans' and, given that the police had told her that there had been no strangers in the area at the time of the attack, she could draw only one conclusion. Deborah Devenney, the failed council candidate, claimed that it had been loyalists and that she had witness statements to prove it. There had been loyalists in the area earlier in the evening but not at the time of the window being broken. Paula was invited on to the radio to debate the issue with Deborah Devenney. I was in Spain at the time and when she rang to tell me about it, I asked, 'Why are they feeling so confident?' So far, Sinn Féin had avoided direct dialogue with us in public and had actually pulled out of radio shows that I had been invited on. Regardless of whether or not Devenney was right about the loyalist, a dialogue could lead to other places and I was surprised that Sinn Féin was taking the risk. Paula rang back within half an hour to tell me that Deborah had pulled out. Obviously she had made the decision to take part without consulting the leadership and her decision had been overruled. We were disappointed.

Despite immense provocation, we had resisted confronting any of the individuals involved in Robert's murder. We could have easily done so, as we knew who they were and where they were. Many of them lived in the Short Strand and others worked in it. Every day we were told of their comings and goings, what they were saying and who they were with. We imagined ourselves confronting them, what we would say or do, but ultimately we knew that such action would do no good. A street fight or catfight would undermine the seriousness of their crime and serve only to release our pent-up frustration for a short time. This aside, however, everyone has a breaking point, and the IRA brought us to ours. July is always a contentious month in Northern Ireland and it is usual for groups of vigilantes to patrol areas such as the Short Strand, watching out for trouble. It is also usual for the IRA to organise these watches, and its members take part. In 2005, the IRA chose as vigilantes people suspected of direct involvement in Robert's murder and, to add to this insensitivity and to our distress, they stood right outside Robert's door, in their job of protecting the area. Every evening they paraded up and down, up and down, parking cars just outside Robert's front door and brazenly standing guard with other IRA men. These same people, according to Adams and McGuinness, were acting out of self-preservation, forcing themselves on the local IRA, or so they would have had us believe, if we had been stupid enough to do so.

Tempers eventually were lost one evening after Paul Brennan — a brave man in a crowd — confronted my partner Ed. This led to the gathering of a crowd and a direct confrontation between them and us. A scuffle involving a local IRA man and my brother-in-law escalated when Paul Brennan intervened and proceeded to hit Gerard with a weapon. Pandemonium broke out, and people ran after Brennan. Women and men were shouting and one local IRA man tried to restore calm by saying, 'There's more important things to be worrying about', referring to the gathering of Protestants at the top of the street.

Paula swung around to face him. 'You don't have to worry about them,' she said. 'It's in here that they murder you.'

It was the first time that we had confronted any of those directly involved in Robert's murder and, as Paul and Dee Brennan swung from their father's coat in an attempt to fend off others, Paula shouted to them, 'Tell your father the truth.'

'They had nothing to do with it,' Frankie Brennan stammered.

'Then why did they go to Killough?' Paula shouted angrily.

'They were ordered to Killough,' he said.

Accusations and denials circled the air but as quickly as it had exploded, the incident subsided. The crowd dispersed, with bystanders shooing people away from the scene and persuading others to 'leave it alone'. Paula, followed by others, went back home. The small confrontation had ignited a volcano of anger and frustration that we could not afford to let boil over. The IRA, however, had been confronted and it was not going to suppress its anger. Within an hour of the minor altercation, a call came through informing us that Jeff Commander had been savagely attacked by a group of local IRA men. Jeff was a life-long friend of Robert's and had been present during the earlier altercation but had only watched, saying and doing nothing. His presence, however, was enough to mark him and seal his fate.

As he and his wife Sinead made their way home, Gwen Brennan — the mother of Paul and Dee — shouted to him, 'Jeff, what was that all about?' obviously referring to the earlier incident. He walked over to her and had no sooner engaged in conversation than eight men set upon him, beating him with sewer rods and fists. He gripped the railings, whilst Sinead tried to fend them off. The attack lasted only a few minutes but he took a severe beating. In the evening light and in full view of the residents, the eight unmasked men felt confident to beat Jeff with weapons. Young teenagers came to Jeff's aid and, attacking the IRA men with bricks, they chased them from the estate.

Now Jeff was left in a dilemma. Did he report the incident to the police? Did he provide statements that would lead to arrests and charges? He knew the men who had attacked him, as did other witnesses. In the past, such incidents would have gone unreported, and the IRA men presumed that this would be the case now, their confidence demonstrated by their failure to wear masks. A close friend of Robert's, Jeff believed that his fear of reporting the incident would only condone the cowardice of those witnesses afraid to come forward in Robert's murder, and so the decision was promptly made to call in the police. Although it was never suspected that the decision to call in the police would be greeted happily by the Provos, we were very soon enlightened as to the degree of influence they exercised over the whole community.

A Community Restorative Justice (CRJ) representative, who had also witnessed the attack on Jeff, visited to impart the advice that drawing media attention to the attack would not be a wise thing to do. Harry Maguire explained that the decision to go to the police was Jeff and Sinead's but said that the community would look poorly on the publicity. Jeff decided to ignore his advice and called in the papers, showing his injuries to reporters and describing the attack. The Provos, much preferring mediation, usually through groups such as the CRJ, attempted to persuade Jeff that it was the best course of action. On one occasion, two local IRA men arrived at the door suggesting that Jock Davison would mediate between them and the IRA men who had attacked him. The IRA's choice of mediator dumbfounded Jeff: the man accused of giving the order for Robert's murder was being put forward as a mediator. The IRA had also claimed that Davison had been expelled from the organisation, an insignificant point the men had overlooked.

As if mediation involving Jock Davison wasn't enough of an affront, worse was to come. With Jeff refusing mediation for a second time, the Provos decided to call upon the Catholic Church. Jeff's wife Sinead received a call from Fr Alec Reid, asking her to consider mediation. Sinead refused, explaining that her husband could have been killed and that the matter was in the hands of the police. The interference of Fr Alec Reid demonstrated the power and influence of the Provos. The unethical interference of the Catholic Church and the ability of the Provos to call upon Fr Reid shed light on the reasons why they ruled areas such as the Short Strand with an iron fist. If such powerful institutions as the church fed into the Provo ethos, what chance did we have? The Provos' access to the church was in stark contrast to our own. We had literally had to beg for a priest to lead the prayers at Robert's vigil, yet the Provos could call on a high-profile priest such as Fr Alec Reid to intervene on behalf of local IRA thugs. We were certainly up against it.

Jeff was undeterred, however, and witness statements were taken and four men were arrested and charged with the assault on him; they were Sean Clinton, Patrick Magee, Gerard Leonard and Sam Caskey. For every action, of course, there is a reaction, and once again the local Provos reacted in the only way they knew how.

THE PICKET

Returning from her mother's house one evening, Bridgeen was dressing Conlaed and Brandon for bed when she noticed a crowd of women beginning to gather on the 'green' across from her house. It was a week after the attack on Jeff, and charges had been brought. Unsure of the purpose of the gathering, she strained to hear what the women were saying, hoping that it was nothing to do with her. From the words she could pick up, however, she was left in no doubt as to the target of the crowd. The women had come to foist their depraved and ugly thoughts on two young children and their mother. Although she could not clearly hear what the spokeswoman was saying, the cheers and clapping of her followers unnerved Bridgeen and the two children. Conlaed asked his mother if the crowd had come to kill them. Bridgeen tried to reassure him, telling him that the people across the road had nothing to do with them. She closed the blinds and turned up the television, hoping to distract the children and drown out the drone of the women's voices. It did no good, however, and Bridgeen's own state of distress alarmed and frightened Conlaed who, already suffering from the trauma of losing Robert, was convinced that the women had come to kill his mother and brother. As the women jeered louder, Bridgeen rang Paula, but by the time she arrived, the crowd had dispersed.

The picketers were not the only ones in the street, however, and we were able to gauge from other local people the circumstances that had given rise to the picket. We were told that a meeting had taken place in the community centre earlier in the day at which it was decided that something had to be done about the McCartneys and their continued intimidation of the IRA. The charges against the local IRA were the last straw and so it was decided that the only way to stop people like ourselves from supposedly intimidating the IRA was for them to intimidate us on behalf of the IRA. People were designated to spread the word of the time and place of the protest. Women went from door to door, asking other women to take part in the picket; some women, disgusted at the suggestion, told them that they ought to be ashamed of themselves. This didn't deter them, however, and at the appointed time a group of women left the community centre and headed for the 'green'. Amongst them was Marie-Louise Davey who we were told had declared at the meeting, sobbing, 'I've known the McCartneys all my life but they are not going to intimidate me.' She took her place amongst the crowd and walked down the Mountpottinger Road.

Some women, uncomfortable with the picket but afraid to say so, slipped away down side streets, and so around fifty women stood across from Bridgeen's. A family friend noticed the crowd passing her home and, suspicious, followed. Realising its purpose, she stood, alone, outside Bridgeen's door, in defiance of the crowd. The crowd listened as Noreen Rooney, the spokeswoman, read out the group's demands. There were three of them, the last one so ridiculous that we refrained from repeating it to the media. The demands were firstly that the charges against Jeff's assailants be withdrawn; secondly that Bridgeen and the children leave the Short Strand; and thirdly that the McCartneys stop intimidating the IRA. The women cheered and applauded her pronouncement. Some children standing close by jeered the crowd. Noreen vowed that they would return every night at the same time until all three demands had been met, and so the crowd dispersed — very quickly once the news reached them that the media were on their way.

The actions of the women were beyond explanation or understanding, not least the fact that former friends stood amongst this crowd. Women who had once been welcomed into our home now stood outside it demanding the exile of Robert's children. These women had children of their own yet they terrorised Robert's. We couldn't believe the sheer audacity of these people. They had no right to stand outside Robert's door and demand his children's eviction. We belonged to this area as much as they did. We were absolutely amazed at their behaviour and bemused by their demands, particularly the last one — that we stop intimidating the IRA. Did they not realise how stupid they sounded? 'Pathetic' is the only word to describe them. Nevertheless, the picket could not be ignored and if these women were intent on returning the following night, we would be there to face them.

We informed the press of the picket and the intention of the women to return every evening until their demands were met. The following evening, at the set time, a crowd of up to 150 local people stood outside Robert's door, waiting for the arrival of the picketers. The media were also in attendance; even CNN, the American channel, had sent a reporter to monitor events. None of the protesters appeared, however, and we were told that Gerry Kelly had met with the ringleaders that day and told them that a similar incident was not to happen again. One woman had protested to Kelly, declaring that 'one republican' had killed Robert McCartney. Kelly told her that he wasn't interested in what she had to say, and insisted that no more pickets were to take place.

Obviously the picket had been the brainchild of the local brigade and, as usual, left to their own devices these people had made a hash of the whole thing by creating more bad press for Sinn Féin and refocusing attention on Robert's murder. This was the last thing Sinn Féin wanted. The picketers attempted to undo the damage, and the following day we received a letter from the Short Strand Women's Group, stating that the crowd had gathered in protest at anti-social behaviour and that they supported our campaign. It was a futile and unconvincing attempt to cover their tracks.

The picket had frightened Bridgeen and the children, particularly Conlaed who had nightmares after it. Although only four-and-a-half years old, Conlaed had felt Robert's loss deeply. He knew how his father had died and so, at a very young age, was aware of what adults could do. The actions of the women that night served only one purpose, and that was to further traumatise a young boy who was already suffering from the loss of his father. A feeble letter from Patricia Johnston and the Short Strand Women's Group was not going to undo that damage.

The picket was the last straw for Paula and Bridgeen. They couldn't live in the Short Strand any more, and so, in October, they left the area for good.

Chapter 4

DECISION TO GO TO AMERICA

THE IRA

Our decision to go to America put us on a collision course with the republican movement who upped the odds in the whispering campaign of vilification against us. The papers were running headlines such as 'Grieving sisters square up to IRA', 'This crisis threatens to halt the advance of Sinn Féin', 'Sinn Féin Count the Cost', 'Justice for Robert: Sister says she may take on Shinners at ballot box', 'Time To Go', 'Adams must come clean over McCartney murder', and so on. Pro Sinn Féin papers like the *Andersonstown News* took a different view of our campaign and the US trip. 'Unionism on Tour' was the headline above an article by Robin Livingstone. A battle of claim and counter-claim was being waged through the press. IRA criminality was under the spotlight and politicians queued up to condemn Robert's murder and also to demand that the IRA disband, decommission, sign up to policing, and whatever else was required to kick-start the peace process again. We were running here, there and everywhere, talking to anyone who we thought could help, whilst giving countless interviews to all of the media.

Meanwhile, Sinn Féin was spouting nonsense about witnesses coming forward to third parties such as priests, solicitors, doctors, even the lollipop man — anyone but the police. The party dismissed our claims of intimidation of witnesses and a cover-up, and argued that the people in the bar that night simply mistrusted the police. Sinn Féin would have us believe that it was because of years of brutality at the hands of the RUC and British crowned forces that Deirdre Hargey, Cora

Groogan and Sean Hayes, along with many others, could not co-operate with the police. These arguments didn't make sense but they went largely unchallenged. 'Why don't they ask them how it works legally and practically?' we would shout at the television screen. The notion that murderers, rapists and other criminals had roamed free for years, or the equally absurd notion that only the IRA dealt with such people, was ludicrous. We would scream at the television whenever another Sinn Féin representative spouted this nonsense: 'He's talking a load of bollix!' It was all political nonsense designed to deflect attention away from the truth of the matter. Sinn Féin and the IRA's stance on Robert's murder was based on nothing more than protectionism. They had closed ranks and were keeping them closed.

Unfortunately for many numbskulls in the Strand, Sinn Féin's propaganda about the police was accepted. 'I'm a republican' was given as an excuse for turning their backs. We were amazed at the stance taken by some people. Friends and neighbours whom we had thought well of for years and had considered to be people of integrity and strength couldn't distinguish between right and wrong. What had stabbing a man, cleaning up the scene, taking witnesses away blindfolded and covering up a murder got to do with being 'a republican'? Of course these people lamented Robert's death and said that they wanted his murderers caught, but oddly enough they didn't turn their backs on those very murderers! Instead, the murderers walked about the district freely, sat in the social clubs and worked in the community centre without hindrance. True republicans? As far as some people in the Strand were concerned, we should have accepted the republican mantra of non co-operation with the PSNI and kept quiet. But that was never going to happen and if we had to travel to the four corners of the world to get justice, that is what we would do.

When we had met with the IRA in February, they had claimed that they were powerless to take any action against their men because of the political consequences. Pádraig and Sean said that the IRA could only assure witnesses that they were free to come forward. Given that Brendan Devine had been taken away blindfolded three times, and other witnesses intimidated, the IRA's understanding of 'freely' was warped, to say the least. The IRA spoke about Robert's murder as if it were an innocent independent party in the whole affair, an impartial body trying to help a distressed family. But the IRA had played a key role in the destruction of evidence and intimidation of witnesses; it wasn't simply a case of people being afraid to come forward because of the involvement of the IRA, but rather that the IRA had been pro-active in covering the tracks of the murderers and their accomplices.

The IRA told us that they knew who had ground down the knife, but where had he got a grinder at that time of night? Where was the grinder now? It could be forensically tested for evidence, but none of this was forthcoming, just a broad outline of the events of that night and as broad an outline as the IRA could give without making it obvious that its members were withholding information. While Robert was being attacked, other IRA members were already co-ordinating the clean-up. Jock Davison was still present at the scene and it can only be concluded that, because of his seniority, the clean-up was sanctioned at his request. The knife and CCTV videotape were taken away, clothes burned, witness names and addresses noted and key witnesses such as Ed Gowdy taken away. This operation required experienced IRA personnel. Women from the Strand washed the clothes of the murderers to help them to avoid detection. These women did so in the knowledge that they were washing away the blood of an innocent man. These same women denounced evil at Sunday Mass!

All of this seemed to go over the heads of those who used the excuse, 'But I'm a republican.' If they chose to turn a blind eye to the beating and stabbing of their loved ones because the perpetrators were Provisionals, that was up to them, but they could not deny our call for justice because of their own misguided loyalty.

We intended to speak to whomever we thought could help, and America was an obvious choice. Of course there were also some people who were resentful of the attention we were receiving. Some of these people had lost loved ones through murder and had never got justice. Although I could empathise with them, I could not understand why their anger was directed at us instead of at those who had created an environment in which justice was used as a political football — a game in which, tragically, victims had to engage. Pitching victim against victim is one sure way of ensuring that no one gets justice. We were aware that Robert was just a name to many people and even to those who were our most ardent supporters. His murder opened a window of opportunity for the political process, and supporting us was politically expedient. That was all there was to it. From our point of view, we also had a window of opportunity, a window closed to many, and it would have been unforgivable and cowardly not to use it.

March was an absolutely crazy month. Not a day went by without something happening. The IRA seemed to be issuing statements daily whilst Sinn Féin was uttering sound bites in response to accusations of a cover-up. The media hype round our trip to America was intensifying and members of the press were constantly milling round outside Paula's house. When the IRA or Sinn Féin issued a statement, journalists descended on Paula's in their droves, waiting for our response. It was a terrible time for us. Exhausted, traumatised and shell-shocked, we had to stand in the court in the Strand and speak to the IRA over the airwaves and through the press. We were inundated with requests for interviews and meetings, and we refused none.

After the rally in the Strand we had hoped that there would be a breakthrough — that the IRA would order its men in or at least that witnesses would start coming forward. We also hoped that three witnesses in particular would start telling the truth, but meetings with the police confirmed that nothing had happened and, in fact, people were still refusing to co-operate with them. 'I don't trust the RUC/PSNI,' was the excuse given by many. However, the silence of the IRA and Sinn Féin was matched by the loudness of our voices. Their presumption that we would tire or make fools of ourselves did not materialise. The leadership underestimated our determination and capabilities. In the very macho world of the republican movement, it was assumed that women would not be able to hold out too long: too emotionally loaded, we would not be able to carry the argument beyond the boundary of sympathy. This inherent chauvinism and social snobbery cost them dearly.

Our trip to America was unnerving quite a lot of people in the Strand and the Provisional movement. We were moving beyond our boundaries. They had tried to contain us in the Strand, and then in the country. Now we were going across the Atlantic. It wasn't going down well. Our motives started to be questioned and it was concluded that we must be out to damage Sinn Féin — nothing to do with justice. Other darker, sinister forces were obviously manipulating us: we were only women after all and from the Strand to boot, so we could not possibly be operating independently; someone must be behind us. We were bemused at the suggestions of manipulation. We were getting help and advice from all sorts of people, some on opposite sides of the political debate, some champing at the bit to have Stormont resurrected, and others who never wanted to hear the word 'Stormont' again. All advice was taken gratefully but ultimately we made the decisions ourselves, which became apparent over the following months.

To keep up the pretence of support, Sinn Féin requested another meeting before its Ard-Fheis celebrating Sinn Féin's centenary. Once again, Gerry Adams, along with Gerry Kelly, arrived at Paula's to discuss the whole saga. The two men's demeanour was cordial, as was ours, but no one could have doubted that we were on opposite sides of the fence. I worked on the assumption that Adams already knew everything there was to know — our informing him of this and that was a waste of time. As far as I was concerned, he knew more than we did. We were hearing details daily, so more than likely there was very little he didn't know — no surprises to pop up for him. Regardless of this, Paula, Claire and I sat in the living room going over once again all we knew of the events in Magennis's that night and who had been involved or who knew what had happened. Paula updated him on what we knew and he asked her to write down the names of the Sinn Féin people whom we claimed were involved. Paula wrote the names down and I remember thinking to myself as she did so, 'What is the point of this? He is only going through the motions.' But then again, one reasoned, maybe this was all part of the process. Maybe Adams had to engage in this charade of ignorance so that he could act against those involved. This line of reasoning was way off course but at the time we considered every possible scenario before assigning it to the dustbin.

Paula handed Adams the piece of paper with six names on it: Dee and Paul Brennan, Gerard and Sean Montgomery, Joe Fitzsimmons and Bobby Fitzsimmons. He glanced at the list and said that he didn't recognise the names of any of the people on it. The discussion continued around what could be done, what was needed, and so on. Adams had the protection of the ambiguity of Sinn Féin's relationship with the IRA to guard him from awkward questions. 'That's a question for the IRA,' he would say when we asked why they were not being handed in. He would discuss Robert's case only within the safe parameters of legality — convenient for him and for the perpetrators. He insisted that he knew nothing of the sanctioning of the cover-up by the IRA and that he knew nothing regarding the latter's actions or thinking.

Adams's 'That's a question for the IRA' was reminiscent of Kelly's 'I can't answer that', a get-out-of-jail-free card. No one was guilty because nothing could be proven, and nothing could be proven because no one was talking, and no one was talking because the IRA had told them not to. But to Adams, this was all 'a question for the IRA'. At one point he expressed annoyance at our pursuance of Sinn Féin and, in particular, himself. Pulling his hands towards his chest, he said in a somewhat offensive manner, 'I didn't murder Robert', and accused us of holding him responsible for something in which he had no involvement. Whether it was a genuine perception he held or a ploy to make us feel guilty and less hostile towards him, it didn't work. We were unimpressed and certainly unsympathetic; in fact, we were quite angry at his declaration. It wasn't the first time we were to witness Sinn Féin and its followers adopting the mantle of victimhood.

Claire looked at Adam incredulously. 'We know you didn't,' she said. 'But it was your people who were involved and you cannot blame us for bringing pressure on you to get those who murdered him.'

It was obvious to us that Adams was treating Robert's murder as nothing more than a mishap. Sitting listening to his utterances of concern, I kept thinking to myself, 'Why, in the name of God, did I ever think that this man was genuine?' The Brennans, Montgomerys, Davison and the rest of the murderous gang had Gerry Adams in their corner — that was obvious. Robert had us. Adams was a formidable opponent; a flirtatious move and he could win over our political supporters at any time, and he had big prizes with which to court the British, Irish and Americans. We had the truth. His party was knee deep in Robert's blood and no number of prizes was going to wash that away.

The real purpose of Adams's visit was twofold: information gathering — he wanted to know what we knew — and a PR stunt. He was probably also curious to meet us face to face, to get an idea of the women who had the audacity to challenge the republican movement. Getting reports on each of us individually was not as instructive as meeting us face to face. He probably had us sussed pretty quickly — albeit wrongly. After an hour or so, the meeting ended. Still everyone was cordial but, as usual, when they left, one of us turned to the others and said, 'Well, what do you think?' and the answer was the same as always: 'Don't know' and then 'A waste of time.'

'Well, we'll wait and see,' Paula said. 'I think that maybe he'll do something.' And she went on to point out how he had 'seemed genuinely shocked' by something we had told him. Her natural instinct was to take people at face value and she always hoped that they were sincere. I was always cynical and had less faith in human nature.

'I think if he was going to do something, there would be no need for meetings,' I said. 'But we'll see.'

The only way we would know whether Gerry Adams was sincere or not was when the police told us that witnesses were coming forward. We could only wait. We didn't have to wait long, however. Over a week later, a picture of Gerard Montgomery standing alongside Gerry Adams was published in a Sunday newspaper, implying that Gerry's claims that he didn't know anyone on the list of names we had given him was untrue. We couldn't understand why Adams would put the republican movement through hell to protect the likes of Davison and Co. It is still a mystery to us, although it must have served some benefit to the leadership.

Adams used the six names given to him by Paula in a PR masterstroke, a move designed to take the heat off our trip to the US and feign proactive support for our campaign. He instructed his solicitor to hand the names to the Police Ombudsman and, on the back of our information, he claimed to have suspended seven members. It was a 'symbolic gesture' which carried no substance whatsoever; for some republicans it was a huge step, and *Daily Ireland* congratulated Adams for showing an example; others saw it for what it was — a 'fruitless move'. As PSNI Chief Constable Hugh Orde commented, he didn't need Gerry Adams to tell him who was involved; it was evidence that was needed not information.

Some Provos, however, were angry at the move, and graffiti appeared in the Short Strand: 'Jerry Adams is a tout' and 'Gerry Adams and Nuala O'Loan are comrades'. *Daily Ireland* used this graffiti to bolster Adams's position, saying, 'Anyone who thinks that republicans haven't gone the extra mile to get the wrongdoers in court doesn't understand the Rubicon which has been crossed by Gerry Adams in handing names over to his solicitor to be passed to the Police Ombudsman.' It went on interestingly, 'They must be blind to the graffiti which has appeared in the Short Strand, effectively accusing the

Sinn Féin leader of colluding with the PSNI.' What it failed to mention, however, was that the graffiti writers were none other than the members of the Third Battalion who, on their way home from a night out in West Belfast celebrating that battalion's history (a part of which was Robert's murder), drunkenly scrawled the graffiti on to the Short Strand bus depot. The *Sunday Mirror* quoted a republican source as saying, 'The new graffiti is a message to Gerry Adams, a two fingered gesture from hard-line Provos who can't stomach SF's decision to throw members out and worse still give names to a policing body'. What these hard-line Provos could stomach, however, was the murder of an innocent man.

Such comments and thinking served only to bring the republican movement into further disrepute; they were comments we would have expected from Johnny Adair and his C company, not the IRA and Sinn Féin. There is nothing republican about protecting murderers, but they persisted because republicanism was no longer the blood pumping through the veins of this organisation. Money and power had replaced ideals and convictions. What interested us was the fact that we had given Adams only six names, not seven. Why did he suspend seven based on our say so? Obviously he was using the pretext of having got the names from us to take some form of decisive action. The fact that he suspended seven instead of six indicated that he knew more about Robert's murder than he was prepared to admit.

The suspension of these members was unimpressive. It was nothing more than a paper exercise, a public cover intended to take the heat out of the US visit. These manoeuvres by Sinn Féin further infuriated us. Everything that was done was for the purpose of public perception. In private, the discussion went round in circles. We told them everything, every little detail; they told us nothing, only theories and possibilities, and so on. Sometimes it felt like nothing more than a therapy session, or telling your boss your frustrations. The boss listens but does nothing. At this time, we were still hoping that Adams and Co. would do the right thing or at least try to ensure that the right thing was done. But in reality these meetings were a strategic part of Sinn Féin's damage-limitation exercise. Contact implied an effort to help, support and listen. It didn't matter what was said at the meetings; it was what the meeting *implied*. It implied that relations were good. In a country where eye contact is regarded as a mark of congeniality, a meeting is regarded as good public relations. The substance is irrelevant. Gerry Adams was speaking over our heads to the bigger and more important audience; his voice carried across the Atlantic to reach the ears of American politicians and grassroots republican supporters.

We were at a disadvantage with regard to Gerry Adams. We didn't have a well-oiled press machine at our disposal, or a strategy team assessing the possible impact and outcome of any move. We never sat down and calculated our next move or message; we reacted to what was happening daily and to what the police were telling us. To a degree, however, we played Gerry at his own game. We went along to these meetings and told every little detail, but it didn't really matter, as Sinn Féin got no more than any journalist coming into Paula's house. Planting people in Paula's house was unnecessary, as we had nothing to hide, no games to play — just the truth and what was right.

The movements of Robert's murderers were reported to us daily. Gerry Adams had said that 'these people didn't act like republicans or on behalf of republicans...' yet there was no evidence that they were being ostracised or exiled from the republican 'family', a term favoured by Adams. Jock Davison was regularly seen in the company of senior IRA men such as Eddie Copeland and Bobby Storey, and his cohorts clung to him like sticking plaster. The press rarely focused on the individuals involved or their activities, so Sinn Féin and the IRA were able to play to the wider public, claiming that they had done all they could, while ensuring that the old adage, 'Whatever you say, say nothing', was adhered to.

And still, every day we hoped that the IRA would decide to give up the murderers. Paula gave Adams the benefit of the doubt, hoping that he would see sense. Like many others, she couldn't understand why he would want those who had not only murdered Robert but also brought the republican cause into disrepute to get off scot-free. This hope eventually waned and when the picture of Adams and Gerard Montgomery standing side by side appeared in a Sunday newspaper, we felt like fools. The republican movement was merely playing a game with us. Robert's murder was nothing to Sinn Féin. Just as our brother had been left like a dog in the street that night, Sinn Féin was treating him like a piece of dirt. This was deeply hurtful but we had to rise above it. So many people had died at the hands of the IRA in circumstances that could not be reconciled with any war. Why would Robert be treated any differently from these other young men? Our disgust deepened and by the time we arrived in America, we were entrenched in our belief that Sinn Féin, far from helping us to get justice, was the main impediment to it.

DAMAGE-LIMITATION TACTIC OF SINN FÉIN AND THE ARD-FHEIS

The forthcoming trip to the US had attracted huge media attention. The American press such as the *Boston Globe, New York Times, Time* magazine, CNN, *Washington Post*, USA and others contacted us asking for interviews. We refused no one an interview. We knew how important it was to explain our campaign in our own words rather than have it interpreted by others. Of course we did not have full control over what journalists wrote, and at times our words were put in a context that distorted our agenda. Nevertheless, we could only do our best and stick to the truth and hope that others would act with integrity. Going to America was a huge challenge, given that Sinn Féin has a lot of support there at base and political level.

Sinn Féin was regarded as having the gift of peace in its hands; the willingness of the leadership to lead its people down the path to peace and concede the principles for which republicans had fought for hundreds of years had bestowed upon it influence that was not to be underestimated. Ireland was on the verge of ending an age-old conflict. Everyone wanted a piece of the credit, but Gerry Adams had had the biggest slice for so long now, and we were coming along and tarnishing his reputation. To add insult to injury, we were only six women from the Strand. Some sections of the press got quite hysterical about it. Robin Livingstone of the *Andersontown News* took it particularly badly and lambasted us from his rag sheet. Was one man's murder going to block the peace process? he asked. Yes, he argued, people sympathised with us, but ultimately we were not the only ones to have lost a loved one in this terrible conflict, and so on and so on. Now that we had cried our tears, we should go back to the kitchen. We were 'unionism on tour', bolstering the position of those opposed to Sinn Féin, he claimed. The murderers came in for no such onslaught, however.

Livingstone never asked for an interview with us. And he wasn't the only journalist keen to undermine Robert's murder and place it in the context of a bar brawl and nothing else. The degeneration of the IRA into criminal gangs was an issue they didn't want to report on or recognise — we were a much safer target. What did it matter if people in areas like the Short Strand were living under a 'green jackboot'; it was green, wasn't it?

The most important thing to the leadership was its political ascendancy — the IRA was a bargaining tool that Sinn Féin leaders were not ready to cash in just yet. Until they were ready, the IRA could not be portrayed in its true light; the illusion of a revolutionary force with soldiers ready to sacrifice themselves for their country had to be maintained to create the impression that there was something to bargain with. Criminal gangs and self-serving thugs do not carry the same bargaining weight, but Robert's murder demonstrated to the leaders that they could not get away with the illusion forever. Time was running out. They tried to conjure up the old mantra of criminalisation of the IRA; the hate figure, Margaret Thatcher, was resurrected to silence the calls for justice. Journalists in Ireland keen to exonerate the Provisional leadership from any wrongdoing in Robert's murder had moved quickly to absolve the IRA of responsibility. Anne Cadwallader, writing for the *Irish Echo* on 15 February, stated bluntly, 'Police clear Provisionals in stab death.' Her opening statement read:

> Attempts by the DUP to blame the IRA for the fatal stabbing of a man in a city centre bar a week ago have been dismissed by police, who say there is no evidence it was anything other than the tragic result of a bar-room dispute.

This inaccurate reporting of Robert's murder enraged me so much that I wrote to Cadwallader:

> Your article is an insult to the intelligence of my family and to the nationalist community. It is one of the most ill-informed or deliberately misleading reports on the incident that I have read so far. You have failed to point out that Hugh Orde did state that those involved in Robert's murder were linked to an 'illegal organisation' and although he did not name the organisation everyone knows it is the IRA. Your use of Alex Maskey as a source regarding the cover-up operation is incredible. How does Mr Maskey know that the allegations are without truth or foundation? The names of these

people are known by police, the community, Sinn Féin and the IRA. Some of those arrested are members of the IRA. Maskey's election workers are implicated as are Martin McGuinness' bodyguards. There is more evidence linking the IRA to Robert's murder than there is linking them to the Northern Bank robbery. There were 70 or more people in the bar when Brendan Devine had his throat cut yet no one has been charged. Why do you think that is? I would suggest that you investigate the details of Robert's murder a little more closely before you so fervently clear the IRA of any involvement. I will be quite happy to give the facts of the case so that you can carry a more balanced version of the events.

It was the last time I took the bother to meet with a journalist in an attempt to inform them of facts. I had learned that it was a waste of time. In fairness, Anne Cadwallader did write a more balanced article after our meeting, but she reverted to form a few weeks later. I didn't respond to this second article — what was the point? We soon realised that there was no such thing as an impartial, truth-seeking press. Between the agendas of the people and parties surrounding us, supporters, opponents, friends-turned-foe, political pundits, journalists out for a story, the IRA, the murderers, the accomplices, the do-gooders, well-wishers, ill-wishers and crackpots, and anyone else who had an opinion on our campaign, at times it felt like we were swimming in a sea of madness. And above all this, the overarching truth hovered. Robert was dead.

From the first days of going public, we knew that we could not let Robert's murder become a story for a few days and then disappear. We could not keep it on an emotional or human level either: appearing on television appealing for witnesses would certainly pull at heartstrings but nothing else. After a day or two, the world would move on, one man's murder of little relevance to their everyday lives. We, on the other hand, were equipped with the truth and could see that Robert's murder impacted not just on us, but on everyone. There was an underbelly of evil lurking in the streets of Belfast, hiding and living in areas such as the Strand. It was present in those who disguised themselves as community benefactors, feeding off the debris of a thirty-year-old conflict and carving out a niche of power and patronage. Its victims could be anyone as long as the community from which they fed continued to sup from the cup of propaganda.

From the beginning, we knew what we had to do and that was simply to put Robert's murder on to the political agenda. The first political move was a small one — a motion passed in the Belfast City Council, condemning Robert's murder and calling on witnesses to go to the police. Claire and I had travelled over to Belfast City Hall and watched from the gallery as the councillors debated the motion. Joe O'Donnell from the Strand was Deputy Mayor; he too had described Robert's murder as a result of a bar brawl. We suspected that Joe knew exactly what had happened that night. He was seated on one of the throne-like chairs at the front of the chamber. Not looking very regal, he seemed out of place and uncomfortable. Alex Maskey was in the Chamber and spoke about how Sinn Féin's amendment to the motion should be included; this would mean the reference to the police being removed and people called upon to come forward to whatever party they trusted. If the amendment were included, he said, his party could support the motion.

Sinn Féin's insistence that people come forward to a third party always vexed me. It was a complete nonsense and everyone knew it, yet no one seemed to challenge the party on it. How does it work? For example, you are walking along the street and witness a crime, serious or petty. Do you go in search of a priest to report it to? What if the priest isn't at home (any time we needed a priest, he was unavailable)? What if the priest doesn't want to take statements from witnesses? If not a priest, then a solicitor — what happens if you don't have one? Would a solicitor take statements from passers-by? Do they charge? Are they available immediately? The nonsense of Sinn Féin's position was never challenged and it was frustrating. Bernadette McAliskey's claim that a third party was a tried and tested method used by republicans for years was rubbish, yet she proclaimed it on national TV and no one challenged it.

Not enough pressure was being put on Sinn Féin in the areas that we would have liked, but unfortunately the politics of the time dictated that Robert's murder was being used for a purpose relevant to *realpolitik* as opposed to justice for one family.

In the event, Sinn Féin and the PUP (political wing of the UVF) were the only two parties to reject the motion. As Claire and I sat in the public gallery listening to the debate and looking at two men, Alex Maskey and Joe O'Donnell, whom we detested and believed were the first to put the political cover-up into motion, we felt sick. I sat taking notes whilst Claire was trying to make sense of the procedures. '

The grandeur of the council chamber implied that it was a place of deliberation and debate, but this impression was undermined by the presence of mavericks like Maskey and O'Donnell, masquerading as civic fathers. I don't believe I've ever heard either of these two utter an original thought, and their desire for respectability and acceptance into the echelons of the political elite was palpable. It brought to my mind the old saying, 'You cannot make a silk purse out of a sow's ear'. Yet Claire and I had to sit and listen while they debated our brother's right to justice. Because by refusing to co-operate with the police, they were obstructing the process of justice, regardless of how they wrapped it up in political jargon. We left the gallery disheartened, angry, and sickened by the hypocrisy and lack of humanity.

Journalists and TV crews were waiting outside and we were asked about our plans for the US and why we were going. We spoke of our disgust at the lack of support from Sinn Féin and explained that we were going to the US to persuade the Americans to bring whatever pressure they could on Sinn Féin. I remember a journalist asking, 'Are you not afraid?'

'Why, what are they going to do? Murder us all?' I replied a bit too aggressively, on reflection. Sometimes it was hard to remember that journalists were only asking questions to which the public might like to know the answers, rather than voicing a personal opinion. What the journalist's question did illustrate, though, was that the Provisionals were doing a poor job of persuading people that they were on our side.

At the time, we regarded going to America as no bigger a deal than meeting with the politicians at home. In fact, we thought the rally should have been a much more poignant and effective action, but it hadn't moved Sinn Féin or the IRA. The news of our upcoming trip to the States, however, did catch their attention and, for the first time, they seemed to take on the board the seriousness of their situation, hence the second meeting with Gerry Adams on 3 March. From here on in, Sinn Féin and we maintained a thin veil of cordiality. We met with the leaders, attended the Ard-Fheis and they uttered public words of support. Behind the veil each knew exactly where the other was coming from. After the trip to the US, after two more meetings with Sinn Féin, contact between us ceased, aside from a few accusatory emails which came my way, as usual in defence of thugs.

There was no doubt that America would prove to be the climax of our campaign. I suppose it would be accurate to say that once you have met the President of the US, there is nowhere else to go. We had no intention, however, of letting the US trip spell the death knell for our fight for justice. In spite of the fact that we were women and from the Short Strand, we did have a reasonable understanding of the nature of *realpolitik* and we could appreciate the bigger picture. We knew that we had to gain tangible support, not just platitudes. We also knew that the only reason we were being invited to the States was that the peace process had broken down in December of 2004 and the Northern Bank robbery had added to the difficulty. Political patience with Sinn Féin and the IRA was running out and, since 9/11, tolerance of illegal violent groups, regardless of how romantically viewed by a large section of the community, had ended. Robert's murder confirmed to people like Senator Ted Kennedy and even Congressman Peter King that the IRA had become the obstacle to peace. The IRA was at a crossroads. We decided to capitalise on this but were always aware that there was a danger that when the IRA chose the only road that was realistically open to it, Robert's murder would slip into history, like so many others. We never lost sight of this, nor did we let the attention or media hype lead us into a false sense of security. Robert's murder was part of a bigger picture: what we had to do was to convince people that its resolution was an essential part of that picture.

We were denied the right to grieve naturally; instead we had to replay, over and over, mechanically, the events of the night when Robert was beaten and stabbed to death. People find it difficult to be around those who are grieving and they also dismiss a lot of what is said as part of the grief. Mitchel McLaughlin actually attempted to do this one evening on television, describing us as a family who were 'angry and grieving', the implication being that our words and actions were understandable but not to be given too much credence. So although we were a grieving family, we had also to be a rational one, and the first thing on our list of priorities was to arrange meetings in the States with the people who mattered.

The idea of going to Washington and meeting with influential people was daunting. Into the bargain we had to organise the visit ourselves. The SDLP offered valuable logistical support and, with a list of contact numbers and email addresses, we set about requesting meetings with a series of influential people. We found ourselves ringing the private secretaries of people like Senator Ted Kennedy and Senator Hillary Clinton. It is the strangest feeling to have to ring a US Senator — or anyone for that matter — and open with the words, 'Hello, my name is … We are campaigning for justice for our brother Robert who was murdered by the IRA and Sinn Féin members….' Having to repeat these words over and over again was nullifying.

From Paula's home in the Short Strand we spoke to some of the most important people in America. It was a surreal situation. Needless to say, they already knew what was happening on the streets of Belfast and were open to meeting with us. We also requested a meeting with the President through the American consulate. We had already met with the Consul, Dean Pittman, and had secured his support. That year the White House was a cold house for all the politicians of Northern Ireland, and community leaders and other civic representatives were being honoured in their place. We fitted perfectly into these criteria. In between making arrangements for America, we were giving interviews from morning to night. I was rarely at home and the only time I was alone was on the journey from Castlewellan to Belfast. It was during this journey that Robert's death would really hit home with me. It was a pain and despair that we could not submerge ourselves in. Regardless of how despondent we felt, we had to keep going.

We had seized upon the opportunity to go to the States — we would have been foolish not to have. There was the small matter of money, however: we were broke. At the beginning it was clear that we could not afford for all of us to go, so a decision had to be made as to who would travel. We were beginning to think strategically and it was decided that Bridgeen, Paula and I would go because Paula and I had been doing the main bulk of the interviews and had inadvertently become the faces of the campaign; Bridgeen was Robert's fiancée and her presence carried the weight of the future of which he had been robbed. It was a purely pragmatic decision; no one was looking forward to the trip.

Exhaustion, grief, stress and anguish were weighing heavily on us, and we were spending little time with our families, so a five-day trip across the Atlantic was not appealing.

The previous few weeks had been gruelling and things looked set to get more so. We were inundated with requests from journalists from TV, radio, newspapers, documentaries and anything else that was a medium of communication. Journalists were even talking about doing fly-on-the-wall documentaries. In the middle of all the mayhem and madness, some wanted us to agree to have a camera follow us wherever we went. It was crazy stuff. On top of this, we had been invited to Sinn Féin's Ard-Fheis on 5 March, and the Irish Labour Party had invited us to the Dáil for International Women's Day on 8 March. That was two trips to Dublin within a week before going to the States.

We had met with Adams earlier that week when Paula had given over the names, and so we decided that our attendance at the Ard-Fheis was unnecessary. At the time, Paula thought that we should go down, as she feared that by refusing we would alienate republican support. I argued that it was unnecessary and probably just a gesture on Sinn Féin's part to show public support before we went off to the States. Eventually it was decided that we wouldn't go in light of our other trip to Dublin on the Tuesday and then America. Paula's instinct had been right, however: checking the internet on the Saturday morning, I found the *Belfast Telegraph* proclaiming, 'McCartneys Shun Sinn Féin'. My immediate response was, 'What are they writing that for?' We had told the press that we wouldn't be attending the Ard-Fheis because we had already met privately with Gerry Adams. Even at this point in the campaign, I hadn't realised the extent to which our every action and word were being assessed and judged by others. It was simply not true that we were shunning Sinn Féin. That party was certainly doing nothing to help us and we would have been perfectly right to shun the Ard-Fheis but at this time it wasn't useful. As it turned out, though, our initial decision not to go held us in good stead for what Sinn Féin had planned. But on Saturday morning we felt we had no choice — we had to go to the Ard-Fheis.

First, we had to phone and ask Sinn Féin if the invitation was still on offer. I also had to look for volunteers to accompany me to Dublin and to set out right away. Ringing Gerry Kelly that morning, I thought to myself, 'What will I say if he asks why we've changed our minds or if he says no?' Now that would have been a dilemma. I could hardly have told him the truth: 'The thing is, Gerry, if we don't come down, it might harm our campaign.' We could hardly have expected a sympathetic response to that! The pressure of the whole thing was immense. If we didn't get down there, Sinn Féin would have a hook on which to hang its victimhood claims. If I had let the party off the hook because of my bad judgment, I would never have forgiven myself. Getting the bastards who murdered Robert was too important to mess up. Jesus Christ, I thought, why didn't I just listen to Paula and agree to go down?

Obviously as far as Sinn Féin was concerned, our presence at the Ard-Fheis was important, too, but for the opposite reasons to ours. Kelly never asked why we had changed our minds. And whether Sinn Féin had seen the headlines or not, we didn't ask. Maybe our presence at the Ard-Fheis outweighed any potential harm we might have done to our campaign by not attending. Whatever the case, travel arrangements were made and, an hour later, Gemma, Paula, Donna and Claire arrived to pick me up for our onward journey to Dublin. From Newry we travelled in two cars that had been arranged by Sinn Féin. They were clearly very keen for us to attend.

We had no idea what to expect and we didn't discuss how we should act or react and what we should say or not say. We were taking it as it came. We had thought that we would enter the hall unnoticed, listen to the speeches and leave. The allegations of shunning Sinn Féin or Sinn Féin-bashing would have no foundation therefore. We did become a little concerned when the driver told us that a group of women had tried to gain entrance to the Ard-Fheis, claiming to be the McCartney sisters. She told us that when the media got wind of the news that the McCartney sisters had arrived, they had charged around to the entrance. That should have given us an indication of how important our attendance was, but we just pondered the absurdity of the whole situation. They were taking this Ard-Fheis thing a bit too seriously, we thought. We had spoken with Gerry Adams a couple of days earlier. How in the name of God the press could deduce from our absence that we had shunned Sinn Féin was really beyond us. It didn't make sense, but then, of course, if people want a certain message put out, they will find ways of delivering it.

Driving up to the RDS in Dublin, we were in an apathetic and resigned mood. We looked out at the press milling around. They were obviously keen for comments; it was cold and they had been waiting for news of something all day. They would have to wait a little longer, however, as we were hurriedly directed into the hall and up stairs behind the main stage. Glad to get away from the mayhem outside, we sat around a low table with Gerry Adams, Martin McGuinness and Gerry Kelly facing us. The journey had been a long one and Paula and I were gasping for a cigarette and cup of coffee. The others were hungry but had to settle for plain biscuits and coffee. The place was a mess and there was nothing pleasant or comfortable about the surroundings. The polystyrene cups, dirty tables and uncomfortable chairs contrasted sharply with the brightly lit and colourful stage. It struck me that it mirrored Sinn Féin's character — all glossy and welcoming on the outside but stained and soiled on the inside.

The conversation obviously focused on Robert's murder and what could be done to get the perpetrators brought to justice. Denial permeated the air and I felt that we were participating in it. Martin McGuinness did most of the talking. He offered his condolences and told us how disgusted he was at Robert's murder. Considered to be more a soldier than a politician, and therefore to have a more direct understanding of the dishonour Robert's murder had brought upon the IRA, McGuinness was accorded a degree of credibility by us. It was possible that he was not part of the dirty tricks being played by the Belfast Provos and was being told only half the story. He told us that it was necessary that Robert's murderers be ostracised by the community (on reflection, he did not say 'exiled'). I can remember Gemma agreeing wholeheartedly with McGuinness and saying that it had to come 'from within the community', or words to that effect. The others nodded in agreement. I sat impassively. I was unimpressed with this show of solidarity but I didn't say so. Maybe I should have but Sinn Féin was playing a very close game, and an outburst and accusations would do no good. Better to play along with them but to your own rules, I thought. McGuinness noticed my lack of enthusiasm and, leaning forward, said, 'Catherine has reservations.'

I hate phoney people and wasn't going to become one for the sake of Sinn Féin and so I decided to tell him where we stood before we went out to the hall. 'The bottom line is this,' I said. 'Robert's murderers have to be brought to account; it is only when this happens that we will be satisfied that you have done all you can, and that's what we will be saying when we leave here.'

'That's fine' said Martin, smiling, his smile as impassioned as his threats.

They then rose to lead us down the steps and into the hall. McGuinness turned to me and said, 'Don't worry; you're amongst friends.'

'It's hard to know,' I replied.

Within twenty seconds of entering the hall, I knew. The hall was in darkness apart from the front. When we entered, the delegates stood up and cheered and clapped. We were taken aback and even more so by the press contingent situated at the front below the stage. Cameras flashed and people milled around, and we were directed to seats at the front. Gerry Adams, smiling as broadly as he smiles, positioned himself between Paula and me as the cameras flashed and flashed. It was overwhelming. We had not been prepared for this. They hadn't mentioned press back stage and we thought that the bulk of the media were outside.

I got a bad feeling; this was choreographed down to Gerry Adams taking the cup of coffee from my hand and taking a drink, which conveyed a good relations message if nothing else did. As soon as he got up to make his speech, Caitriona Ruane filled his seat. She clapped enthusiastically at the appropriate points of Gerry's speech and the pictures give the impression that the McCartney sisters are applauding.

We felt really disappointed at Sinn Féin's behaviour and I was incensed at the audacity of Caitriona Ruane: as Sinn Féin's Human Rights spokeswoman, she hadn't yet uttered a word of condemnation of Robert's murder. And she still hasn't to this day. The right to life is the first cited in the UN Declaration of Human Rights, the most fundamental of principles, yet Ruane has never felt compelled to speak on how Robert's right to life was taken away. Instead she played along with Sinn Féin's little PR stunt, and in the process discredited her own reputation as a human rights advocate.

At first, my sisters didn't realise what was going on. Uncomfortable anyway, they were sitting bemused by the whole proceedings. To make sure that they didn't in any way appear to be supporting Gerry Adams's empty utterances of condemnation of Robert's murder and statements of support for us, I leaned across Caitriona to Paula and said, in not too hushed tones, 'We've been set up.' She was genuinely shocked. She looked appreciatively at the delegates who had stood and applauded us

Mother and Father were married in April 1963 at St Patrick's chapel.

Holidaying at Coney Island caravan park. (*Clockwise from back left*): Gemma, Paula, me, Gerard, Robert, our mother (who was pregnant with Claire) and Donna.

Robert on his First Holy Communion day, outside St Anthony's chapel.

Robert on his Confirmation day. Mother knitted his Aran jumper. We all boasted one, at one time or another.

St Matthew's Boxing Club. Robert is in the middle row, second from right. (*John Conlon*)

St Matthew's Football Club. Robert is in the back row, second from left. (*John Conlon*)

Robert and Bridgeen on a night out.

Robert as proud as punch, with Conlaed and Brandon.

Magennis's bar where the Provos returned to after marching in commemoration and solidarity with the families of the Bloody Sunday victims. (*Pacemaker Press International*)

Up to 1,200 people attended Robert's funeral, testimony not only to his popularity but also to the wrong committed by the IRA. (*Pacemaker Press International*)

The first vigil, held on the Friday night after Robert's death. The community's repulsion was palpable. (*Pacemaker Press International*)

The rally in the Short Strand was attended by up to 600 people demanding justice. (I am in the foreground.) The people's plea to the IRA fell on deaf ears. (*Pacemaker Press International*)

Bridgeen with Conlaed and Brandon just before the rally. (*Topfoto*)

Brendan Devine, the man Robert died trying to protect. Devine had a history with the IRA, and his presence in the bar that night sealed Robert's fate. (*Pacemaker Press International*)

Written on the walls of the Short Strand shortly after Robert's murder. It is still there today.

At the Sinn Féin Ard-Fheis, March 2005. Gerry Adams and Caitriona Ruane are strategically positioned amongst us for the purpose of the cameras. The stern and contemptuous faces of those applauding belie the rapturous applause. Seated (*from left*): Caitriona Ruane, Paula, Gerry Adams, me, Donna, Gemma. (*Topfoto*)

Bridgeen, Claire and Paula with the Taoiseach, Bertie Ahern. Although supportive, the Irish Government did little to push Sinn Féin on Robert's murder. (AFP/Getty Images)

Outside Leinster House, Dublin, on International Women's Day, March 2005. (*From left*): Joan Burton, Mary O'Rourke, Mary Hanafin, Róisín Shortall, Bridgeen, Gemma, Claire, Paula, Donna, Liz McManus. (*Photocall Ireland*)

Paula, Bridgeen and I at our meeting with President George Bush, March 2005. We met with the President on two further occasions. The support of Irish America was vital to our campaign.

Paula (*right*) and I outside the White House, March 2005. (*PA Photos*)

Donna (*centre*) and Gemma (*right*) pictured with Senator Hillary Clinton, March 2005. They look on as Senator Ted Kennedy makes it clear to Sinn Féin that it is time for the IRA to go. (*Getty Images*)

Paula (*left*), Donna (*centre*) and I, at a vigil outside Magennis's bar in April 2005. We couldn't get a local priest to say prayers at the vigil, but fortunately a Jesuit priest stepped in. (*PA Photos*)

(*From left*) Myself, Paula and Sinead Commander outside 10 Downing Street in December 2005. Like the Irish, the British Government was reluctant to push Sinn Féin too much. (*PA Photos*)

Paula and I (*second and third from right*) at the Policing Board meeting, June 2007. This was the first public meeting since Sinn Féin had signed up to supporting the PSNI. (*Pacemaker Press International*)

Outside Paula's house in the Short Strand. (*Clockwise from back left*): Claire, Bridgeen, Paula, me, Donna and Gemma.

when we arrived in, and her expression towards Ruane had also been friendly, but in a second it turned to horrified disappointment. To the left of me, Donna's face was already one of bemusement so when I told her what I thought, she simply rolled her eyes. The message was passed on to Claire and Gemma and so, feeling disgusted and angry, we all sat through Adams's speech, listening impassively as Gerry spoke of the IRA's right to commit crimes for political ends and said that the group could not be 'wished away, or ridiculed or embarrassed or demonised or repressed out of existence'. 'We know that breaking the law is a crime,' he said. 'But we refuse to criminalise those who break the law in pursuit of legitimate political objectives.' Addressing Robert's murder, his speech continued:

> His murder was dreadful, not only because of the way he died and not only because it robbed his family of a father, a partner, a brother, a son. His murder was dreadful because it is alleged some republicans were involved in it. That makes this a huge issue for us.

'As president of Sinn Féin or as an individual I could not campaign for the victims of British or unionist paramilitary thuggery, if I was not clear and as committed to justice for the McCartney family,' he added. 'Those responsible for the brutal killing of Robert McCartney should admit to what they did in a court of law … others with information should come forward. I am not letting this issue go until those who have sullied the republican cause are made to account for their actions.'

It was reported in press that a motion supporting us had been passed at the Ard-Fheis. Apparently a significant number of delegates abstained, probably more than abstained from the motion supporting the PSNI two years later.

I have never felt as uncomfortable sitting amongst supposed friends as I did sitting at the Ard-Fheis that year. The whole episode was a choreographed farce, and, although the delegates gave us a standing ovation, there was a sinister element to it. The scene with the child-catcher in *Chitty Chitty Bang Bang* comes to mind when I think of the 2005 Sinn Féin Ard-Fheis. To counteract Sinn Féin's PR strategy, we couldn't afford to applaud the good work of the international guests present. We felt awkward not applauding; however, our failure to clap was not a snub or a rebuff of the guests but rather a need to ensure that applause would not be misconstrued or misrepresented as applause for Adams. We couldn't afford to give Adams the picture he wanted simply because others might have been offended.

As Gerry Adams droned on, his lack of oratorical skills struck me. He was quite simply boring and I found it difficult to understand how he enthused his listeners. The content of the speech equalled its delivery. I felt sick with anger listening as he spoke about Robert and pretended to support us. The temptation to walk out was overwhelming but it wouldn't have done any good. At last his speech came to an end and we were once again rushed out of the hall; obviously our presence during Adams's speech was all that was required. It suited us: an hour was long enough at the Ard-Fheis; what any of the other delegates had to say was of no importance or interest.

With relief, we left the hall and quickly made our way to the cars. The media were still milling about and some reporters were shouting towards us, asking for a comment. 'You don't have to speak to them…' McGuinness said.

'It's OK,' I replied. 'I'll go over.' When we were asked why we had come to the Ard-Fheis, I repeated the line about 'seeking the support of republicans on the ground'. One journalist asked if attending the Ard-Fheis wasn't sending out mixed signals. 'Mixed signals!' I snapped, again forgetting that he was only expressing a wider view and not a personal opinion. 'No … this is a social justice issue. Mixed signals. No.' It angered us that we were being treated like professional lobbyists or politicians. People seemed to forget that we were an ordinary family seeking justice, not political players or pundits. People said things like, 'You know that going to the Ard-Fheis may have lost you support amongst such and such a section of the community or politicians …' or 'I think going to the Ard-Fheis was a big mistake; up until then I thought you were doing the right thing but …', and so on. And when we went to America the criticism became: 'Going to America was a step too far for me. Up until then I supported them, but….'

What absolute hogwash! It shouldn't have mattered where we went or to whom we spoke. Justice should not be qualified. But then again we knew that the only reason Robert's murder was getting any attention at all was that it could be used to put Sinn Féin under pressure. It was impossible for us to remain outside of this if we had any chance of justice. What we needed to do was to make sure that Sinn

Féin did not ride the crisis out without delivering justice. The fact that it was we who were coming in for criticism for attending, rather than Sinn Féin for attempting a PR coup, was more telling.

Courtesy of Sinn Féin, we went for a meal at a local hotel before travelling home. Adams and McGuinness arrived to bid us farewell and thank us for coming. For our part, we thanked them for the invitation and the meal. Clearly content with the way things had turned out, they were in a light-hearted mood. We exchanged pleasantries and off they went, Martin with a book entitled *Ireland and Europe* tucked under his arm. Eventually we travelled home, exhausted and disgusted. More convinced than ever of Sinn Féin's insincerity, when home we discovered that Deirdre Hargey had spoken at the Ard-Fheis. This absolutely sickened me; if I had known that, I would have proved the *Belfast Telegraph* headline right: I would have shunned them and would have had a very good reason for doing so. It seemed that Sinn Féin was determined to flaunt these people in front us.

As mentioned above, many people were curious about our decision to go to the Ard-Fheis and feared that it would take the impact out of our campaign and weaken the support we had galvanised up to then. At the time, Sinn Féin's main concern was the American lobby, not the British or Irish governments. Both governments were keen to have the process back on track and, although they wanted to press Sinn Féin, they didn't want to apply pressure; nudging and coaxing the leadership in the right direction was more suited to their strategy. Sinn Féin was in a strong position in regards to the two governments but the Americans were less convinced that Sinn Féin's hands were tied regarding the IRA. Less inclined to court and flatter, the Bush administration took a hard line, and, more importantly, so did long-term allies of Sinn Féin.

It was our trip to the States that Sinn Féin had been trying to head off by inviting us to the Ard-Fheis. Many suspected that the photographs would be used to cast Sinn Féin in a good light. The pictures would show that the McCartneys and Sinn Féin were at one on the issue and that Sinn Féin's support was solid. However, I had taken on board the wise words of a journalist who had followed the Provos for years: 'Don't let them take ownership of it; responsibility yes, but not ownership. You'll be running to meetings with them for years.' This piece of advice stuck with me throughout the campaign, and the Ard-

Fheis was proof that they would use every dirty trick in the book to deceive.

In hindsight, I don't think that going to the Ard-Fheis was necessary to our campaign, as the support of the republicans on the ground didn't make a difference one way or the other: too many in the republican movement were too mealy-mouthed to press the leadership on Robert's murder. But more importantly, it did not harm our campaign either. The trap set by Sinn Féin failed — the party gained nothing from it even if it didn't lose anything either. Robert's murder had shifted the political goalposts of the day. It was no longer about one man's murder but about the IRA itself and Sinn Féin's commitment to democracy. In the midst of this, little PR stunts such as the Ard-Fheis showed that Sinn Féin hadn't caught up with the rest of the world yet. Its leaders were completely thrown by our campaign and their usual stunts were proving ineffective.

Some commentators interpreted our attendance at the Ard-Fheis in the way that Sinn Féin had hoped they would. Mark Davenport reported on 7 March:

> ...the newspapers' images of the sisters at the Ard Fheis will confound those who portrayed their campaign as part of a 'popular revolt' against the IRA. Although the McCartney sisters have made it clear that they will judge republicans by results, their attendance at the Ard Fheis looks likely to take some of the sting out of their forthcoming visit to the United States. They no longer appear to provide quite such a symbolic contrast to the Sinn Féin president as he embarks on his new look St Patrick's tour.

At the time, I did not read many of the newspaper articles written and, on reflection, I am sure that this was the right thing to do. Northern Ireland is such a complex place that straightforward events become embroiled in complex issues of culture, conflict and history. Reading such comments as Davenport's could have led us astray in the sense that if we became concerned about how we were being perceived, we would have become circumscribed and eventually silenced. To try to counteract such arguments would have caused confusion and again deflected from the issue. But his comments are interesting and give an insight into how difficult it can be to get heard in Northern Ireland.

Davenport's observation was right in that some had tried to portray our campaign as part of a popular revolt against the IRA, the rally seemingly confirming this. To dissuade other republicans from supporting us, republicans in the Short Strand had spread it around that the rally was an anti-republican rally, but it was a weak argument set against the facts of Robert's murder, and the attendance at the rally proved this. The people of the Short Strand were lambasting not the republican movement but the murderers of Robert who for years had been lording it over the place.

On the one hand, we had to digest such interpretations designed to destroy our credibility amongst one section of the community, yet on the other we had to listen to others imply that we were in some small way complicit in Robert's murder because of where we came from. One instance of this was Gail Walker's article, ironically in support of us, which claimed in brackets that our campaign had an 'element of the biters bit' about it.

No matter where we turned, we were confronted with an interpretation of our campaign. No one seemed able to stay focused for too long on the reality of the circumstances surrounding our brother's murder. That was fairly straightforward. I even had one journalist who asked me if I thought 'the middle classes' would find it 'disconcerting' that Robert was drinking in a bar on a Sunday. I felt the anger bubbling in the pit of my stomach at such pretentiousness. Even to ask the question warranted a slap in the face and I had to use all my strength to prevent myself from screaming at this man for his insinuation that Robert was partly responsible for his own murder by virtue of the fact that he was in a bar on a Sunday. I suppose if he had been at a golf club, it wouldn't have been an issue.

Davenport's prediction that our attendance at the Ard-Fheis would take the sting out of our visit to the US was unfulfilled, thanks to the IRA and its 'offer to shoot the murderers'. On the back of this, Senator Ted Kennedy announced that he would not be meeting with Gerry Adams, and a spokeswoman stated, 'Senator Kennedy has decided to decline to meet with Gerry Adams, given the IRA's ongoing criminal activity and contempt for the rule of law.' She went on to say:

The IRA murder of Robert McCartney and subsequent calls for vigilante justice underscore the need for IRA violence and

criminality to stop and Sinn Féin to co-operate with the police
service of Northern Ireland.

Kennedy's decision was a diplomatic slap in the face for Sinn Féin and
particularly for Adams. The Senator had been a fervent supporter of
the peace process, and ten years earlier had lobbied President Bill
Clinton to give Gerry Adams a visa, which bolstered Adams's position
within republicanism and mainstream politics. Over those ten years,
Sinn Féin had built up an extremely important political and financial
base in America; the party had also moved from the streets *per se* to the
corridors of power, courted by presidents and hailed as 'peacemakers'.
But IRA criminality was undermining Sinn Féin's international
credibility and, more importantly, damaging Adams's persona and
ability to deliver peace. US spokespeople warned that Adams was
beginning to be held in the same disdain as the White House held
Arafat: 'Just as the President labelled Arafat not a partner for peace, the
same now goes for Gerry Adams. The President does not want to meet
him.'
    The President was not meeting any of the political parties — they
were all paying the price for Sinn Féin's misbehaviour. Refusing to meet
Adams was a diplomatic tactic and nothing else, and we knew it.
Refusal to meet with the other parties also indicated this; Sinn Féin was
not completely out in the cold, or at least it was not alone. Strong words
and forceful actions were temporary measures designed to get the
peace train going again. It is politicians who decide who is the obstacle
to peace and who is conducive to it, and they treat each accordingly.
The noises coming from America, however, could not be ignored by
Sinn Féin. The party was in a different era. It had joined mainstream
politics where pomp, ceremony and power appeal more than ideals,
unachievable goals and the 'Soldier's Song' being sung in backstreet
bars. It had come a long way in ten years. What was the alternative to
sticking two fingers up at the US, sulking back in Ireland and planning
a return — and a return to what?
    Privately we were delighted by Ted Kennedy's refusal to meet Adams.
It seemed that our message was getting through, with help from the
IRA. However, all the time we had to steer clear of becoming embroiled
in the bigger issues. Sticking only to our message was a difficult and
nerve-racking exercise. Every TV and radio interview was dissected.

'What did I say that for?' 'Did I say that?' Or 'I should have said that', and so on. Our fears were not ill-founded and, while at times we over-reacted to our mistakes or worried unnecessarily about something we had said, our opponents did use some remarks in an attempt to undermine our campaign, although they sometimes shot themselves in the foot in the process. In hindsight, whilst we were being blamed for or credited with the actions of Kennedy and others, the part played by the IRA in weakening Adams's hand, by offering to shoot the murderers just before we went to America, seemingly went unnoticed.

Why did the IRA make such an apparently stupid move? Or was it so stupid after all? Reflecting on how far Adams has brought the IRA in the two years since Robert's murder, it seems that every move — regardless of how apparently insane — had a purpose and one that benefited Sinn Féin. At the time, we never had time for reflection or analysis; we reacted to day-to-day events. Interviews and meetings, interviews and meetings were our diet for weeks. Our preparations for the trip to Washington were made in the midst of media mayhem. Some interviews were as early as 6.00 a.m. We would travel to television studios at all times of the day to record interviews for British, North American and United States television, repeating over and over what we wanted to achieve by meeting with President Bush.

Others in America were less than enthusiastic about our trip and campaign. Writing to President Bush, the Unity in Action Committee of National Irish American Organisations expressed concerns at the pressure being exerted on Sinn Féin:

> We ask that the U.S. government demand that the parties to this conflict, as well as the two governments, stick to the realities of conflict resolution, not allegations and petty politics; we also hope that our own government avoids jumping on the anti-Sinn Féin bandwagon based upon politically motivated speculation. (Quoted in the irishecho.com).

This group whose representatives included the Ancient Order of Hibernians, Brehon Law Society, Irish American Unity Conference and Irish Northern Aid regarded the IRA's right to murder and cover up murder as 'petty politics'. What would it take for such people to recognise the truth? If murder was 'petty politics', then what was the rest of it? The naivety of these groups was no excuse for their arrogance or contempt for the lives of citizens in another country.

SECOND MEETING WITH THE IRA

The second meeting with the IRA revealed less than the first. Summoned once more to a neutral meeting place, we met again with Sean and Pádraig. We had decided that we were not spending any more than an hour at this meeting. The last one had dragged on for five-and-a-half hours and had been totally fruitless. Anyway, Donna and Gemma had arranged to meet a guy about renting an office and they had only an hour to spare.

For us, meeting with the IRA was no different from meeting with anyone else. In hindsight, we gave Sean and Pádraig a very easy ride. I suppose it was because at the time we didn't blame them personally for what had happened; we knew that they were only the messengers. Thinking back on it now, we didn't grill them enough about the IRA's role. However, it was only five weeks after Robert's murder and we didn't know everything at that point. Today would be a different matter altogether. A quiet anger bubbled in each of us and the IRA's ruthless reputation and the fear we were supposed to have of the consequences of speaking out washed over us. We simply didn't care. We knew only too well what they could do, and that was why we were there. Robert was dead because of what the IRA could do. 'Let them do it,' we replied, when asked if we were afraid. One policeman even expressed the opinion that he was 'afraid we may find one of their children in the River Lagan in six months' time'. But we were not about to be bullied.

The meeting room was smaller than the previous one and we sat around a table where tea and coffee had already been placed. We joked about the improvement in the biscuits on offer: McVitie's chocolate digestives instead of the fusty Hobnobs at the previous meeting. Nothing new was told. Sean and Pádraig claimed that they had spoken to some of the witnesses and assured them that they could come forward. Gowdy and Devine had been spoken to and assured of their safety. (According to Devine, he and Gowdy were also meeting with the IRA at the same time and in the same place, but separately.) It seemed strange to us that Gowdy and Devine had to be visited or taken away so many times to be convinced to tell the truth, and in Devine's case taken away blindfolded. The IRA's obsession with the witnesses rather than the perpetrators was an attempt to pass blame. The only hope we had, they argued, was that witnesses would come forward, and the IRA had assured the key witnesses of their safety. Nothing more could be done. Once again, they alleged that Jim McCormick was the knifeman. They denied that Jock had been present when Robert was being attacked. Terry Davison was never mentioned, and they had claimed at the first meeting that he wasn't one of theirs.

Bridgeen asked them if they had asked McCormick why he did it. Sean looked at her solemnly and said, 'No reason.' Some of us began to cry. I don't know what we wanted to hear — no excuse given would have made it easier, so the answer 'no reason' should not have been any more upsetting. According to Pádraig and Sean, the IRA had ordered Montgomery and McCormick in but they were refusing to comply. They insisted that there was nothing that the IRA could do about it. They were playing the peace process card. In the light of this, they were powerless to do anything else apart from assure us that witnesses had nothing to fear from the IRA. Elaboration on any of the others involved in the cover-up was not forthcoming. They were denying that to the end.

There was a very good reason why the IRA was focusing its attention on Robert's three friends. They were telling us that if only these men would tell the truth, the crime would be solved. At the same time, they were threatening the men and ensuring that they peddled a version of events that suited the IRA. It was a cynical mind game. This was the last meeting we had with the IRA and, apart from confirming what we already knew, it was useless.

Thinking no more of the meeting with the IRA, we travelled down to Dublin the following day to attend an International Women's Day event hosted by the Labour Party. This was our second visit to the Dáil. On the previous occasion, we had had a round of talks with the political parties and some government ministers. The pressure of the weeks since Robert's murder was beginning to take its toll on us individually, and inevitably at times tempers flared and disagreements arose, particularly over media attention. Gemma in particular got hot and bothered about the media and argued that our attendance at events such as this one was unnecessary. Paula and I saw it differently. For us, media attention was essential, and every reasonable opportunity had to be taken to highlight Robert's case, plus important contacts could be made at such events.

Needless to say, relations between ourselves weren't very good and the tensions bubbling below the surface were beginning to rise.

After a long day of barely speaking to each other, and nitpicking when we did, we went to a restaurant where news of the release of the IRA's statement reached us. The statement was generating excitement amongst those at the table as it was rumoured that it said something pretty drastic. With the excitement in the air, we were hopeful that it said something substantial — maybe we were coming to the end of this ordeal; maybe the IRA had seen sense. Maybe it was all over. The meeting we had had with Pádraig and Sean hadn't indicated any change. Was it possible that they had had a change of heart overnight? We chatted amongst ourselves, each talking to those we were on good terms with, whilst officials went out of their way to get us a copy of the statement. We hoped and prayed that this would be the one to put an end to it all and that it would also be an end to the media attention that was causing some of us distress.

Instead, what we got was a convoluted account of that night and an untrue claim that they had offered to shoot the perpetrators. We were disappointed and angry. Was this what everyone was getting so excited about? Now the reason for the meeting the night before became obvious. It was a pretext for the statement and the dramatic offer. Shooting or hurting anyone had not been discussed at the meeting; we were never asked if we wanted the murderers shot. The IRA was obviously up to something, and the notion that it was a mistake was also nonsense.

The media and politicians responded as one would expect, lambasting the IRA for its murderous and brutal offer. What planet were they living on? Justice Minister Michael McDowell said that they must be living in the 'twilight zone'. No one listened when we explained that the IRA hadn't offered to shoot anyone. The truth didn't matter, though — the statement said that it had, that was the story, and it served a better purpose. The offer highlighted the need for the peace process to work, as the alternative was unthinkable. The supposed offer to shoot focused attention on the IRA and its continued existence, and Robert and the murderers were peripheral to this. Our protestations went unheeded, the offer to shoot deemed much more newsworthy and interesting than analysing the IRA's deceit or motives for deceit.

Paula and the others believed that the offer to shoot the perpetrators was aimed at undermining our campaign within the republican community; the offer to shoot them would be interpreted as the IRA showing its disdain for criminals within the community and being prepared to take action against the offenders; continuing with the campaign was proof that we were campaigning against the IRA itself. Although this seemed plausible, it was difficult to believe that republicans would not see through this: surely the IRA took action by itself not at the behest of others? How many people would have been saved from death or punishment beatings if the IRA had asked the victims' families if they wanted the perpetrators of crimes shot or beaten? No such onus would have been put on families in the past, and claiming to have done so now should have raised more questions than answers for many republicans. The fact that we never mentioned to the media an offer to shoot is testimony to the truth that it was never made. I also knew that there was a strategy behind the IRA's apparent madness. Some people commented that it had made a big mistake. 'The IRA don't make mistakes like that,' I replied. 'They're up to something. I don't know what it is, but there is a motive in their madness. That was no mistake.' So why lie and take so much flak? we asked amongst ourselves. Whatever the reason behind it, the statement put us in a stronger position at home and abroad, but no closer to the arrest of Robert's murderers.

If our visit to the Ard-Fheis had undermined our position, the IRA's offer to shoot the murderers revived it. There was widespread condemnation and disbelief at the IRA's offer to shoot them. The effect reverberated around the world and, of course, the media once again descended on Paula's house to hear of our reaction to the statement. I arrived there the following morning to find a press contingent in the courtyard at the back of the house. What has happened now? I wondered. When I got in, Paula told me that the press had been ringing all morning asking for our response to the IRA statement. 'There's nothing for us to respond to,' I said. 'That statement isn't addressing us.'

'You may say something,' Paula said. 'They've been here for over an hour.'

In the meantime, a cameraman was in the kitchen, following my every move. I sat down to write a response to the statement. The house was chaotic with people everywhere, a camera in my face, the phone ringing. I could hear Paula say, 'We'll be out shortly, no more than half an hour.' Eventually I asked the cameraman to turn off his camera as it was too distracting. It was only afterwards that I realised the absurdity of the cameraman following us. It was absolute madness: we were reacting on instinct, discussing things that couldn't go out into the public domain, not to mention the fact that the mental strain of the whole affair was at times unbearable. The last thing we needed was a camera pointed in our face every step of the way. The agreement to such a thing in the first place illustrates the depth of shock we were in.

I wrote out a statement: the offer to shoot was irrelevant to us, the IRA's account was wrong and we wanted the IRA to stop protecting the murderers. Claire had to read it to the waiting press. The IRA statement had done nothing but add drama to the situation. We knew that it was engaged in some sort of game and that bringing Robert's murderers to justice wasn't part of it. That over with, we went back to making arrangements for the States.

THE 'ADVISOCRATS'

I simply didn't have time or the inclination to go shopping for the clothes or other things I would need for the US. We had secured tickets to the American Ireland Fund Dinner, one of the key events in the St Patrick's Day calendar, and this would require evening wear. The round of meetings would require a suit, and so on. Donna and Claire did the honours regarding the clothes shopping, whilst other family members sent over coats, and other items that were riffled through. Thanks to the generous donation of €10,000 from a Southern donor, we were now all travelling to the States. As expected, some sections of the press were keen to promote the idea that we were being controlled by others, and Colm Heatley, a *Daily Ireland* journalist, reported that the SDLP had not only paid for the trip but had organised it also.

This was a deliberate attempt to discredit our campaign by implying that we were not in control but were being used by others. 'The McCartneys are SDLP puppets,' was scrawled on the walls of the Short Strand, Heatley's allegations providing succour to the supporters of murderers. Who was in control of us became a fixation with Sinn Féin. Unable to grasp the notion of people like us working autonomously, Sinn Féin searched fruitlessly for our string-pullers. Its lack of faith in ordinary people is telling. When the press reported that Paula was thinking about standing for the local election, Martin McGuinness issued a veiled threat: 'To step over that line, which is a very important line, into the world of party politics, can do a huge disservice to their campaign' (BBC Radio Ulster). He added that we could lose the support of hundreds of thousands of republicans. His remarks attracted widespread criticism and he retaliated by refuting the remarks but again implying that we were being used by others: 'I at no time warned the family about entering the political arena,' he claimed. 'What I was cautioning against was them being manipulated by others for ulterior and political purposes and I intend to take this matter up with the Press Complaints Commission. I am fully in support of the McCartney family and I believe that bringing those responsible for their brother's death to justice is their sole motivation but I also believe that they are surrounded by some people who have a very different agenda.'

This was what we were dealing with, at the highest level of Sinn Féin, while Jock and his men were being provided with cover. McGuinness's threat once again caused a ripple in the press and in those political circles where being seen to act and speak democratically is regarded as important. Despite his protestations that his meaning had been misinterpreted, it was pretty clear to others and to us. We were stepping on territory claimed by the Provos and, in turn, the latter reverted to form — intimidation. The threat, however, fell on deaf ears as far as we were concerned.

It was ironic that Sinn Féin should criticise us for seeking help from the SDLP in pursuing justice. Sinn Féin had been active for many years in promoting the cause of families seeking justice, yet now it lambasted us for doing the same. By isolating and circumscribing us, Sinn Féin was trying to weaken our campaign, hoping that we would be straitjacketed and therefore limited in what we could do. It was true that the SDLP had helped us with logistics and were on hand if we needed any advice, but we also discussed what was happening with others. One of these was Anthony McIntyre — a former blanket man and an outspoken critic of the 'process' but not the peace — and he was a tower of strength. But never did we seek advice on what we should or shouldn't do. We took the decisions ourselves and, given that Anthony and the SDLP were poles apart politically, it is difficult to see how we could have been controlled by both at the same time.

The language of the peace process had created an illusion that anyone not in favour of the process was not in favour of peace, and was labelled a dissident. This label was adopted from Sinn Féin by the British and Irish governments and was used to isolate anyone who had an opposing view of the peace process. Anyone could fall under this wide, sweeping generalisation — from justice activists to Continuity or Real IRA bombers. We had to prove strenuously to some US figures and British ministers that Robert's murderers were not 'dissidents'; that is, they were not mavericks out to destroy the peace process by getting Sinn Féin into trouble. Sinn Féin had been touting such nonsense and it is an indictment of people such as former Secretary of State Peter Hain that such claims were given an ounce of credibility. But unfortunately they were because politically it suited the peace process for them to be believed. Anthony McIntyre earned the label of dissident because of his criticism of the direction of the Provisional leadership, using nothing more than intellectual argument. In an article in *The Blanket* ('The Advisocrats, It's All Their Fault', 22 March 2005), McIntyre scoffed at McGuinness's allegations that he had claimed he was a McCartney advisor:

Two months ago Joe Pilling was the subject of McGuinness's ire when, desperately trying to plug a leaking credibility, he flailed around in search of a convenient scapegoat on to whom he could pin the rapidly depreciating label 'securocrat'. Now to explain away his party's failings in its handling of the McCartney murder, he has cast his line again, this time in hope of hooking an advisocrat.

Anthony summed up McGuinness' intentions:

What does McGuinness hope to achieve by churning out porkies? Seemingly, he reckons that if the McCartney women's campaign can be tainted with the shadow of the 'anti-peace' lobby, it might bring a few much needed alms of sympathy his way. Unfortunately for Sinn Féin, it has not been too adept in manipulating a wider public into believing that opposition to the peace process and violently dissenting from it are essentially one and the same.

Our treatment at the hands of Sinn Féin's propaganda machine was both insightful and shameful. I felt ashamed of myself when I realised how easy it was for the party to vilify and demonise those whom it opposed. I had lived in a community that had listened to Sinn Féin's mantra of fighting for equality, yet how it treated those who seemed to threaten it was more indicative of its belief in such principles. If the IRA didn't physically coerce silence, Sinn Féin tried to destroy credibility and character and turn the community against you. How many people had they destroyed without a murmur of protest? Our campaign of justice seemed to enrage Sinn Féin and its supporters; it attracted so much venom and anger, and the line that others were controlling us was pushed by Heatley: '*Daily Ireland* has also learned that Ruarai McKenna, who acted as the McCartneys' media officer during their stay in Washington, is a former SDLP activist.' The insistence that we were being helped by others seemed to be of more importance than the murder of a man. Our decision to go to America was really pissing off these so-called republicans, and they were firing their guns. Their lies and spin just served to anger us further; they didn't deter us or make us rethink, and Robin Livingstone's *Andersonstown News* article about 'unionism on tour' was so disgusting that I had no choice but to email him and tell him what I thought of him.

In the days leading up to our trip to the US, one thing after another seemed to happen. The Ard-Fheis, the meeting with the IRA, followed by the statement about offering to shoot the perpetrators, Ted Kennedy's refusal to meet with Gerry Adams, the graffiti slur on the walls of the Short Strand designed to intimidate us, and then the news that Cora Groogan had been in the bar on the night when Robert was murdered. Despite the fact that Robert was with his friends that night, not one of them had told the police anything that could be translated into evidence. We were completely devastated by this but, more so, we were deeply hurt for Robert. Since he was a child, he had always had a deep sense of loyalty to his friends and naturally supposed that they had the same loyalty to him. Letters written to Robert by Brendan Devine expressed how good a friend Robert was to him, and the strength of Robert's friendship was undisputed by the many who paid their respects after his death. Ultimately, however, this friendship meant nothing in the throes of death.

Robert did have one friend, however, who in a small way was able to reveal the hypocrisy of Sinn Féin. My partner Ed had been a friend of Robert's for many years before we met. On the night of Robert's murder, he was working from a taxi depot on the Ormeau Road. It was the same depot that the IRA phoned to order a load of cars to come down and ferry people away from the bar. Ed was completely unaware of what was happening and was told by the taxi operator to go to Magennis's and pick up a fare. The police were already at the bar when he arrived but he was oblivious to the reasons for their presence. He picked up two women who were in an agitated state, and so witnessed the conversation recorded in the first chapter in which one of the woman responded, 'So fuck!' on being informed that she was leaving the scene of a crime. It was only the following day that Ed realised why the police had been outside the bar, but the importance of his taxi pick-up wasn't realised until we discovered who the woman was who had said to the policeman 'So fuck': it was Cora Groogan.

We checked with the police and, as expected, Groogan had not made any statement to them or to the Ombudsman, despite Adams calling on people to come forward. Once the press got hold of the story, Groogan issued a brief statement:

> I got to the bar about 10 pm that Sunday. I was there for a short while. There was a commotion in the bar but I witnessed nothing and left shortly after 11 pm. I have given a full statement to my solicitor.

Groogan's, Hargey's and Hayes's conduct was particularly sickening. These three people had been put forward as potential candidates for election. The Northern Ireland public was going to be subjected to these hypocritical, unprincipled and amoral people preaching about the importance of human rights and justice. To top it all, Hargey was standing in May as a candidate for the local council. People who refused to co-operate with the police or the Ombudsman in a murder enquiry were seeking election as civic representatives.

Sinn Féin's behaviour was a disgrace and arrogant. Did these people have no conscience? Were these the type of people who could possibly be put in charge of the country in a couple of years' time? People who despite knowing that a man had been brutally stabbed and beaten yards from where they sat didn't feel the moral need to provide the police with the smallest details? 'Morally defunct' was the only way we could describe them. The whole thing reeked of depravity and evil.

As the trip to the States drew closer, Sinn Féin tried once more to placate us. Gerry Kelly arrived at Paula's house in a fluster to tell her that Montgomery was going in to make a statement to the police. Gerard Montgomery had been named by the IRA as being aware of who was responsible for providing the murder weapon and destroying the key evidence. By this stage we had lost complete faith and trust in Sinn Féin. Nothing that party said could be taken at face value; only the outcome of actions could determine the sincerity of its leaders. As it turned out, the police refused to interview Montgomery and he sat in the car park for eight hours. Sinn Féin was outraged at this and issued a statement condemning police inaction:

> Republicans have suspected that the PSNI is tailoring their investigation into the murder of Robert McCartney to cause maximum damage to Sinn Féin. Today's revelations that the PSNI turned away a key witness and a key suspect adds further weight to this suspicion.
>
> In such a high profile murder investigation it beggars belief that the PSNI would reject an offer of an eyewitness statement from a key witness and the opportunity to interview a key suspect who they claim to have been searching for.
>
> But this is what happened today. It is also clear that eyewitness testimony which identifies some of those involved in the attack on Robert McCartney has been ignored and that a decision has been made not to arrest and charge those identified by the eyewitness. The normal police practice of quickly putting suspects into an identity parade has not happened despite the fact the PSNI know who was involved and has eyewitness evidence about this. This underlines the fact that politics rather than justice is driving the PSNI investigation. All those who have been vocal in support of the McCartneys need to put some searching questions to the PSNI.

We did question the police on its failure to bring in Montgomery — maybe the IRA was eventually coming clean, we thought. The police informed us that they knew what they were doing and that Montgomery had no intention of talking to them. Whether this is true or not, we will never know, but ultimately we had to trust someone and, as the IRA and Sinn Féin had done their utmost to cover up Robert's murder, we did not trust them. Given that all the other suspects had picked a spot on the wall and stared at it, we had no reason to believe that Montgomery had any intentions of doing any different.

Chapter 5

BRINGING THE CAMPAIGN TO WASHINGTON

I am amazed at how, after five weeks that had passed in a blur of interviews and meetings, we still got the strength and energy to go on — it must have been the adrenaline flowing through us. Adrenaline produced by anger and grief. The six of us headed to Dublin to catch our flight to Washington, unaware of what awaited us and with no idea how we were going to handle the whole thing. We had been in the thick of a media and political whirlwind for five weeks, and the flight turned out to be a welcome respite. As we sat in our economy seats prior to take-off, a stewardess approached us and asked if we were 'the McCartney sisters'. We nodded apprehensively, expecting bad news. She asked us to follow her to the front of the plane where the captain had made seats available to us. We were pleasantly stunned by this gesture of kindness. Gemma had been convinced that we were being escorted off the plane. The glass is always half empty for us!

Our notoriety unnerved us, though. In one way we were grateful that people knew who we were, because then they knew about Robert, but on the other hand it could be a little embarrassing. In any case, we were very grateful to the captain that day and we travelled to Washington in comfort. For the first time in six weeks, we were able to rest without being disturbed by the phone ringing or journalists calling to the door.

The strain of the whole thing was beginning to take its toll on us physically and emotionally: I had lost weight, leaving me looking like a 'chicken', according to Donna; everyone's nerves were frayed and we argued amongst ourselves. Gemma and Donna were less patient with the press and politicians, Gemma concerned about the media intrusion and Donna angry at having to travel across the world to get justice. None of us knew if going to America was going to help or hinder our fight for justice. There were no guarantees and we were fumbling in the dark. I relied on gut instinct, and if something felt right, we did it. This was the force that guided the campaign rather than strategies and discussions. Outcomes could not be specified or measured and this lack of clarity or guarantees created a tension within the family. Were we wasting our time? Were we being used? Did these people really care? These were just some of the questions constantly asked.

And then of course there was the truth that all this didn't make any difference to the fact that Robert was dead. It wasn't going to bring him back, and at times it seemed that we were using the campaign as a way to run from that truth. Not ready to face the fact that Robert was dead, concentrating on the campaign provided an escape — or did it? I had thought about this on a few occasions when things got really tough. Were we using the campaign as a way of grieving? Was it possible that we could pick up the pieces without bringing anyone to justice? But the answer was always 'no'. The image of the men pursuing Robert down that street would haunt all of us forever. I could see their faces and Robert's, could see them beating him, saying things to him, ignoring his pleas for mercy. I could see the women mopping the floor, washing the clothes, could see the scene in the bar with the gang standing around him. There would be no closure until these people had faced their crimes. If we stopped, we might as well have been present that night, too, so nothing was a waste of time. It didn't matter if other people didn't care; we did and that was all that mattered.

For me, it was important to get our message heard in the States where many Irish-Americans still had a romanticised notion of the republican struggle. In one interview, I explained that we wanted 'to dispel the romantic vision of the IRA' and to let Irish-Americans know that 'the IRA of today is not the IRA of ten to fifteen years ago'. The comment was welcomed by some and greeted by others with anger. Robin Livingstone's anger was vented through his 'Unionism on Tour' article, mentioned in the previous chapter. I was unaware of the effect my comment had had back home in Ireland, but apparently it had police officers and ex-IRA/Sinn Féin members alike jumping with delight.

We arrived at Dulles Airport in Washington and queued up at the immigration desk. I had an irrational fear and sense of guilt as if I were trying to enter the country illegally. The stern demeanour of the security staff didn't help. We had filled in the visa waivers on the plane and had written that we were on business, so of course when I approached the immigration desk I was asked by the officer, 'What is the nature of your business?' I wondered to myself, *Now how do you explain this one?* 'What's the purpose of your visit?' she repeated.

'Meetings with Senators and Congress people and the President.' I cringed, thinking to myself, *How stupid does this sound!* I tried to explain quietly that we were there to meet the President of the United States as we were fighting a campaign of justice.

The officer looked at me bemusedly.

Meanwhile, Donna and Gemma were at other desks and Claire, Bridgeen and Paula were waiting in the queue. I heard Donna shout over, 'Catherine, why are we here?'

I turned towards Donna, whose face was blood red and was exuding an air of annoyance. 'To attend meetings,' I replied, wanting to add, 'Don't be cheeky to them; you'll just make things worse.' But I just thought to myself, *So much for discreet!*

'Who with?' Donna persisted.

'Hillary Clinton, Ted Kennedy and others,' I responded as quietly as I could. I didn't want to say 'the President'. The other travellers were looking on and our explanations must have sounded ludicrous.

'There you go,' Donna said to the officer, her face flushed with anger.

The officer attending to me then asked, 'And how do you intend to get to the White House?'

'Taxi,' I replied.

'And how do you intend to get in?'

'My passport,' I explained calmly.

Unconvinced by my explanation, she directed me to the holding centre, Donna and Gemma following in quick succession. Gemma had initially passed through immigration unhindered even though she had also explained that she was there to see the President. However, when the officer noticed the reaction of his colleagues to us and realised that she was one of our party, he followed his colleagues' lead and directed Gemma also to the holding centre. This was not a good start to the trip and, suppressing an irrational fear, I went up to the desk to explain again why we were there. Luckily I had my file that contained the itinerary and the direct numbers to the offices of the private secretaries of Senator Kennedy and others. The immigration officer went off to dial one of the numbers. Meanwhile, Bridgeen came bursting in, shouting and waving her hands about, her long nails exaggerating the motion.

'Where's the letter, the letter?' she said.

What letter?' I asked.

'The letter from the White House saying we were invited.'

'I didn't get a letter,' I said.

'Paula had it.' Bridgeen was very flustered and was panicking, and I started to panic, too, at the notion that we had forgotten to bring our invitations with us. *Jesus Christ!* I thought. What would happen if we couldn't meet the President because we had forgotten the letters? Paula, meanwhile, was sitting impassively, Donna was angry, Claire was a little afraid and Gemma was amused at it all; after all, she had got through with no trouble.

'Paula, did you get a letter from the White House?'

'No,' she said. 'Just from the consulate outlining the programme, no letter of invitation.'

'What are we going to do? My kids!' Bridgeen exclaimed in despair.

'Look, give it over. The officer is away to check out our story. There's nothing to panic about; there were no official invites, so stop panicking.'

Just at that, the officer came back and smiled and said that she had rung Senator Kennedy's office and been told to 'let us go'. What a relief!

We thanked the immigration officers and headed for the exit where we were met by dozens of reporters and film crews. I was still panicking about the letters and rang the consulate as soon as we hit the hotel to check that we didn't need an official letter to get into the White House. I was assured that we didn't but they faxed us through an invitation anyway to reassure us. We laughed at Bridgeen's story of her experience at immigration.

'Who are you here to see?' she had been asked.

'The President,' she had replied, matter-of-factly.

'What President?'

'George,' she had drooled, bemused by the fact that the officer didn't know the name of his own President!

On future trips to the US, we ticked the leisure box on the visa waivers — a lot easier.

At last we arrived at Jury's Hotel, Dupont Circle, in downtown Washington. We checked in and were shown to our rooms, where we ordered coffee and tea but had little time to drink it as the phone started ringing with requests for interviews. A mood of foreboding hung over us. Recounting the experience in the holding centre and laughing at the antics of Bridgeen demanding, 'Where's the letter, the letter?' had lifted it a bit but we had little time to relax; our schedule was full and the media were eager for interviews.

Media interest in our campaign reached its climax during our trip to America. It was absolutely crazy and took us by surprise even though we had given up to 600 interviews in the previous six weeks. We had been on radio and television, at the Ard-Fheis, in the Dáil and at the rally. But nothing could have prepared us for the media scrum that was to take place in the States. We were inundated with requests for interviews and were rarely 'journalist free', and in between meetings we were running back and forth to television studios so that the pictures could be sent back home in time for the news bulletins. We were grateful that the SDLP had put us in touch with Ruarai McKenna whose help, drive and professionalism proved to be invaluable during this time. He was from Ballymena and had been working in Washington for the previous three years. A go-getter and enthusiastic about politics, he was genuinely interested in our campaign, and acted as our press officer for five days for nothing more than a 'thank you'.

The media attention was overwhelming and at times it could get pretty aggressive. Although we were over in the US to lobby the politicians, press coverage was also important and so we didn't refuse any interviews. Overexposure was always a fear but we knew that it was going to be temporary, a window of opportunity that we had to use. Of course, the press could be unrelenting, and at times this caused friction amongst us. Newspapers and magazines wanted their own pictures to go with their story. 'Why can't they take one from the archives?' some said, exasperated. But magazines such as *Time* were very influential and we had to remember that Robert was special to us but to no one else; justice wasn't going to fall on our lap because it was our brother who had been murdered. Every interview and meeting was important, even if it produced nothing substantial. We just had to keep going and hoping. Grief, exhaustion and irritability could all wait.

The five days in Washington were very busy: we had meetings during the day and then social occasions at night. In between these, we had radio, newspaper and television interviews. We had become accustomed to the interviews although we were always nervous. We were overly cautious about saying the wrong thing and were very hard on ourselves if we didn't say this or that. The meetings with the senators and congressmen, however, were our reason for being there and we had to impress upon them the facts about Robert's murder and to counteract Sinn Féin's version of events. Over the previous weeks, Sinn Féin sympathisers had been pushing the bar-brawl line and claiming that those involved were dissidents, people whom Gerry Adams was having difficulty with in bringing on board the peace train. It was our job to convince people like Senators Ted Kennedy, Hillary Clinton and others that Sinn Féin and the IRA had created a climate wherein gangs within their organisations were committing crimes and being protected by the Provisional movement, including Sinn Féin. Refusal to co-operate with the police was a pretext for a much deeper underlying culture of criminality.

Our first scheduled meeting was with Senator Kennedy, Senator Hillary Clinton, Senator Chris Dodd and Senator John McCain. Kennedy sent a car to the hotel to pick us up and as we drove up to the Senate buildings, the media were waiting outside. As we emerged from the car, we realised that Senator Kennedy himself had come out to greet us, and this was not only a kind gesture but also a deliberate political message. Given that he was refusing to meet with Adams publicly, greeting us accentuated the difference in approach to both parties. We symbolised the obstacles to the peace process — IRA criminality and contempt for the rule of law. Of course we had to bear this in mind also as we sought justice for our brother.

Senator Kennedy was a warm and charismatic man, his paternalistic manner welcomed by us, given the pressure we were under, and his natural approach put us at our ease. After the press photographers had got their pictures, he led the way to his office for a private meeting. His office walls were covered in pictures of his family: J.F.K. and Robert looked out from frames, alive and smiling faces looking down on the proceedings; other photographs depicted them in a more serious contemplative mood, conveying the seriousness of their positions. His loss of his two brothers was mirrored by our loss of two brothers; we shared the brutality and devastation of murder. Needless to say, we felt strange sitting in the small office whilst Senator Kennedy poured coffee and tea and offered us shamrock-shaped iced shortbread. We seated ourselves on the comfortable couches, nervous and apprehensive. The last thing one wants to do is to look foolish in front of such people.

Getting the points across clearly was important, as was impressing on them the truth that Sinn Féin held the key to justice. Senator Kennedy sat in a chair facing us, and three other chairs awaited the arrival of our other hosts. The atmosphere was very relaxed, although we were all nervous and a little overwhelmed. Hillary Clinton then entered the room, followed by Senators John McCain and Chris Dodd. All three expressed their condolences. We discussed the circumstances surrounding Robert's murder and impressed upon them the grim reality of the IRA's hold on areas such as the Short Strand. Sinn Féin's determination to protect murderers from justice was undermining the development of peace in Ireland, leaving ordinary citizens vulnerable to thugs and bullies such as Jock Davison and his crew. Kennedy, Clinton, Dodd and McCain were aware of the issues and did not buy into the Sinn Féin line of a bar-room brawl or dissidents. From the discussions it was evident that the IRA's criminal activities had been concerning those in Washington for some time. Robert's murder appeared to be the last straw and the last piece of evidence they needed to prove that the IRA was becoming the obstacle to peace. Referring to the IRA, Kennedy said, 'There's a time to hold them and a time to fold them.' Obviously in his eyes the time had come to fold them. Gerry Adams had ridden two horses for too long. Ultimately it had led to the death of men such as Robert; there could be no more.

We were all in agreement about what the problem was and the solution, but I was always aware that people like ourselves are only details in the political arena. Although Robert's murder was pivotal to highlighting the realities of IRA criminality, bringing his murderers to justice was not necessarily required in order for the peace process to get back on track. What we had to do was to try and put those politicians who claimed to support us in a position wherein they were prepared to demand delivery from Sinn Féin, not just words. As the months rolled on and our campaign achieved for others what they could not achieve for themselves, it was frustrating to listen to politicians gratuitously congratulating themselves on their efforts and talking about how the

IRA had made historic moves that would progress peace. Justice for families like ours was of academic interest.

We informed Senators Kennedy, Clinton, Dodd and McCain of the reality of living on the streets of the Short Strand; we told them about how the IRA and Sinn Féin operated in such areas, controlling people through violence and fear. We had brought a dossier with us containing photographs and the names of those connected with Robert's murder. The picture of Gerard Montgomery and Gerry Adams and the positions of the others in the community refuted Sinn Féin's line that those involved in and with direct information concerning Robert's murder were on the fringes of the peace process. They were at the very heart of it, and had benefited since 1996 from the peace dividend and the flow of monies into areas like the Short Strand. To aid in the development of peace and reconciliation was used as a form of patronage. Robert had been murdered because the courting of the IRA by the peace lobby had created an environment in which IRA men could operate freely in crime. Governments had turned a blind eye to murder and other serious crimes of the IRA, and this had created a criminal comfort zone around IRA units. In turn, members of the IRA and Sinn Féin believed that they could get away with murder. And they were right.

After half an hour or so, the meeting came to a close, for which we were all relieved. To a degree the fact that the meeting had taken place rather than what was said was the key factor — we could have talked about the weather. These people were statesmen and women, and meeting with us was designed to send a political message to Sinn Féin. The US had stiffened its resolve against illegal organisations, the courting was over, and decision time had come. The details of Robert's murder were also of academic interest. This is not to say that, as individuals, they didn't care or were not sincere in their condolences, but rather that it is the nature of *realpolitik* that getting bogged down in details can stop the advance. This was and still is the most difficult thing to come to terms with: the fact that a man's life — Robert's life — could be conceded for a perceived bigger prize. What was probably more frustrating was that Sinn Féin also knew this, and the smugness of its leadership and members was galling.

The most nerve-racking part was still to come, however: a press conference had been arranged and I was pushed forward to speak for the family. I stood with Senator Kennedy, Senator Hillary Clinton (possibly the future President) and Senator McCain (another possible candidate for the Presidency) as they sent a clear message to the IRA that it was time to go. I spoke only of the need to bring Robert's murderers to justice. Of course Kennedy's refusal to meet with Adams and standing with us was a point of interest for the press but it was one that it would have been foolish for us to comment on. It was important that we stayed within our boundaries, as commenting on the wider political debate could undermine or campaign. We were not the only ones concerned about this. We were asked what we would be saying if the press posed a question about Kennedy's refusal to meet with Adams. I said that I would not be commenting on it.

I was very anxious and nervous about the press conference, as I knew that the press would ask difficult questions; I had to think on my feet. It was incidents such as these that demonstrated how difficult it was to fight for what seemed to be a straightforward cause — justice. If you're from Northern Ireland, justice is politically loaded and one wrong word can set the tide against you. We were not politicians and could not comment on the political actions of others. We had to engage with the politicians but not politically; at times it was difficult but we managed to do so fairly well. The dreaded question did come up at the press conference but I replied that Senator Kennedy's decision was a matter for him and he could answer it. This went down well with everyone, apart from the press, of course, who would have preferred meatier answers. We were aware that Kennedy's strategy was a temporary measure, whereas to applaud or condemn would have long-term consequences for us. We had to tread a very thin political line.

After the meeting and the press conference, we headed over to the Congress buildings to meet with Congressman Peter King. Peter King was a fervent supporter of Adams and Co., but he needed little convincing about Sinn Féin's ability to help us to get justice. Another fervent supporter of Adams, Congressman Jim Walsh, was in full agreement with King and the others regarding the IRA. Unfortunately when we met with Jim Walsh on a return trip that November, he was a little less enthusiastic about our campaign. We made the trip in the aftermath of IRA decommissioning, to refocus attention on what we believed really mattered — justice. Robert had been killed not with a gun but with a knife; the only way his murderers would be brought to justice was if Sinn Féin were forced to co-operate. However, by then, the tide had changed against us. IRA decommissioning in September had captured the imagination of the press and politicians: once again the IRA had taken a historic step and it had to be rewarded. Details such as justice paled into insignificance. That November, Walsh asked us directly if the British were behind our campaign and, by the following March, Walsh and King had completely dismissed Robert as a 'microscopic' detail. This was for the future, however.

The first day of meetings over, we went back to the hotel for another round of interviews. We had been invited to the American Ireland Fund Dinner, a gala event held every year and apparently the highlight of Washington's St Patrick's Day celebrations. We were all seated at different tables at the dinner, something that made some of us nervous. Just the thought of an evening of small talk and polite conversation was exhausting, and the fact that we had a whole night of it ahead of us added to the sense of despondency. Gemma and Donna were in a gloomy mood and asked if it was necessary for them to go. I was exasperated at this and told them that people had gone to an awful lot of trouble to get us the tickets for this dinner; they had cost money and the media were going to be present. In my view, we all had to go. No one was enjoying any of this, and we were all equally exhausted, traumatised and grieving, but we were in Washington for a purpose and going to this dinner was as important as the meeting with Bush and others.

Even while we were getting dressed, we carried out interviews with journalists in the hotel room and on the phone. On reflection now, some of this was unnecessary and we could have given ourselves some time by saying no, but there was a sense of urgency about the whole thing and so no one was turned down. As expected, the media were waiting for our arrival and, as we walked into the hall, they milled around, pushing and shoving, trying to get the best picture. It is the most uncomfortable position to be in. Trying to act naturally and ignore them was hard, and we just wanted to get to our seats as quickly as possible. As we descended the stairs, Gemma slipped and fell to her knees, nearly bringing Paula with her as she attempted to save herself. The panic and shock on both their faces was comical. Fortunately no pictures of Gemma falling with a glass in her hand appeared in the papers, but it gave us a brief respite from the formality of the gala.

We were seated at tables with American patrons of the event. I was seated beside a very nice family whose father had donated over a million dollars to the American Ireland Fund. It was strange sitting at the table listening to this family laugh and joke with each other. They were very friendly and included me in the conversation, but — given what I had been through in the previous six weeks, with the murder of my brother, and subsequently being plunged into a reality far removed from normal family life — it was difficult to immerse myself in the conversation fully. I smiled and chatted casually but I couldn't wait for the whole thing to be over. It was so out of place with our reality, and sitting amongst the guests intensified the awfulness of our own situation. These people were out for an evening of entertainment and light conversation. Catching up on old friends and family was the essence of the event for them. We, in contrast, were there because the worst thing in the world had happened to us. We were in the depths of despair, and we envied the people sitting with their families, just having a night out. We would have given anything to have been one of them, but we were not.

The hosts gave a summary of the different projects back in Ireland that the money raised at these events went to. Film clips of children back home, Protestant and Catholic playing together, were shown; integrated education was a key theme and Lagan College was hailed as a great example of this system. Patrons were brought up to the stage and cheered for their efforts in bringing peace to Ireland. Gerry Adams sat in the audience, as did Taoiseach Bertie Ahern, Foreign Affairs Minister Dermot Ahern and other political and community figures from Ireland, applauding the American benefactors. There was no doubt that the donors were generous to the Ireland Fund, but there were signs that they were beginning to question Ireland's need for handouts. A year later, I attended the same event and one of the benefactors sitting at my table commented that he and his co-benefactors were beginning to question the need for such fund-raising events. 'We are beginning to realise that while we are giving money to help those in need in Ireland, there are many of our own people living in poverty who could do with a helping hand from us,' he said. 'These events may be coming to an end.' A fair point, I thought.

Senator John McCain was called to the podium to address the gathering and he didn't disappoint. His speech was hair-raising, and he pulled no punches, lambasting the IRA; the audience was a little taken aback by the vociferousness of his language. Adams sat coolly sipping his Guinness and leaning back, appearing bemused. I am sure that he felt the full blast of McCain's reproach. The Senator congratulated us on our bravery, which made me uncomfortable; Adams sat impassively as the crowd clapped and cheered. He couldn't have been expected to clap, of course — he was the leader of the movement singled out for the harshest criticism, and it was neither surprising that he didn't clap nor disappointing.

The grand finale was a song from the Ulster Scots play, *On Eagle's Wing*. Unfortunately the American patrons at my table were less than impressed, but rather highly amused at the performance. At one point, the guy sitting next to me stuffed his napkin in his mouth, his face crumpled with laughter and tears in his eyes. His wife tried to constrain her laughter but eventually joined in. I sympathised with the singer but part of me thought the response deserved, given the depiction of Ireland to which we had been subjected during the evening.

The gala dinner over, we returned to the hotel for yet more interviews. It was exhausting but there was no escape. The next day was more of the same: interviews and meetings. The St Patrick's Day calendar is full of events and receptions, which are an effective way of highlighting campaigns and getting the ear of influential people. But there is also a sense of the abstract about them — endless talking and explaining. Our story was attracting attention from as far away as New Zealand, and on one occasion I had to stand outside the hotel and do an interview for New Zealand television with a cameraman who didn't have a clue about us. The arrangements had been made by phone and I was told that a film crew would be waiting outside the hotel at five o'clock. At five, I headed outside and approached a cameraman.

'Hi,' I said. 'I'm Catherine McCartney. Are you here for New Zealand television?'

He looked at me confusedly. 'I'm waiting on a Sister Catherine,' he said.

'I'm Catherine. You're the guy for New Zealand television?'

'Yeah, but I was expecting a nun.'

I burst out laughing. 'A nun?'

'Yeah, they said I was to film an interview with Sister Catherine.'

'They probably said, "the sister Catherine",' I explained.

He still looked confused, but it became clear to him as I gave the interview that there were six of us, and why we were there. He shook his head in disgust as I relayed the story of Robert's murder once more, and, turning to Paula, said, 'Dirty bastards.'

PRESIDENT BUSH

Although the meetings with the Senators and Congressmen were important, the key focus of our trip was meeting with President Bush. Because it was the White House, we were expecting all sorts of security checks to be undertaken. We were surprised, however, at how relaxed the process was. We stood in a queue alongside other guests including Ann McCabe, also on a mission of justice for her husband Jerry, a garda who had been shot dead in cold blood by the IRA during a robbery. Ann had been promised that the men responsible would not be released under the terms of the Good Friday Agreement, and a personal letter from Bertie Ahern a year or so previously had reassured her of this. But Ann, like us, had been catapulted into the campaigning world by the warped nature of Northern Ireland politics. Sinn Féin had been negotiating hard on behalf of the men responsible for Jerry McCabe's murder and, as part of a peace deal, it was close to securing the men's release under the Agreement. Ann was having none of it and had galvanised the support of the Irish people. As a result, Sinn Féin and Ahern backed away from the issue and the men themselves issued a pathetic statement from prison, claiming that they didn't want their plight to be used as an obstacle to the peace process.

Ann was at the White House to ensure that another U-turn was not employed in any future talks on Northern Ireland. We had the pleasure of meeting her again back home in Ireland at an award event; like us, she was driven by nothing more than love for her husband and a conviction that justice should not be politically expedient. And so she and we stood outside the gates of the White House, thousands of miles away from where the injustices had taken place. Why we had to do this was a sad reflection on the powers that be at home. As we queued up outside, we were interviewed by the press and asked what we expected to get out of the meeting. We repeated ourselves again and again. One Irish journalist asked what I thought of the 'backlash back home in Ireland'.

'What backlash?' I asked.'

'Well, many people are unhappy that your family are being given access to the White House,' the journalist explained.

'Those people should ask themselves why they have a problem with ordinary people walking the corridors of power,' I replied. 'We have as much right as politicians — that is what democracy is all about.' I was angry at this assertion that people in Ireland were resentful towards us because we were meeting with powerful figures. We were in America not to seek fame or recognition but because our brother had been murdered and his murder had been covered up by the IRA and Sinn Féin, a party that had been courted by America for over ten years. There was resentment towards our campaign but it emanated mainly from those republicans who chose to focus on us rather than on those who had murdered our brother. Instead of asking their republican leaders why they were not doing more to help us to get justice, they preferred to hide behind the cry of 'Sinn Féin-bashing'. It was a much more comfortable position to take, and didn't require any great analysis or challenge to the thought processes that republicans had adopted for thirty years. Others resentful of our campaign but outside the republican circle should have been questioning why we had to travel so far to ask for justice, instead of slamming us for seeking it in the first place. One thing we did learn about human nature is that it can be irrational, fickle and selfish, as well as courageous, kind and empathetic. No backlash could succeed in silencing us.

It was a cold but crisp day and, as we moved up the queue, I envisaged getting to the top and being told that our names were not on the list. My fears were not realised, however, and so we entered what is probably the most iconic building in the world, and the residence of the most powerful leader. I was surprised therefore that what I could see of the interior was neither glamorous nor awe-inspiring; it was obviously the section reserved for events such as today's. There was a buzz in the air and people chatted about the reasons for their presence. Some had been before and commented that Bill Clinton threw a much better 'do'. We mingled with the other guests while we waited to be called to meet the President. Paula, Bridgeen and I were to represent the family, and we were quite nervous at the prospect of meeting with the President.

After about ten minutes, we were brought to another room which was empty of furniture apart from lamp tables and a couple of small couches back against the wall. On the floor were place names. We found ours and stood in a semi-circle around the oval rug, waiting for the arrival of George W. Bush. Security personnel in military uniform stood around, as did plain-clothes security. American security men and women are very stern, their demeanour and stature sending out the message, 'Don't even joke let alone mess with us.' It can be intimidating.

We didn't really know what we were going to say to the President that would make an impact. We knew that Mitchell Reiss, Bush's Special Envoy to Northern Ireland, was our man in terms of being focused on Northern Ireland. President Bush, I suspected, took his lead from his advisors on this one, and the whole St Patrick's Day thing was something he did because it was on the calendar. Bertie Ahern had advised us to speak concisely to the President, and give him a clear message.

A bugle sounded and the arrival of the President was announced. Everyone stood at their place name and waited to be greeted by the most powerful man in the world. President Bush entered the room, accompanied by the Taoiseach grinning from ear to ear like the man of the moment. Bertie had something to feel smug about — very few political leaders get such access to the United States President and even fewer small political players like Ireland. This relationship is not to be scoffed at: in terms of international politics, Ireland is in a privileged position regardless of whether we like it or not. This privilege, however, has a downside: it inflates the egos of Irish politicians and provides them with a sense of self-importance that is out of proportion to the reality of their positions.

Making his way around the room, President Bush spent a few minutes chatting with each guest, laughter drifting from whatever company he was in. As he made his way towards us, I got more nervous. How could you make sense of our story in a few short minutes or say something that would have an impact? Eventually the President and Mitchell Reiss approached us, along with the Taoiseach who introduced us and explained who we were. The President's face was smiling as he shook each of our hands in turn, offering his condolences and congratulating us on the stand we had taken. We nodded in appreciation of his words and I said something about the importance of pressurising Sinn Féin into handing over Robert's killers. He talked briefly about how the IRA had become an obstacle to peace and how upholding law and order was essential to democracy. Still smiling, he nodded towards Mitchell and said, 'And how's this guy doing?' I uttered some words about how Mitchell had been a great help. 'Yeah, he's a good guy,' he replied. He then spoke to Bridgeen about Robert and the boys. He told her to stay strong and said that the road to justice was a long one but that he would be doing all he could to help us. Before they moved on, they posed for a photograph with us. The President decided to move around the back and stood with his arms around Bridgeen's and my shoulders. We were relieved when it was over; Bertie leaned back towards us as they moved off and said, 'Well done.'

The meeting with President Bush was the pivotal moment of our campaign: you cannot go to a higher office in the world. What I said or what he said was unimportant. The fact that Robert's murder was an issue in Washington demonstrated what effect it had on the political arena. Sinn Féin and the IRA's attempt to contain it within the Short Strand had failed dismally. Unlike so many other murders, they were unable to pass it off as 'internal housekeeping' or a tragic incident. The IRA's criminality had become too blatant and arrogant. Our campaign provided the peace process politicians with the moral high ground and they used it to coerce Sinn Féin in the direction of endorsing the PSNI.

After the President had finished meeting and greeting his guests, we sighed with relief and talked amongst ourselves about the encounter. Did we get our message across? we wondered. At this time we thought that it mattered; time would teach us differently.

After our short encounter with Bush, we were directed to another room where an Irish reception was being held in honour of the President. The theme was typically Irish and the only thing missing was the leprechaun. It wasn't the most entertaining of receptions and probably less so for President Bush who is less endeared by Ireland than his predecessor. A small, heavily built woman from Brooklyn enthusiastically played the tin whistle for her President and then two Irish dancers did a jig or a reel in the little space afforded them. The President then approached the podium and spoke about his guests and the relationship between Ireland and the US. He singled us out for special recognition, explaining to the audience the reason for our presence and declaring, 'You are going to change the world'; he then instructed us to stand up and take a bow. The audience clapped loudly and we were absolutely mortified as we stood to the applause of the room. We wanted the ground to open and swallow us up.

Bridgeen, Paula and I were seated on the left-hand side of the room; Claire, Gemma and Donna were on the right. Recalling the event later, we rolled with laughter at Gemma's account of the congratulatory scene. As we stood up on one side of the room, Gemma, Claire and Donna followed suit. All three stood, but the audience, not as familiar with their faces, was applauding and looking in the direction of Bridgeen, Paula and me, obviously following the President's lead. The other three quickly realised that no one was clapping in their direction; they slowly skulked back into their seats, embarrassed but in a fit of giggles. The reception drew to a close and the President rose to leave the room. As he marched down the aisle, he stopped very briefly at our row and mouthed a 'thank you' to us. There was no doubt that in terms of Northern Irish politics the IRA was at centre stage, as were we at this point.

By this time, Paula and I were gasping for a smoke. The whole episode had frayed our nerves and the only thing we could think of when the reception was over was having a cigarette. The others went off to get food whilst Paula and I went outside. We could see the press standing in a group at the top of the street, waiting for us. The reception wasn't over yet and, with our bodies replenished with nicotine, we turned to go back in. The security man had other ideas, however, and simply refused us entrance. So much for 'changing the world' — VIP guests one minute, not allowed back in the next! How quickly things change. We were not bothered really, though. The most nerve-racking meeting was over and a quiet cup of coffee and cigarette were very appealing.

Appealing as they may have been, they were not to be had, though, as the press corps was in full swing and anxious to get a story. 'What did the President say?' 'How did you feel meeting with the President of the US?' 'What did you say to him?' 'What was the Oval Office like?' 'What do you think of the President?' and so on — relentless questions.

One journalist asked Paula, 'What was it like sitting in the Oval Office with the President?' She said something about it being very nice. 'We weren't in the Oval office,' I interjected.

'Well, it had an oval rug,' she replied. We laughed at her naivety when she said that she had been wondering if the desk and other office paraphernalia had been removed for the occasion.

The press wanted pictures of us in a more congenial setting and asked if we would walk through Lincoln Memorial Gardens. Being in the middle of a media scrum is not a pleasant experience. The pushing, shoving and confusion are disconcerting and frankly make you feel like an object rather than a person. The media surrounded us for photographs, and Donna got hit on the head with a camera, the wrong person to be hit. Impatient with the media at the best times, being assaulted — regardless of how unintentionally — was the last straw for her. We had to take it in our stride, however, and after an hour or so we eventually made our way back to the hotel for that well-deserved cup of coffee and smoke. We were feeling as elated as anyone could be, given the circumstances, that the day was over. We had nearly completed our heavy schedule, and the support we received from the Americans had given us hope that maybe Robert's killers would be caught.

Back in the hotel room, Paula rang home and was informed that Bobby Fitzsimmons and Dee Brennan had led the St Patrick's Day parade out of the Short Strand. These two men were suspects in Robert's murder, Sinn Féin was aware of this and, in fact, had claimed to have suspended both. This was proof that the suspensions were no more than a damage-limitation exercise, designed to create the impression that the party was doing something constructive and decisive. Leading the parade out of the Short Strand would appear an insignificant thing to many people unfamiliar with street dynamics of communities such as the Short Strand, but it spoke louder than any UN declaration or Presidential address. We were not only sickened and disgusted by this news, but also hurt by it. We had to bear in mind, however, that the organisation of such parades stemmed from the community centre, a Provo support base. It was like inhabiting two parallel worlds — the streets of Washington and the streets of the Short Strand were poles apart. We switched back and forth, from one to another, in turn.

The last official engagement of the week was the Irish Ambassador's reception. A more informal occasion, it was a welcome opportunity to make important contacts in a more relaxed atmosphere. Gemma and Donna decided to stay at the hotel as they had had enough of meetings and small talk, so Paula, Bridgeen, Claire and I went along. What was surprising was the number of people in important government positions who knew exactly what the IRA was up to back home. Stories were told of harassment and intimidation, even murder, by the IRA, for reasons far removed from the 'war'. Robert's murder didn't shock these people — they had heard it all before. It was this realisation that woke me up to the fact that it was possible that Sinn Féin was not going to be pressurised into handing over Robert's murderers. It would be pressurised into doing something about the IRA generally, but not about Robert's killers. These people needed Sinn Féin on board and, although they would apply pressure to ensure that it stayed on board, they would not push the party on cases such as Robert's; he was a minutia. This was disheartening and probably did justify the question some journalists asked about the attention we were receiving; however, some of them asked this question in the wrong vein. After an hour or so at the reception, we returned to the hotel. The last engagement was over and we could finally relax and catch up on some sleep.

The following day, we sat around in the hotel, waiting for our departure time. We hadn't seen much of Washington, having spent most of our time travelling to and from events in taxis or cars. We had no interest in sampling the many tourist attractions on offer, and the last day was the longest we had stayed in the room apart from sleeping. The media attention had subsided and, as we lay about, we reflected on the five days and what — if anything — they had achieved. The fact that there was no further news from home confirmed that nothing had changed, but we hoped that the whole thing hadn't been a waste of time. As I looked out the hotel window on to Dupont Circle, a very lonely and empty atmosphere filled the room. With no rushing about to do, the reality of our situation was taking hold. It was hard to believe that we were in Washington, had met the President and Senator Kennedy and others. Hard to believe that Robert had been murdered and that that was why we were here. The 'Why us?' and 'Why Robert?' questions swirled round in my mind as I looked out the window at the passing traffic and pedestrians down below. We left for the airport early, preferring to sit in more busy surroundings, and at last boarded our flight back to London.

It was economy seats on the way back but we weren't bothered — the less attention, the better. From London, we flew into Dublin and, as we walked through the arrivals lounge, people began clapping. Once again, I wanted the ground to open up and swallow me, as did the others. Although we appreciated the support, the open show of affection and warmth was embarrassing and not something we were used to or would want to get used to. Arriving at our hotel, I went to bed and never rose until the next morning. The past weeks had eventually caught up with me, and I was run down and suffering from a bad cold. The others had a welcome relaxing meal and a quiet drink. I slept solidly for eleven hours but was still groggy the next morning, when we were due on the *Marian Finucane Show* once again.

Again, we explained to the nation the details of our trip and Robert's murder. By this stage we were slightly mummified by the whole experience. Exhausted after the five-day trip to Washington, we were mentally and physically drained by the strain of the whole affair, and afraid to dwell too long on Robert's loss in case we broke down completely. Our lives were in a complete mess, but life made no sense and to keep going seemed pointless unless we succeeded in our campaign. The desperate need to see Robert's murderers brought to justice dwarfed everything else.

The fall-out from our American trip was to manifest itself in different ways over the next few weeks. We had already been issued with death threats, bomb threats and obscene hate mail, but the intimidation was to intensify over the coming months. For the less insightful republicans, Gerry Adams's exclusion from the White House was our fault, as was his supposed humiliation. The portrayal of Gerry being humiliated bolstered Sinn Féin's depiction of us as engaging in a 'Sinn Féin-bashing exercise'. This was absolute nonsense, of course, but what did truth matter to the idiots who regarded us in the same light as Cromwell? The hatred some self-styled republicans had for us ran deep and was bizarre. We were told that in a bar one night a football match was in full swing on the television. Celtic, one of the teams, scored and a man sitting at the bar cheered and shouted, 'Fuck the McCartneys!' How Celtic scoring was an affront to us, I don't know, but that was how much sense some of those opposed to us made. However, if anyone thought that we were finished, they were to be disappointed. We had been making plans to take our campaign to Europe and, when we got back from the States, we set about organising this and other things.

Chapter 6 ⌒

| THE IRA CLOSES RANKS

W e returned from Washington hopeful of a breakthrough, but it was a hope that was quickly dashed by the IRA statement issued on 22 March. In it P. O'Neill declared:

> The IRA has spelt out its position in relation to the killing of Robert McCartney. It was wrong. It was murder. But it was not carried out by the IRA, nor was it carried out on behalf of the IRA. The IRA moved quickly to deal with those involved....

The statement went on to criticise those who refused to accept the IRA's lies, bemoaning the fact that regardless of what the organisation did, 'some people' would never be happy. The question was, what had the IRA done apart from destroy the evidence and intimidate witnesses?

The statement was followed up by a death threat, delivered to us by the police with some advice and the reassurance that, 'It's the ones who don't warn you that you have to worry about.' Although we treated the threats with nothing more than contempt, they proved that the IRA's own supporters or volunteers didn't believe in its statements of support either. But they were obviously nervous at the possibility that just maybe the pressure brought upon the 'Provisional leadership' would force them to yield a little to justice. They decided to try to take matters into their own hands; hence the threat. We were more concerned, however, with the threat coming from more sinister and powerful quarters: the threat of *realpolitik*.

The US had sent a strong message to the IRA and Adams — they were now regarded as the main obstacle to peace, particularly IRA arms and the refusal to support the rule of law. The old mantra of unionist intransigence no longer held up in the face of the Northern Bank robbery and Robert's murder, and criminality could no longer be ignored. Neither could the existence of a private army. Although the politics of all of this was of little interest to us, it was of huge importance. By Easter, Adams was calling on the IRA to follow 'exclusively peaceful democratic means', and to give up its arms or to decommission. If these demands were achieved, it would be a huge step forward for the peace process and would remove a boulder from the road to peace. How important would Robert be once this was achieved? We guessed not very, but defeat was not an option.

Davison and his men still walked freely and the 'Provisional leadership' had the power to bring them to justice. If its claim were true that Robert's murder was a 'civil crime', what was the boulder on our road to justice? Of course we knew what it was but the Provos refused to acknowledge it; the IRA had retrospectively sanctioned Robert's murder and so had bound itself to a code of honour, willingly. The move towards decommissioning was a combination of Adams giving in to the pressure that he had been under for the previous few months and the reality that the Sinn Féin strategy of 'armalite and ballot box' had run its course and was no longer plausible or acceptable. The IRA had become the obstacle not only to the peace process, but to Sinn Féin itself. It had to go. Perversely it seemed that our campaign created an environment that allowed Adams to move more freely in this direction than would previously have been the case. Robert's murder had lost the IRA a great deal of sympathy and the liability of the organisation was exposed for all to see. We could also see, however, that when the IRA went, we would go as well.

We watched and listened as the politics unfolded throughout the election campaign. Many media pundits had predicted our demise after the US trip and, although they were correct in the assertion that the trip to the US was the climax of the campaign, we were adamant that it would not spell its death. It wouldn't have been surprising if the campaign had dwindled out at this point because of natural and practical causes. We were all exhausted and traumatised. We had campaigned hard for nearly two months, hadn't rested at all, and had spent little time with our families. Resources were non-existent, and the time for returning to work was looming.

Donna had returned to work weeks previously because she ran a newsagent's shop, but the rest of us had taken time off. In February, just a week after Robert's murder, I had been offered a few hours' teaching at a college. I accepted, surmising that being at work would help me to cope with what had happened better than sitting at home. I was completely unaware of what was ahead of us, however, and within a few weeks, I had to give it up. It was impossible to work on the campaign and teach; apart from the practical considerations of teaching, I was in no mental state to teach, particularly Irish History. Gemma was still on compassionate leave from work and was the least able of us all to campaign. She found it difficult to stave off her grief, which physically and mentally disabled her most days. Claire had to return to her job as a teaching assistant, for financial reasons — not being able to pay rent wouldn't help anyone. Paula never returned to Queen's for the rest of the year and her attempts to do so the following year failed. Eventually she gave up her studies. Bridgeen looked after Conlaed and Brandon, leaving them only to serve the campaign.

Our spirits flagged regularly, but giving up was never discussed or indeed thought about. It would take only news or a sighting of one of the murderers to re-ignite our determination, and throughout April there were plenty. It was reported that Jim 'Dim' McCormick was frequenting the community centre and Jock Davison was manning a 'Provisional' Easter stall on the Mountpottinger Road, selling Easter lilies and tricolours. Gerard Montgomery, who lived in the Short Strand, was regularly seen mowing his lawn. Davison's stall companion was Bobby Storey, reportedly the IRA's intelligence officer.

The IRA had claimed that it had expelled all three men. Indeed, it had proclaimed to the world that it had been prepared to shoot Montgomery and McCormick. A statement talked about having 'moved quickly to deal with these people'. The nonsense of this was thrown in our faces every day, but proving that the IRA is lying is not easy. The people living in the Short Strand and Markets knew the truth about the IRA claims but this didn't matter to the Provos; they were unlikely to tell it. The IRA's arrogance was breathtaking, its hypocrisy a constant topic of conversation; for years the Provos had railed against British cover-ups and murders but they had no qualms about doing the same. What was the difference between the British Army covering for its soldiers when they had murdered innocent Catholics, and the IRA covering for its volunteers when they had murdered innocent Catholics?

Only a handful of people from the Short Strand were courageous enough to ask these questions loudly enough for others to hear. Even those disgusted at Robert's murder easily swallowed the IRA's lies, for reasons that only they know. Highly respected residents fed into the Provisionals' propaganda by accepting the IRA's claims that it wasn't involved in Robert's murder. A local man told a reporter, 'What the IRA said in its statement should clear up the confusion that there was any kind of political connections to the killing.' He warned that elements of the media had an agenda to turn the murder into a policing issue. Such easy acceptance of the Provisional line by intelligent people with integrity was disappointing. A glimpse at the facts of Robert's murder made it clear that the IRA and Sinn Féin were responsible because not only were their members involved but both organisations had provided cover. IRA statements were not Moses's tablets. McCormick's visits to the community centre, Davison selling tricolours on the Mountpottinger Road and Montgomery mowing his lawn were proof of this alone, but this proof seemed to escape the notice of seasoned and veteran Provisionals.

We were due to meet with Sinn Féin prior to going to Europe to lambast them there. I decided that a test of Sinn Féin's support for us was needed, and what better show of support than holding the meeting in the community centre? Up until this point, we had been meeting with them in Paula's home, allowing Adams and Kelly to sneak in and out unnoticed. The community centre had become the focal point of Provisional discontent with our campaign. It was from here that the first murmurings of hostility towards us had been voiced.

A crèche worker at the centre had arrived at Paula's home a few days after Robert's murder, when Paula was having a lie-down, and had informed Paula's husband that the poster appealing for information on Robert's murder greatly offended her. She told Jim that she had covered up the PSNI badge at the bottom of the poster because her brother had been killed by loyalists and the RUC had failed to find his killers. Paula was furious at her sheer audacity. 'She should have been looking at Robert's face not badges,' she fumed. The crèche worker's stance didn't correlate either to her membership of the Justice for Relatives group, campaigning for the resolution of their loved ones' murders through the Historical Enquiries Team operated by the PSNI. The woman's attitude didn't surprise us, but her callousness did. However, as is common, the contradictions of the Provisionals were to catch up with her. A few months later, her uncle, Denis Donaldson, was unveiled as a British agent, and she was told by one resident of the Short Strand to 'go and ask uncle Denis who killed your brother'. Sensitivity is not the strongest of traits in such communities.

Some of those involved in the events in Magennis's that night were also heavily involved in the community centre. Sean Montgomery, a brother of Gerard's, worked from the centre. The IRA alleged that he had arrived on the scene that night and had driven people away. When Paula had gone to the community centre to put up the poster, he had taken her hand, kissed her cheek and offered his condolences. 'Sean Montgomery shook your hand? Sure he's one of them,' I said to Paula a little curtly.

'He seemed genuine enough,' she replied.

I shook my head — I doubted it very much. My doubts were confirmed when we met with the IRA a few weeks later. His kiss was that of a Judas.

In light of all these things, I decided that a meeting with Sinn Féin in the community centre would be of symbolic importance. As a focal point of Provisional activity, it was the pulse of the community, and it was from here that the Provos controlled the community. Messages via the Provos to the community were pumped through the centre. It was my judgment that if Sinn Féin were genuine about supporting us, meeting us in the centre would illustrate this. I got the unexpected opportunity to make this request to Adams himself. His response was interesting and confirmed what we already knew — that Sinn Féin's support contained no substance.

We were not long home from the US when the phone rang and I was informed that Adams wanted to speak to me. Naturally I was a little excited; a call from Adams could signal only that something of importance was going to happen, or so I thought. For a few seconds, I allowed myself to hope that this call was signalling the beginning of the end to our campaigning ordeal. Once again, Sinn Féin managed only to raise false hopes. After cordial greetings, he told me that he was ringing in connection with my continued accusations that Davison was in the IRA.

'How do you know he is in the IRA?' he quipped. 'Was he wearing a beret?'

Cheeky bastard!, I thought, but said, 'You and I both know, Gerry, that walking about with Bobby Storey is enough for people to know.'

'Well, I can assure you he is not.'

'Well, that's not what it looks like.'

Although not nasty or particularly intimidating, his tone was dry and passively aggressive. He went on then to ask me if I had known, at the time of our last meeting, that Cora Groogan had been in the bar.

'No,' I said, the temperature rising. 'Did you know?'

'No, it was an embarrassment to the leadership,' he claimed.

'Well, I know what I would do with her if I was the leadership.'

'And what would you do, Catherine?' he asked bemused.

'I'd expel her.'

'Due process,' he replied.

'Takin' awful long,' I answered.

Little else was discussed apart from arranging a meeting sometime soon. 'I think we should have it in the community centre,' I said. 'It would show that Sinn Féin fully supports us at ground level.'

'Too contentious,' he replied.

'How's it too contentious?' I asked.

'Look, I don't like speaking on phones. I'll talk to you at the meeting.' And that was that.

I came off the phone and thought to myself, *What was all that about?* We had been claiming for weeks that Jock was still in the IRA and that that organisation and Sinn Féin were liars. Why would Adams take the trouble to ring to refute this in person? Was it possible that our US trip had made more of an impact than we had expected? The US Senators we had met may still have been putting pressure on Sinn Féin. Adams's anger about Groogan was palpable, or, more accurately, his anger at our knowing about her was palpable. The thought that we had known this at our last meeting must have disconcerted him. Had we deliberately withheld this piece of information from him with the intention of using it strategically to further damage Sinn Féin?

Adams's interest in Groogan intrigued us. Was he being honest when he claimed not to have known that Groogan was in the bar? Was it possible that his subordinates had withheld this information from him? I doubted it. Although it was a possibility, I couldn't imagine that withholding information from Adams would do anyone's career within Sinn Féin any good. On the other hand, if he hadn't known, why hadn't he? Did Groogan withhold this information from Adams? Was she advised to do so by others? Groogan's presence in the bar became known six weeks after Robert's murder and it was more than likely that had the taxi driver been anyone other than Robert's brother-in-law, it would never have come to light. It would not have been implausible for Sinn Féin to conclude that her presence could remain unknown. After all, over seventy people had been persuaded to remain silent. We will never know whether Adams was being honest with us or not about Groogan, but one thing we were sure of was that it wasn't her lack of moral fibre that concerned him, but rather our knowledge of it.

The more we thought about Adams's refusal to meet us in the community centre, the angrier we got. Initially we agreed to meet once again in Paula's house but then we decided that this was allowing Sinn Féin off the hook. I decided to force the issue of the community centre. Speaking with Richard McAuley, Paula once again reiterated our request for a meeting there and I emailed Richard outlining our reasons for the request:

> …we feel that the only contentious aspect of the community centre is that those involved in Robert's murder are freely entering the community centre on a daily basis, particularly the main suspect. Robert was a member of the community and as such the community centre as a venue is regarded by us as a much more appropriate setting. A meeting in the community centre would be a public indication that we have Sinn Féin's 100% support as actions speak louder than words.

This appeal fell on deaf ears and Sinn Féin refused to budge on the issue. Gerry Adams and Sinn Féin were unable to stand with us in the Short Strand simply because they didn't support us. It was as straightforward as that. Small incidents such as this spoke louder about the true nature of Sinn Féin's support than any amount of lip-service to the public.

By coincidence, Congressman Peter King rang me at home one evening to ask how things were going. I informed him of Adams's refusal to meet in the community centre and outlined my thoughts on this. He said that he would speak to Adams and get back to us on it. I stood in the kitchen after this phone call and felt hopeful that Adams would begin to relent. It was obvious that Sinn Féin was still being put under some pressure and I hoped that King could persuade Adams to show us support with substance. I was to be bitterly disappointed yet again. Peter King never did get back.

We discussed among ourselves Adams's refusal to meet us in the community centre and whether or not we should call off the meeting altogether. I leaned towards calling off the meeting: if Sinn Féin and the IRA were determined to protect Robert's murderers, meeting with them was unlikely to change this. Paula felt that meeting with them would give us a chance to put our concerns to them and that refusing to meet them would achieve little — 'Keep your enemies close' and all that. The others had mixed feelings, and so we agreed to meet Sinn Féin leaders once again; only this time we would do it in their offices on the Falls Road.

Denis Donaldson was in this office the day we met; Gemma recalls seeing him as we went upstairs. Originally from the Short Strand, he would have known of our family. We wondered what he thought of the situation. Was he leaning on Adams to do the right thing? We were led upstairs to the attic, painted green unsurprisingly. Gerry Adams, Gerry Kelly and Richard McAuley sat facing the six of us. Nothing of substance or consequence was discussed at this meeting or any others. They were cosmetic exercises for Sinn Féin. We would ask questions and Adams and Kelly would guess at the answers. They were carrying out an internal investigation into the presence of its members in the bar that night. We were told that we would be informed of the outcome. They asked about the police investigation and questioned the lack of arrests and progress. Adams enquired as to whether we had a good lawyer. We told him that we didn't, and he suggested that we get one. Gemma asked in all seriousness if he could recommend one. He said that he didn't think a recommendation from him would be a good idea. I agreed.

There was a sense of farce about these meetings: we were accusing Sinn Féin of harbouring criminals, of obstructing the course of justice and providing political cover to murderers, but we never spoke about these accusations directly. They went unspoken at these meetings; I don't know why. Maybe we were unconsciously engaging in the game that Sinn Féin was playing — fudging the issue to the degree that even we couldn't see it clearly enough to face it head on. Then again, maybe we were just an ordinary family seeking the truth from an organisation that had spent the previous thirty-five years dodging it. The farce reached an absurd height when Gemma asked Sinn Féin to contribute to a fund for a civil action that we intended to take in the future. We had met with a lawyer the previous week and he had advised us that the cost of such an action would be approximately £350,000. We didn't allow the implausibility of this price tag to dampen our enthusiasm for the project, as the thought of laying a writ on Jock Davison or Alex Maskey provided a much-needed sense of pleasure. Adams said that he would have to speak to his lawyers about the legality of such a contribution. I laughed at the pretence: Sinn Féin contributing to a fund designed to bring to justice people it was trying to protect. When would this farce end? I wondered.

The meeting ended with promises of continued support and contact. I always took a note pad and pen to these meetings but never wrote anything down. There was nothing said that was important enough to record, although I remember on this occasion Adams had asked us to keep something to ourselves. When we got outside, we had forgotten what it was. I joked that I should have recorded what it was that we were supposed to remember not to disclose. Standing outside on the Falls Road, I turned to Donna and asked, 'Well, what do you think?'

'A load of bollix!' she replied, and I agreed.

Adams wasn't the only one to raise concerns about the police. We ourselves were not so naive that we didn't contemplate the idea that the police might have been protecting informers. Adams's concerns were political in nature. He claimed, like many Provisionals, that the police were dragging their heels to allow the political establishment and us to pressurise Sinn Féin into signing up to policing. Our suspicions derived from a more traditional nationalist mistrust of the police. Were informers being protected?

On the first day of meeting with the police, the liaison officer foolishly claimed, 'We don't use informers any more'. It was an attempt to allay our fears but this overly simplistic explanation raised more suspicions than it allayed — the PSNI would be the only police force in the world not to use informers; we were not stupid. The principle of using informers wasn't being questioned; it was protecting them when they themselves had stepped outside the law, particularly into serious crime, that caused us our concern. There had been up to thirty Provisionals involved that night and it stood to reason that there were informers amongst them; the question was, would this impede the investigation? This question plagued us throughout the campaign and when we studied the details of Robert's murder and exactly how much we and the police knew, we found it difficult to believe that so little of the vast amount of information could be turned into evidence. The police had arrested ten people, all of whom, we were told, had 'picked a spot and stared at the wall'. When we questioned the plausibility of this explanation, we were told that their training by the IRA enabled them to do so. We were unconvinced about the impregnability of the Brennans, Montgomery and the others, but it always came back to who was responsible for getting rid of the evidence — the IRA and Sinn Féin.

At times, our heads were spinning with conspiracy theories and, coupled with trying to second-guess the motives and possible agendas of everyone we met, it was enough to drive anyone crazy. Some days it seemed that the whole world was conspiring against us; every word and action was analysed and nothing and no one was accepted at face value. 'I wouldn't trust him/her/them…' was the frequent remark throughout the whole campaign. The actions of some didn't help and only increased suspicions. One incident demonstrated this more than others.

According to newspaper reports and street-talk, Jock was a member of the Northern Command (the IRA's power base) and remained so even after Robert's murder. We believed that he was the reason the IRA was protecting murderers and had sanctioned the cover-up. Such a high-status officer would also be useful to the security services, however. Was Jock a 'tout'? We raised this question with the police repeatedly and were reassured repeatedly that the issue of 'informers' was irrelevant to the investigation into Robert's murder. The question for us was, did we trust the police enough to believe this? Were we being foolish and naive in accepting police denials regarding informers? According to many observers, we were. Journalists, former Provos and even politicians raised the question of police incompetence or compliance. It was Northern Ireland after all, we were reminded. It was a dirty war and the police had protected informers in the past, and many people were not convinced that the police were no longer doing so. For us, this caused a great deal of upset and tension. Paula and I met regularly with the police and questioned them closely on all worrying aspects of the investigation. Although never happy with the responses, we were satisfied that they were behaving professionally and within the law.

More often than not, it was the law we raged against, as it seemed to protect the criminal more than the victim. The human rights of suspects were so well protected that the police could not go near them. We also found it sickening that witnesses could not be compelled to speak to the police. It was perfectly legal for witnesses to refuse to answer questions asked by the police. This seemed ludicrous to us. 'Why don't the police arrest them for withholding information?' we asked. 'We need proof that they are withholding information,' was the response. We seemed to come up against a brick wall every time. These meetings always left us in a despondent mood — the police and we were getting nowhere. The whole system was weighted in favour of the perpetrators at the best of times, but when the latter had the IRA and Sinn Féin also covering their tracks, the possibility of a breakthrough was disgustingly slim. Discussing this with others, of course, always met with the same response: 'I don't believe that; that sounds strange to me. The peelers are up to something.' Paula and I would leave the meetings satisfied that the police were doing what they could, but this satisfaction would soon lapse into suspicion and doubts, once we engaged with others less convinced of police impartiality. We had to decide to trust the police because, if we didn't, it was likely that we would sink into complete despondency. At times, however, the police left us questioning this trust.

In December 2005, Paula and I pre-recorded an interview for *Newsnight*. Three days before it went out, Denis Donaldson went on RTÉ television and declared to an astounded Ireland that he had been working for British intelligence for over twenty years. Shock at the news reverberated around the world. Donaldson was a senior Sinn Féin figure and a key strategist within the party, although Sinn Féin denied this after his 'outing'. The notion that the British had guided the Sinn Féin strategy was something that the Provisionals didn't want to take hold. Just days before this revelation, charges against Donaldson for running a spy ring within Stormont on behalf of the IRA had been dropped. The reason given was that it wasn't in the public interest to pursue them. He had emerged triumphant with his two co-defendants, talking of British dirty tricks and so on. Three days later, he was on national television, confessing to 'informing' on comrades for years, but insisting that the British had fabricated the spy-ring allegations. One of the iconic pictures of Bobby Sands includes Donaldson, his arm around Sands in comradely fashion. Donaldson's confession and the whole Stormontgate affair dominated the news for days. If such a high-profile figure as Donaldson had been working for the British for years, who else within the Provisionals had been working for the British? Former Provos talked of how the British had led the Sinn Féin peace strategy and reflected on the ousting from key positions of IRA and Sinn Féin personnel who were against the strategy. Jock, we were told, had participated in ousting those regarded hostile to the 'peace process', or hardliners. This was all conjecture, however, and proved nothing, but once again our suspicions were aroused and strengthened by the fears of the police themselves.

Before the *Newsnight* interview was due to go an air, the BBC ran a short trailer advertising it on radio. It featured a few sentences of mine that included a reference to Jock Davison, '…we have heard that he is going to America.' This news had reached us via the rumour mill, like most news of their movements. We were unaware of the trailer until shortly after eight in the morning, when Paula received a call from the police asking if they could come up and speak to us. They explained briefly that it was about the interview with *Newsnight*. I felt sick when I was informed of the police's concern. Had we said something that could prejudice the trial? We didn't think so. We certainly hadn't said anything that we hadn't said a hundred times before, so why the panic? I dressed quickly and arrived at Paula's to await the police. We went over what we had said but could think of nothing, but still we feared that we had in some way jeopardised the case. 'Jesus Christ, that would do it, wouldn't it? It'll be us who destroy any chance of justice,' we moaned. 'We'll have done the Shinners' job for them.'

We waited eagerly but fearful of the arrival of the police. They arrived shortly after nine and began tentatively to draw from us what we had said during the interview. The senior officer told us that his phone 'went mad' when that trailer went out. 'The boys upstairs are panicking that you may have connected Jock with Stormontgate,' he explained.

'Connected him with Stormontgate?' we queried. 'Why would they think that?'

'You said on radio this morning that he was emigrating to America and they thought you were implying that he was getting off side.'

'I was explaining how he and the others were just getting on with their lives as if nothing had happened,' I said. 'And anyway that programme was recorded last week before Donaldson was outed.'

'We didn't know that; we thought it was going out live tonight.'

We all exhaled a sigh of relief — Paula and I because we hadn't said anything to prejudice the trial; and the police because we hadn't connected Jock to Stormontgate.

The dropping of the charges in relation to Stormontgate had raised speculation that the British were trying to protect a more important informer than Donaldson. As was normal in Northern Ireland, conspiracy theories were rife and swirled round for weeks. The police fears that we were publicly going to connect Jock to Stormontgate indicated that there was some substance to our suspicions regarding Jock Davison. The police had reassured us constantly that informers were 'not an issue' in Robert's murder investigation, but it was difficult to believe this in the light of such incidents. However, we had to place a degree of trust somewhere and we decided to place it in the man in charge of Robert's case, Kevin Dunwoody. He had told us that he would resign if he got a 'whiff' of interference of any sort. We took him at his word and hoped he meant it.

TRIP TO EUROPE

We decided to bring our campaign to Europe for the simple reason that the European Parliament was an important focal point for the articulation and upholding of human rights and justice. Robert's murder and the cover-up were in direct contravention of both these principles. Sinn Féin had two MEPs sitting in the European Parliament, Bairbre De Brún and Mary Lou McDonald. Although Europe couldn't exert the same political or financial pressure as Washington, it carried an important moral weight. We hoped that Europe's support would send a strong message to the Provisionals. As there was an election campaign in progress at home, going to Europe gave us an opportunity to keep our campaign in the spotlight. We sought the help of Irish MEPs for our European trip, and Gerry Adams offered the help of the party's two MEPS; no such offer had been forthcoming in relation to the US trip, and it indicated his lack of concern about the pressure Europe could apply. We declined his offer as the hard work had already been done and, anyway, the offer of help could be interpreted as nothing more than mockery.

During the US trip we had lobbied those who had an interest and insight into Northern Irish affairs. People like Kennedy, Clinton, Walsh and King were well-informed of the current situation in the North and could easily separate 'criminality' from 'political conflict'. Although the Europeans were aware of the IRA and its ruthless reputation, they had less clarity over the issues surrounding Robert's murder. Our campaign was seen in very simple terms of 'terrorism versus human rights and justice'. We met with the political groupings in Europe and appealed for their support in calling upon the IRA and Sinn Féin to deliver justice. Most of the meetings consisted of small groups of MEPS — no more than fifteen — and they listened attentively and with compassion. They questioned us closely on the details of Robert's case and some showed interest in the state's role: even in Europe they had their suspicions about the police and the British. We assured them that Robert's murder and the cover-up were the responsibility of no one but Sinn Féin and the IRA. It was disheartening to listen to MEPS tell us that if the state had failed us, we could have sought redress using various mechanisms. The perpetrators had the European Courts of Human Rights to turn to if they believed that their rights were being violated. Robert's rights, however, were near impossible to exert when confronted by the IRA and Sinn Féin who were accountable to no one.

The most nerve-racking experience was the address to the Party of the European Socialists and the European People's Party and European Democrats. Used to small groups by this stage, we wandered into the committee rooms of the European Socialists expecting a small reception of a few MEPS. Instead, we encountered a packed conference hall of over 200 people. The members sat with their earphones and there was a buzz of expectancy in the air. We were greeted by a rapturous welcome as we walked towards the front. An MEP motioned towards the raised platform where the leader of the party sat, together with a couple of others. Gemma and I made our way to the allocated chairs. All the time, I was thinking, 'What are we going to say?' and I chastised myself for not being better prepared. Explaining the details to a small informal gathering was completely different from this very formal and intimidating environment, even though everyone in that room was sympathetic to us.

The leader of the party welcomed us and addressed the group, providing everyone with a background on our campaign and highlighting the justice and human rights principles at the heart of it. He then passed over to me and, pressing the sound button, I pleaded with God to make sense come out of my mouth, not a flurrying babble. Although it felt as if I was speaking forever, in reality it was only a few minutes. Gemma then called upon the grouping to support our fund for a civil action, stating that it appeared that the only way we were going to get justice was through the civil courts. She had made the request at the last minute. We hadn't previously discussed it but it turned out to be a positive move, regardless of whether the money materialised or not.

On our second day in Brussels, Gerry Adams called upon the IRA to abandon its 'armed struggle' and, during press questions, one European journalist asked us whether 'in the light of his comments', we thought 'that the IRA should disband'.

'Whether the IRA exist or not is irrelevant to us,' we answered. 'Robert's murderers will still exist and it is them we want brought to justice.' Such broad political questions were difficult to answer — there was no such thing as a simple 'yes' or 'no' when it came to the IRA. By remaining focused on the facts of Robert's murder and cover-up, we avoided any major hiccups, but the constant pressure of this took its toll.

Our trip to Europe was more successful than Sinn Féin had hoped. Our lobbying in Brussels resulted in a resolution being put forward to the European Parliament not only supporting our call for justice, but also contributing to the civil fund. Paula and I travelled over to Strasbourg to listen to the resolution debate a few weeks later. The Irish MEPs put forward to the Parliament the arguments in support of the resolution. Proinsias De Rossa from the Party of European Socialists, scoffed at the IRA's offer to 'murder the murderers'. De Rossa's statement deserves to be quoted in full:

> The sole purpose of this resolution is to achieve justice for the McCartney family by insisting that normal policing and judicial procedures be allowed to take their course in relation to the murder

of their brother Robert. Sinn Féin claims that Robert's murder was not politically motivated. But we won't know that for sure until and unless the case is heard in a court of law. What is a fact is that the forensic clean-up of the murder scene, the intimidation of witnesses, the IRA's offer to murder the murderers, the refusal to co-operate with the PSNI, *is* politically motivated and cannot be separated from the murder itself. What is also a fact is that the so-called IRA is the most active and politically driven perpetrator of violence and intimidation in Northern Ireland. That it engages in widespread criminality in Northern Ireland, in the Republic of Ireland, and in Britain, to enforce their 'rule of law' and to fund their activities. Until that criminal activity has stopped definitively, and the iron grip that the republican movement exercises on various communities in Northern Ireland is ended, there is little possibility that ordinary citizens in Northern Ireland can hope to have their human rights vindicated. The European Convention on Human Rights, echoed in the new European Constitution, enshrines the right to life, to freedom from torture, to freedom from punishment without law, to freedom of expression, to an effective legal remedy, and the right to liberty, security and a fair trial. All of these rights are denied by the IRA by word and by deed. And Sinn Féin perpetuates this by its continued integral link with the IRA. By seeking to spread the blame for this monstrous murder the GUE/Sinn Féin resolution, and the Greens' amendment, naively allow Sinn Féin and the IRA to wash their hands of the known complicity of their members before, during and after the murder of Robert McCartney.

We listened as MEP after MEP unequivocally supported this resolution calling on the IRA to stop its intimidation of witnesses. The resolution, reproduced in full in Appendix II, also included the following:

3. Calls on the leadership of Sinn Féin to insist that those responsible for the murder and witnesses to the murder co-operate directly with the Police Service of Northern Ireland and be free from the threat of reprisals from the IRA;...

6. Proposes that, if the Police Service of Northern Ireland is unable to bring a prosecution in relation to the murder of Robert McCartney, the European Union grant a financial contribution,

in conformity with the Financial Regulation, toward the cost of legal fees incurred by the McCartney family in their quest for justice, by way of civil proceedings;

The GUE group to which Sinn Féin was affiliated was the only group not in support of the resolution. We had met with this group, which included Bairbre De Brún, during our visit to Brussels, and it was clear from the MEPs' questions that Sinn Féin had briefed them. The Italian MEP talked of the 'conflict' and the continuing difficulties. We emphasised that Robert's murder had nothing to do with the conflict; indeed, it had more to do with the peace process. The justice vacuum created by Sinn Féin because of its refusal to co-operate with the police had nurtured a 'mafia' culture within republicanism. De Brún was at pains to emphasise Sinn Féin's contribution to the peace process. We challenged Sinn Féin to show commitment to real peace by delivering justice. After this meeting, we had a real sense from the MEPs that they were clearer on the circumstances surrounding Robert's murder, but unfortunately a few weeks later the clarity had evaporated again. We were not surprised by this and listened from the public gallery as the German leader of the GUE explained the reasons for his party's refusal to support the resolution. He sounded unconvincing and his voice didn't carry any of the conviction of the previous speakers. He appeared to be delivering a verdict on behalf of others but didn't fully understand why and wasn't completely comfortable with it.

Nonetheless, the European Parliament was not convinced by the GUE's protestations and, on 9 May, twenty-five countries were asked to vote in favour of recommending a financial contribution to the civil action, in addition to fully supporting our campaign and calling on Sinn Féin to co-operate with the police. It was an uplifting feeling to be present when over twenty-five countries declared their support for us. They recognised the value of Robert's life and supported the call for justice. The GUE and Sinn Féin were defeated, a small victory but an important one. It was an excellent result for us but the hard work wasn't over yet. A joint press conference had been arranged at which the President of the European Parliament, Josep Borrell, and we were to answer questions on the resolution.

We had been dealing with the press for a few months by now and were not too concerned about a few questions. A few questions, however, was not what we got — a 'journalistic grilling' would be a more apt description. As we entered the room, we realised that this wasn't going to be a few random questions with brief answers. We joined President Borrell at the front table, and, with earphones on and buttons poised to press the sound on, we looked up at the thirty or so journalists sitting, gazing down benignly. Just another job to them. They grilled President Borrell on the legitimacy of the resolution and particularly the support for a financial package. Paula and I listened nervously as the President answered coherently and calmly. We were less calm and could only hope that when we did speak, it would be coherent. Paula and I waited anxiously for our turn. When the President had finished, the journalists turned their attention to us.

When the first question was asked, I unfairly looked at Paula, my eyes telling her to answer it. It was a political question and she was uncomfortable with this type of questioning, as I was normally the one who dealt with political questions. On this occasion, however, I couldn't find the words and I froze. Looking at Paula, however, the look of nervous fear on her face galvanised me into action. Her expression said clearly that she wasn't going to answer. Although the questioning was more aggressive than normal, it was justified and gave us an opportunity to concentrate on Sinn Féin's responsibility rather than the broader point of the existence of the IRA. The press conference lasted only ten minutes but it felt like hours. Paula had broken out in a rash, by the time it was over, and she said that the experience was worse than giving birth! We had felt the pressure but we had held our own and I was proud of that. We had withstood the scrutiny of the press because we were speaking the truth.

Sinn Féin was less comfortable answering direct questions on Robert's murder and cover-up. Mary Lou McDonald criticised the Parliament's decision to support a financial package because, she said, it wasn't 'a political murder'.

'His murder wasn't political,' I agreed. 'But the cover-up was.' And Europe had agreed.

We returned to Belfast with the support of twenty-five countries, all of which had condemned Robert's murder and agreed that Sinn Féin's refusal to co-operate with the police was politically motivated. They had condemned Sinn Féin's refusal to co-operate with the investigation and proclaimed that it was abuse of human rights and justice. Ireland, the US and now Europe were behind us. We were not long home from Europe when the Provisionals gave their response.

We interpreted any response from the Provos as proof that we were making headway in putting them under pressure. Throughout the campaign, they had adopted a strategy of avoiding the subject of Robert's murder and, when challenged about it, had reiterated the mantra of support for the family. They refused to be drawn on the details surrounding the cover-up and deflected blame by continually claiming that they were the victims of a political conspiracy. So when they spoke voluntarily on Robert's murder and our campaign, we always interpreted it as evidence of pressure. After the resolution was passed in Europe, Mary Ellis, a Sinn Féin councillor from Derry, was quick to condemn the promise of financial support. To bolster her argument, she used other victims as a comparison, arguing that others had to raise the money themselves for rewards and such. Why were we being given financial help when it was clear that Robert's murder was not 'a terrorist act', one of the criteria that had to be met before money could be released from the Victims of Terrorism fund? She argued that Robert's murder had been a crime, not a political act. Sinn Féin remained intent on portraying Robert's murder as a bar brawl and nothing else. It was obvious that the party was unhappy with the clarification from Europe.

The IRA also criticised the European resolution and responded in its own way: we were each visited by the police and informed of threats against us. We could safely say that our campaigning in Europe had been a success.

Chapter 7

RAISED HOPES
AND FALSE TRAILS

The election campaign for Westminster and the local councils was in full swing throughout April. The political pundits and observers were predicting a triumph at the polls for Sinn Féin. Each election had seen a steady growth in its vote and a strengthening of its appeal to the electorate. The impact of the Northern Bank robbery was unlikely to have a significant negative impact on its vote (the general attitude being one of: After all, who cares? The banks?) but Robert's murder was cited as the episode that might cause them some difficulties. We watched and listened to Sinn Féin representatives consistently deny that the party was impeding justice by refusing to compel its members to co-operate with the police. The obstacles to the restoration of Stormont were central to the election debate and, of course, Sinn Féin's refusal to endorse the police and the IRA's refusal to decommission were the two most cited obstacles. Robert's murder easily illustrated the farcical position of Sinn Féin regarding the police but it always seemed to us that the interviewers would ask the wrong questions. The obsession with Sinn Féin's refusal to call upon people to go 'directly to the police' overlooked the important aspects of Robert's murder and the cover-up. It was rarely mentioned that its call upon its own members and other witnesses to give information to a third party had produced very little; it wasn't as straightforward as calling on people to go to the police. Paula's living room buzzed with questions from visitors and family. 'Why don't they ask about the cover-up?' 'Why don't they question them on Groogan, Hayes and Hargey's failure to come forward?' and so on. There were a number of questions that could have been put to Sinn Féin that would have put them under pressure. 'I wish they would stop pussyfootin' around them,' was one of the milder criticisms directed at the interviewers.

As was usual in Northern Ireland, the obsession with language obscured the reality. Sinn Féin's refusal to articulate 'co-operation with the police' was portrayed as the main obstacle in the investigation, when in reality it was Sinn Féin's endorsement of the police that political and media pundits were more concerned with. The substance of our campaign was simply fiddled with. It was a reality that we had to face, Robert's murder was just another illustration of a bad policy that needed changing if Northern Ireland were to move on. Once the policy was changed, the illustration would no longer be relevant or useful. Our frustration and realisation that Sinn Féin would not be pressed too much on Robert's murder was compounded by the discovery that Deirdre Hargey was standing in South Belfast for a council seat. We were consumed with anger. This was Sinn Féin sticking two fingers up at our family and saying that they didn't give a damn about Robert or what had happened to him. Parading Hargey, in the Markets of all places, was nothing more than spitting in our faces. If Sinn Féin could run candidates such as Hargey, then we, too, would have to stand, we concluded. By April, however, Sinn Féin had decided that Hargey was an electoral liability, this time round anyway, and on 13 April she was deselected. Sinn Féin confirmed that Hargey was 'not standing as she was one of the 7 currently suspended pending an outcome of internal investigation' (PA).

It was news to us that she was 'one of the 7 currently suspended'. Adams had claimed that we had given him the names of the original seven suspended, but Hargey wasn't one of those on our list. Sinn Féin's deceitfulness didn't end with Hargey, and its claim that it had suspended ten members in total and expelled two was dismissed by most as a paper exercise that fooled no one. Speaking with a woman from the Markets one day, I was told, 'I don't mean to offend you, but if you think that any of them are suspended, you are a fool.' I didn't. The tone of the conversation was of resignation at the Provos' impregnability.

We decided to abandon the idea of standing because it was becoming clear that seeking justice in Northern Ireland was far from straightforward. Justice was soaked in sectarianism and, regardless of how many times we said that we were not interested in politics, we were categorised according to people's politics. Sinn Féin was fomenting an 'anti-republican' perception of our campaign, whilst Ian Paisley was advocating Paula's candidacy. It seemed that people supported or opposed us depending on their tribe. Justice came a poor second to their considerations. We decided that the 'whataboutery' of Northern Ireland politics was not the best avenue to take. We would continue lobbying and challenging Sinn Féin in other ways.

Sinn Féin, of course, continued to flaunt its hypocrisy in our faces during the election. As if Hargey's candidature wasn't enough of a demonstration of the party's wafer-thin support for us, the news, that Jim 'Dim' McCormick was the treasurer for the South East branch of Sinn Féin came hot on its heels. The thought that it could be the same McCormick suspected of murdering Robert and whom the IRA had offered to shoot two months previously was unbelievable. We wondered if there could be two Jim McCormicks or indeed whether Sinn Féin was so unconcerned about the negative message it sent out regarding its attitude to alleged 'murderers'.

The IRA had named McCormick as the 'knifeman'. Sinn Féin had claimed that it had expelled him, yet four months later he was still holding an official position within Sinn Féin. A journalist rang the press office of Sinn Féin and asked if it was the same Jim McCormick. We decided to ring Sinn Féin ourselves and ask. After a few hours, Gerry Kelly rang Donna with the answer: 'Yes, it's the same McCormick. He is no longer the treasurer and his name on the register is just an oversight.'

'This isn't looking good for you, Gerry, is it?' Donna replied.

He agreed that it didn't look good but insisted that it had been an oversight. Again, this was a lame excuse: Sinn Féin had returned its registration form only a few weeks previously and had made no changes to it. Sinn Féin's excuse of poor administration was unconvincing — it seemed to us that failing to remove McCormick from his post as treasurer was just another example of the party's duplicity. And it wasn't only Sinn Féin's duplicity that was highlighted but the very strange nature of Northern Ireland politics. In any other democracy, this would have caused a 'scandal', but the media didn't even pick up on it, or simply ignored it. A shrugging of the shoulders, a resounding sigh and the reflection 'it's Sinn Féin' was an attitude we came across time and again, from tabloid journalists to the British Prime Minister. Sinn Féin's semi-democratic nature was not only expected, but also accepted. We often reflected that it was no wonder the Provos believed that they were invincible and untouchable.

Robert's murder was still raw in the memory of the people of the Short Strand, and Sinn Féin knew that its success or failure at the polls would be an important indicator of its standing within this small community. If Sinn Féin support remained intact, it could be safely said that the people of the Short Strand had either forgiven the party or indeed absolved it of any responsibility in relation to not only the murder of a local man but also the concerted cover-up of that murder.

Sinn Féin had won the seat for the first time four years previously and the community had celebrated its success. It was the first time that Sinn Féin had gained a seat in the Protestant-dominated East Belfast. That election campaign was memorable because of the feeling of possibility and excitement in the Short Strand. Sinn Féin had pushed the message home that if the people came out and voted, it was a candidate from the Short Strand that could be sitting on Belfast City Council. For the first time in its history, the Short Strand would have representation. The people heard this message loud and clear. The voting system was discussed in shops. It was impressed on people that every vote counted, and they responded. Joe O'Donnell was duly elected as councillor.

Four years later, circumstances on the ground in the Short Strand had drastically changed in a way that no one could have predicted or foreseen. Deborah Devenney defended the Pottinger seat but her election canvassers did not get as easy a ride as they would previously have expected. The cohesive community had been torn apart by Robert's murder, and many people did not shy away from speaking their minds. Sinn Féin didn't stop trying, however, and the place was saturated with posters and election paraphernalia. Bridgeen and I were in the house the day the posters were going up.

'I wonder will they put one on that lamppost?' Bridgeen asked, gesturing towards the lamppost situated just at the bottom of the path.

'I wouldn't like to think so. They'd have a cheek!' I said.

They did, though. Before we could stop them, two Sinn Féin election workers had the ladder against the lamppost and were putting the poster up.

'Jesus Christ! They're putting that poster up there,' said Bridgeen.

'I don't think so,' I responded.

Bent over with back pain, I hobbled to the door and shouted to the men, 'Excuse me!'

The men looked towards me.

'Do you not think that it's a bit insensitive putting up that poster here?' I asked.

They were taken aback as the last thing they expected was to be challenged about posters. 'This is Robert McCartney's house,' I continued. 'Would you take that down?'

'No problem — sorry about that!' they replied. They were not local men and took the poster down immediately. Once again, Sinn Féin had managed to dumbfound us with its brazenness.

The party hadn't finished, however, and in an attempt to bolster Devenney's election chances, a rally was organised at which Martin Ferris and Bernadette McAliskey were drafted in to speak to the assembled crowd, which included Jock and other members of his gang. McAliskey and Ferris told the people of the Short Strand that Sinn Féin was the only party that could be trusted to deliver people's rights and create equality. When the crowd was told that gaining 'collective human rights' was important, cheers and applause went up. Jock and his gang contributed to the sound. The words of the 1916 Proclamation were revisited to ignite the 'republicanism' of the crowd, and the long line of 'brave Irish patriots' was resurrected to remind all of the 'struggle'. The rallying point was the Mountpottinger Road, the road on which Robert had lived all his life, yet not one speaker mentioned the fact that his most fundamental of human rights had been violated. Robert's right to life had been taken by some of those who cheered and applauded Ferris's and McAliskey's pronouncements on human rights. What had happened to the Short Strand? we wondered

Despite pulling out all the stops, Devenney failed to retain the seat and blamed it on the outgoing candidate, O'Donnell. It was widely accepted, however, that Robert's murder had been the main cause of her defeat, and some people had destroyed their ballot papers by scrawling 'Robert McCartney' across them. Maskey's vote also dropped, although he managed to get a seat, but again he was tarnished with the stain of Robert's murder. The election proved to be a success for Sinn Féin, but it was not the victory the party had hoped for. Sinn Féin's desire to emulate the DUP who decimated the UUP was not fulfilled, and the SDLP survived.

BEHAVING JUSTLY

Although our campaign had been widely supported, it was accepted by many observers that our goal was unachievable. Apart from us, few people believed that the IRA would hand in 'their own', regardless of 'crime' or 'political act'. Anthony McIntyre wrote in *The Blanket*:

> Despite their best efforts it may well turn out that the family of Robert McCartney will never get the justice they pursue. Their sole recompense could be to end up living with the knowledge that they behaved justly. For that reason some observers have begun suggesting that the campaign should be wound up. (28 April 2005)

He went on to say:

> Few campaigns for justice have succeeded after only three months. Relatives of the Bloody Sunday victims are now in their thirty-third year of campaigning. For the Finucane family it is year sixteen. Even if the McCartney women's endeavours to put killers in the dock fails, an inability to obtain justice does not preclude campaigning against injustice.

Anthony and I had spoken on numerous occasions and, despite the fact that I knew his opinion was based on an in-depth insight into the Provisional mindset, I refused to accept his conclusion as truth. I chose to interpret his premise as 'defeatist' rather than 'realist'.

Deep down, however, I knew that his assessment might be right. We could continue campaigning, in the knowledge that the likelihood of the IRA and Sinn Féin either 'handing over' or allowing information to flow freely to the police was remote if not non-existent. The pressure bearing down on Sinn Féin was not necessarily directed towards delivering on Robert's murder but was related rather to the broader *realpolitik* and the obstacles on the path to Stormont — decommissioning and policing. None of these required delivery on a specific case. By late April, we were at our lowest ebb and knew that, unless the focus was placed on Robert's murder and what Sinn Féin and the IRA could do, 'behaving justly', as Anthony had said, would be our only recompense.

The nationalist electorate had mildly slapped Sinn Féin on the wrists at the polls, over the issue of IRA 'criminality'. Sinn Féin was regarded as the IRA's conscience. The people's message to Adams was to try harder, to go to the IRA with a huge electoral mandate and tell its leaders that Sinn Féin's strategy was best. Of course, Adams played up to the part and claimed that Sinn Féin was trying to persuade the IRA to adopt 'exclusively democratic means'. This excited the media and political establishment. They knew what it meant: a statement on decommissioning was expected soon.

We looked on as Sinn Féin began its recovery from the political fall-out from Robert's murder. Upbeat talk about the prospect of decommissioning that could kick-start the peace process issued from the mouths of politicians and media pundits. The doomsday talk that had accompanied the aftermath of the Northern Bank robbery and Robert's murder evaporated. Minister for Foreign Affairs Dermot Ahern had commented back in February that it could be years before the peace process recovered from the two incidents. All this changed with the tantalising prospect of decommissioning. The IRA was moving in the right direction and Sinn Féin was making the right noises.

We sat discussing the possible reality that those responsible for beating and stabbing Robert would never have to face a court, let alone prison. The mention of the names involved in Robert's murder stirred a feeling of nausea and anger in us. A day rarely went by without a sighting of one of the gang members. Bringing to justice those involved in Robert's murder and the cover-up obsessed us daily. We had been told by Devine that, as he lay on the street that night, the last image he saw before he drifted into unconsciousness was of Terry Davison 'clawing' at Robert's face. He told us he had shouted out to Davison, 'not you', and drifted off again. That phrase haunts me to this day: 'clawing at Robert's face'. At this point, my brother had been beaten and stabbed, and was unconscious on the ground, unable to fight back and defend himself. Davison had clawed at his flesh like a dog, oblivious to the inhumanity of his behaviour.

Every day the image of what had happened in Market Street haunted us. We saw the faces of the men and women who helped clean up the bar, heard the men in the street as they attacked Robert, and listened as people debated the righteousness of our campaign. Our whole lives had been turned inside out by the events of that night, and Sinn Féin and the IRA had destroyed any possibility of our rebuilding our lives without Robert. We could not contemplate giving up on the hope of getting justice. Settling for 'behaving justly' was not an option. Even if we tried to consider the reality that the Provisionals would never hand over their own to justice, a mention of Davison, Brennan, McCormick and the rest would quickly bring us back to our reality, and justice was the only thing that could bring us peace. The IRA and Sinn Féin could not be as immovable as they presented themselves or others assumed. They could move on anything if they chose to, and it was our goal to move them on Robert's murder. We hoped that the politicians we had met would fulfil their commitments and keep pushing for us. As April and May trundled on, the likelihood of this began to evaporate.

We had lobbied TDS, Senators, Congressmen, the President of the United States of America and MEPs in Europe, but the Provos continued to hold out. Decommissioning was getting closer and, if delivered, Sinn Féin would certainly reap the benefits. This would take considerable pressure off that party to deliver justice to us. Despondency began to creep in and a sense of foreboding and inevitability. Depressive and defeatist moods would come and go constantly and we would have to delve into the deepest recesses of our reserves to sustain us. Our campaign for justice wasn't falling off only the political radar but also the public one. We were never so naive as to think that the public would maintain as keen an interest in our campaign as they had done in the beginning; after all, we were also the public, and we had only to assess our own attitudes to what was happening around us, past and present, to realise that people move on quickly. It is natural to do so, particularly when there is little one can do about an event or cause and when one doesn't feel connected to it in some way.

However, when met with the reality of this, I was left feeling sad for Robert and for us. I had gone back to work as a part-time tutor and, during a tutorial session, a young girl told me that she had recently taken a group of young people over to Westminster to listen to a debate in the House of Commons. She complained that she was disappointed because the debate seemed to concentrate on 'that man who was murdered. That's all they seemed to be talking about...'. I just looked at her sadly. 'He's my brother,' I told her gently.

I tried to ease her discomfort and embarrassment — she had meant no malice and was expressing an opinion many held. I was disappointed, however, that Robert's murder was spoken about with such a lack of empathy but also simplistically. The cover-up raised fundamental questions for our society yet this message didn't seem to have got through. Sinn Féin, a party seeking to govern Northern Ireland, had facilitated the cover-up of Robert's murder. The contradictions of the party's stance seemed to go over the heads of many people, or in most cases people shrugged their shoulders and said, 'It's Sinn Féin' in a 'what do you expect?' kind of way. My upset at the girl's remarks and her lack of understanding was compounded by her use of the term 'that man'. Sinn Féin councillor Joe O'Donnell had used the term on the day Robert had died. 'The death of that man...' he had said. This choice of words — 'that man' — depersonalised Robert. He was not 'that man' to us: he was a father, brother and son. Stripping him of his identity disempowered him even in death and it was made worse by the fact that Joe O'Donnell was fully aware of his name.

Giving in to defeatism would serve no one but the Provisionals. If we started to believe that the IRA would never do this or that, then we might as well stop trying. As Anthony McIntyre had said, 'an inability to obtain justice does not preclude campaigning against injustice.' We decided to organise a vigil outside Magennis's bar and to attend the May Day rally in Dublin. Keeping busy and making preparations for meetings and events was the only thing that kept us sane. In a perverse way, the campaign was sustaining us through our grief. It was what got us up in the morning. Sometimes the desire just to lie in bed and drown in a sea of misery and despair was overwhelming. Not being able to do so at times felt repressive; there was always something to be done, someone to see or to speak to. Having to keep going when you just felt like giving in to the grief was a burden, but equally the fear of grief spurred us into action. Depression disables people and we couldn't become disabled.

Fed up with the Sinn Féin leaders' persistent claims that they had done all they could and had taken action against those members in the vicinity of Magennis's that night, we decided to try to get clarity about what exactly it was that they had done. I drew up a list of eighteen questions and, although we didn't expect Sinn Féin to answer them truthfully, we felt that it was important to ask them. We decided to hand them in to Sinn Féin headquarters whilst we were in Dublin for the May Day rally, during which we marched through Dublin carrying our banners. As usual, the wording on the banners was carefully considered, and family members mulled over possible slogans for days beforehand: should we directly attack Sinn Féin or have a broader and more inclusive message? We decided on 'Justice and Human Rights For All' and a quote by Caitriona Ruane: '…violation of due process and the law does not resolve conflict; it just creates more conflict.'

Ruane had been referring to the situation of the Colombia Three but the meaning was as relevant to our situation and the circumstances surrounding Robert's murder. The IRA's right to commit and cover up murder was in direct contradiction to Ruane's claims, yet as Sinn Féin's human rights spokesperson she had yet to give support to our campaign. The quote was chosen and put on the banners for its ironic value.

We marched to Sinn Féin's headquarters with the banners held high and were met by an official who was as polite as we were. It was nothing but a media stunt, of course — no substance to it whatsoever — but at least Sinn Féin couldn't pretend that it hadn't received the questions. Paula handed the Sinn Féin official the letter but the photographers were unhappy with the angle. He asked if they could do it again. They both obliged. Three times they exchanged the letter to satisfy the photographer. This added a farcical element to the proceedings. However, the issue of the unanswered questions was raised again in the press and that was what was important. As predicted, we never did get answers despite Gerry Adams's insistence to this day that we did.

RAISED HOPES AND LET-DOWNS

Every day we hoped for a breakthrough. Every day we hoped that someone who had been in Magennis's bar that night would go to the police and tell them what they knew. We prayed for arrests and charges. We were amazed at the number of people whom we knew who were refusing to co-operate with the police. People who claimed that Robert was like a brother to them also refused to tell the full truth: 'He has told what he is prepared to tell,' was the consistent answer from the police in relation to Gowdy and Devine. We interpreted this as, 'They are not telling the whole story.' We already knew this, of course, as the accounts they had related to us didn't add up, but still they insisted that they had told all they knew. Gowdy and Devine were not the only ones holding back, however. Others refused point blank to speak with the police at all, some out of fear and others out of cowardice. Others refused to tell the truth simply out of loyalty to the IRA, and many because they were involved in the attack itself or the cover-up. Our desperation for a breakthrough or any titbit of information attracted the attention of people whose motives could only be described as bizarre, and the result was an emotional roller-coaster ride for us.

One evening in Castlewellan, I received a call from someone who described himself as a 'well-wisher'. Before he would explain what he wanted, he insisted that I answer a series of security questions to confirm my identity. As bizarre as this was, I conceded and tentatively answered his questioning, questions of my own running through my head at the same time, along the lines of who is this strange person at the other end of the phone — friend or foe or 'nutcase'? And more pertinently, what right did he have to demand answers from me? Satisfied with my responses, the man claimed that he was ringing from a hotel foyer in Glasgow and had actually travelled there for the purpose of making this phone call. He was using the public phone to ensure that his call could not be traced.

He went on to talk about our campaign and, in an accusatory tone, he criticised our claims that the IRA was protecting Robert's murderers and insisted that it was simply a 'policing issue'. I got angry at this: who did he think he was? The truth was plain for all to see — I reminded him of the cover-up and asked who had got rid of the evidence and intimidated the witnesses. The IRA could undo a great deal of the damage if it chose to. He argued that this wasn't the case, insisting that it was purely a 'policing issue' and advising me of a piece of legislation that had recently been passed that allowed anyone from the North to report a crime to the Garda Síochána. We could ask for the investigation to be headed by a garda. He advised me that we should speak to Michael McDowell, then Minister for Justice, about this. If he agreed and the arrangement were made and Sinn Féin still refused to co-operate, then it would be clear that Robert's murder was simply a case of Sinn Féin and the IRA protecting his murderers. Of course, this notion intrigued me, as it could be used to prove that mistrust of the police was not the primary reason for the failure to make arrests and charges.

'Listen carefully,' the caller commanded authoritatively. 'It's a policing issue, nothing else.' He said that he would ring back in a couple of weeks' time to check up on progress and he also told me that I wasn't to tell anyone about the phone call.

The following day, I mulled over the phone call with the others: was the 'well-wisher' a Sinn Féiner telling us of a possible solution, one of the infamous 'securocrats'? Was he a genuine individual trying to help, or just simply a 'nutter'? Given the circumstances, we didn't dismiss anything or anyone. We allowed ourselves to hope that the 'well-wisher' was genuine and that this would lead to the breakthrough we had been hoping for. We would soon find out. We met with McDowell and discovered that the legislation did allow for co-operation between both police forces but couldn't be applied to Robert's case.

The 'well-wisher' never rang back to check up on progress or to find out how the McDowell meeting had gone. The caller himself was relatively harmless, but in our situation the impact of his eccentricity had a demoralising effect. We were in a desperate situation and small incidents and events got blown out of proportion. The slimmest of possibilities were pursued rigorously and, in most cases, ended in profound disappointment. One example of this was 'the witness'.

The refusal of witnesses to speak to the police or sign statements was the cause of the lack of evidence, as the IRA had destroyed all forensic evidence. Witnesses who possibly held the key to justice refused to divulge anything to the police for fear of reprisals by the IRA. We knew of one such witness who the police told us 'could break the case'. He had held Robert as he lay dying but had fled when the police had arrived. For months, we hoped that he would go to the police. We were understanding of his fear but believed that his conscience would eventually dictate to him to do the right thing. We waited and waited but still nothing happened. We were tempted to go and speak directly to him but didn't want to apply emotional pressure. He had, after all, tried to help Robert that night. Although we were desperate for a breakthrough, the decision to go the police had to come from him. He had to be prepared to live with the consequences of doing so.

The police had arrested and charged Terry Davison with Robert's murder in June, but they had no evidence against the others. Some witnesses from the bar had provided police statements but the information was limited, as most claimed to have been in the toilet or on their phone. The truthful statements contained nothing of substance. Of those in Market Street during the attack, most were suspects and therefore unlikely to talk. Apart from Devine, Gowdy and McKay, this witness was the police's only other hope of getting information that could be translated into evidence. The police told us that this witness's information was crucial but that they could not force him to talk. He had to go to them voluntarily and they reminded us that giving a statement was only the first step. He would have to stand over his statement in court, he would be cross-examined by the defence — a daunting prospect — and the shadow of the IRA would be hanging over it all. These talks with the police left us feeling frustrated and angry. The process of justice at times appeared to be the main obstacle aside from the Provos.

We could only hope that this witness would have a change of heart. He had explained to Robert's friends his fear and that the safety of his family was his main concern and worry. He simply didn't trust the Provos and had seen too many instances of their brutality to be convinced that they would leave him alone if he testified. We couldn't contradict this. In early summer, however, we happened to be at the same holiday camp as him and got the opportunity to speak with him. It was clear from the way he spoke that he had been traumatised by what he had seen.

He stammered as he recalled the events of that evening and his voice broke from time to time, and he cried. It was hard to listen to the details. He had seen Robert after the gang had finished with him. He described the damage to Robert's eye, saying 'His eye was lying on his cheek'. I brushed over this quickly. The injury to Robert's eye hadn't been confirmed to us. The police had told us that Robert hadn't lost his eye, but it was obvious from the reports we had heard that substantial damage had been done to it. I preferred to accept the police interpretation, so quickly dismissed from my mind the witness's description. At some point we would have to digest the injuries inflicted on Robert but for now our minds could deal only with the vague details of the attack, the outline.

The witness told us that Devine was lying not far from Robert and called out to him, 'What about me? Help me!' The man showed little sympathy for Devine, telling us frankly that he believed that Devine had brought his injuries upon himself. He wouldn't elaborate but this suggested that he had witnessed something of what had happened in the bar. He talked confusedly at times, but it was obvious to us that his evidence was important and should be given to the authorities. He admitted that he was afraid to go to the police. Adams's and the IRA's words meant nothing to him. He recalled Frank Hegarty's fate over twenty years earlier. 'You know what these people are like,' he said. 'They don't mean what they say. I have to think of my ma and da!' He knew the people involved in Robert's murder and, reading the street, he could tell that they were far from expelled.

'What do you want?' I asked. 'A guarantee of your safety, from Adams?'

He perked up a little at this suggestion and we said that we would do all we could to get assurances of his safety. He didn't want to change his life or to leave; he just wanted to know that he would be safe. We were in no doubt that his fear was real and we told him he had to make his own decision. He in turn told us that he would think about speaking with the police and he left, a little lighter for having spoken with us, but still carrying a burden, one placed on him by the IRA and Sinn Féin, but one that only he could lift from himself.

This witness had brought to life the events of that night; he was the closest we had been to what had happened, and talking with him was profoundly difficult. Robert's pain and trauma seemed to come alive as he spoke and at times I had felt like telling him to stop. I didn't want to hear and watch the events of that night unfold. The inability to intervene and change the story's outcome was distressing. We didn't push him on details because it was too upsetting. I reflected that Adams's call for people to bring information to the family had been callous and unfeeling.

When we met with Adams a few weeks later, we raised the issue of the safety of the witness but his response was, as usual, evasive. Despite this, the witness decided to go to the police and we anxiously awaited the outcome. We expected arrests and charges as, after all, it had been the police who had told us that his evidence was crucial. Once again, we were left deflated. According to the police, he had 'told what he was prepared to tell' and it wasn't sufficient to lead to more arrests or charges. Our disappointment was tangible. The reality was that this was going to be the case until the IRA and Sinn Féin disowned the gang.

Around April 2006, the tantalising prospect of justice was dangled in front of us once again. One day, a stranger called into Donna's newsagent's and asked to speak to one of Robert's sisters. He left his name and number with the girl behind the counter and left. A week or so passed, and once again he went into the shop. Bridgeen was serving this day and he rambled on to her about the IRA gang in the Markets and Short Strand and claimed that they were intimidating him. He left her, naming one particular individual as the weakest link. 'If they get him in, he'll break like a plate. His nerves are wrecked.' Once again, we dismissed it as rambling for we were beginning to learn from our previous experiences that people said and did things for reasons that only they understood. If people genuinely wanted to help, they should have been speaking to the police; giving us information was pointless and only caused more frustration and upset.

A couple of weeks later, the man came back into the shop and again left his phone number and asked if we could call him urgently. Paula decided to ring, arguing that it would soon become clear if he was a fraud. We had become quite adept at assessing people's character. In fact, just before this man appeared on the scene, another man had claimed to have important documents in relation to Robert's murder. He had tracked Paula through a local journalist and claimed that he knew who had killed Robert and had the proof of it. He asked us to collect the information from his home and claimed that his life was in danger because he possessed the documents. Paula asked the police to check him out and, whilst she was waiting for them to get back, he rang again. Once again, he rambled on about the documents and, when Paula told him to hand them over to the police, he responded, 'The police did it.'

'The police did what?' Paula asked, agitated.

'The police murdered Robert.'

'Ah for fuck's sake!' shouted Paula and hung up the phone.

Now, once again, we were faced with someone claiming to know something. We decided that we couldn't ignore the claims and could only hope that he was genuine. We had nothing to lose in any case. The initial conversation with Paula sounded promising. He was naming people and describing events that fitted in with what we knew to be true. Paula invited him to speak face to face in her home. There was a sense of anticipation surrounding his first visit. The house was cleared of excess people and we decided that only Paula and Jim should talk to him. We didn't want to frighten him off, after all. He arrived up at Paula's and spoke at length about what he knew of the events on the morning of Robert's death. According to him, the gang had met in a house in the Short Strand and it was from here that the cover-up had been orchestrated. This man claimed that the disposal of the tape had been discussed in the house that morning, along with other things. 'It'll blow over,' someone had commented.

'Oh, this will not blow over,' another reportedly replied.

We were suspicious of this man's motives and tales. Why was he telling us this now, a year later? He said that his conscience had got to him and that what had happened to Robert was wrong. He had wrangled with his conscience all this time but had eventually decided to do the right thing.

He showed us text messages that contained threats and jibes, such as 'PSNI tout', to prove his claims of intimidation. His story sounded convincing but was useless if he wouldn't relate it to the police.

For weeks on end, he arrived up at Paula's and talked of his family and the Strand, and so on. He was angry about his treatment at the hands of Bernie and said that he was going to tell the police all he knew. We waited for this to happen. We conjectured that his statement and willingness to stand over it could lead to arrests or at least the questioning of some people who had refused to speak to the police. It could lead somewhere, we thought and hoped. We got excited at the prospect of a breakthrough but, as the weeks went by and he continued to visit but made no suggestion of going to the police, we began to get angry with him.

'What does he think he's doing?' I asked. 'Does he not realise we've gone through enough without people telling us details of what happened but refusing to tell the police? It seems to me that he is using us for some kind of therapy. He's no intention of goin' to the police. He's playing some sort of game. I would tell him to fuck off. He either goes to the police or pisses off.'

Jim argued that we should be patient with him as he was afraid.

Eventually he made his way to the police station and made his statement, and we breathed a sigh of relief. Someone had eventually come forward. Even if it didn't lead anywhere, someone had stood up. Paula rang round the family to tell them that he had gone in, and the first glimmer of real hope shone through. We could feel the weight being lifted off our shoulders by this one small step forward, and we could only imagine how we would feel if there were a real breakthrough. The weeks of waiting and listening had eventually paid off, and we waited anxiously for the response from the police.

When it came, it was devastating. The man had withdrawn his statement as quickly as he had made it. Within twelve hours, he had changed his mind. He explained to Jim that he was frightened for the safety of his family. He claimed to have left a copy of his statement with the *Irish News*, with instructions to open it on his death. Jim placated him. 'You should have told him to fuck off. Cowardly bastard!' was our response. The *Irish News* claim just added insult to injury. We wondered if it had all been lies. What type of person preys on the vulnerability of a family whose loved one has been murdered? He had used our situation either to satisfy some freakish and perverted trait or to satisfy his desire for revenge against those who had offended him. Either way, it had nothing to do with his 'conscience' or a desire to do 'right'. Once again we had been shown the twisted face of human nature. We never heard from him again. We didn't doubt his information, however, and were not surprised at the people he named.

The 'well-wisher', the witness and the storyteller all led to dead-ends. We felt as if we were living in a maze. The emotional energy we invested in the hope such people kindled in us left us completely drained when it was dashed. We had dismissed no one and followed the remotest of possibilities. Even when the insane presented themselves to us, we still searched for a more rational motive behind their crazy behaviour. One such person was the Cora Groogan look-alike.

Maire Hendron of the Alliance Party, recently elected councillor for the Pottinger Road, was visiting Paula's home one evening in early May. She had arrived with her husband and, after a few minutes, she asked Paula if her friend, who was sitting in the car, could join them. Paula gently chastised them for leaving their friend in the car, and Maire's husband went out to get her. As Paula looked out the back window in anticipation of the arrival of Maire's friend and the return of her husband, her mind briefly registered the presence of two women who followed Maire's husband up the path. 'I thought she said "friend",' she said to herself. The two women entered the room and the older woman extended her hand to Paula, saying, 'Pleased to meet you'; the younger woman hugged her enthusiastically. They sat down but within minutes the behaviour of the younger woman began to arouse Paula's suspicions. Her skeletal frame, protruding teeth and limp shoulder-length brunette hair drew the company's attention towards her, but her imposition and incoherent strands of conversation raised eyebrows and furrowed brows.

She claimed that she was a barrister and had been in the bar on the evening of Robert's murder. That day, she had gone back to the bar and had sat crying over her drink. She told Paula and the others that she was distraught at what had happened and wasn't coping with it too well. She claimed to know everything and said that, despite what we thought, the Provisionals were not covering up Robert's murder. Her behaviour became more erratic and aggressive as the minutes passed and from time to time she reached into her bag.

In a ranting fashion, she said that we should stop blaming the IRA and that the law would eventually get to the truth. Paula excused herself from the company, on the pretext of making some tea. There was a sense of danger emanating from the woman and Paula was surprised that Maire and her husband were not intervening to calm her down. It was obvious that she had been drinking and was agitated about something. She also wondered why Maire hadn't warned her that the woman had been in the bar on the night Robert had been murdered. Claire, who was also there, quickly followed Paula into the kitchen, and they discussed the woman's behaviour. Maire's husband was sitting at the window overlooking the yard. Paula went outside to peek into the living room. She could see from the expression on his face that the woman's behaviour was concerning him. Catching Paula's eye, he mimed, 'Who is she?'

Paula mimed back, 'Is she not with you?'

He shook his head from side to side in response.

Alarm bells went off in Paula's head. No one had any idea who this woman was. She had walked into Paula's uninvited, pretending to be in Maire's company. Had she waited outside for an opportunity to enter? Paula and Claire began to panic.

At that, the phone rang and Tommie Gorman, RTÉ's Northern Editor, jovially greeted Paula. 'Well Paula, how's it going?'

'Jesus, Tommie, we can't talk now — a woman has walked in here and we think she has a gun.'

'A what? What's going on up there? Phone the police.'

Just at that moment, there was a knock on the door and Paula could see two policemen. 'It's all right, Tommie' she said. 'The police are here. I'll ring you back.'

Uncannily the police had arrived to warn Paula of the existence of a second threat. Their arrival was pure coincidence but their appearance was greatly welcomed. The woman had also spotted the police and had grabbed her bag and fled from of the house. Paula quickly reported what had happened and the police went after the woman. They returned soon after and told Paula that they had caught up with her and she had provided them with identification. She was the worse for drink and was a little bit unstable, but essentially harmless; she didn't have a gun or any other weapon.

Paula's description of the woman fitted a description of Cora Groogan, and once again we wondered if this was a breakthrough. Had Groogan broken under the strain? Had she given the police a false name? It turned out to be another dead-end, however, when the police confirmed that the woman was who she said she was. We still wondered, however.

One thing the false hopes did confirm was that the only people who could deliver a breakthrough were Sinn Féin and the IRA. Despite the fruitlessness of previous meetings, we decided to meet with Sinn Féin again in July, to raise the issue of McCormick's and Davison's placement on the republican wing of Maghaberry prison.

We sat, once again, in the attic of the Sinn Féin office on the Falls Road. We didn't revisit the venue issue, as there was no point. Paula, Claire, Bridgeen and I went along to the meeting. By this stage, Donna and Gemma had decided that meetings with Sinn Féin were a waste of time. In fact, there was a general feeling that meeting with anyone was a waste of time. It was still difficult for us to accept why we had to campaign so publicly and strenuously — what gave the Provos the right to murder our brother and then cover it up? Why did we have to go begging for justice whilst the grotesque people who had carried out the macabre act were wrapped up in the blanket of Irish republicanism? They were mothered and protected by the jaundiced interpretation of ideals and principles and a polluted republicanism, while we had to go to the custodians of the same and beg for justice. It was demeaning but we had to do it. We also sensed that because we were women, Sinn Féin had adopted a condescending approach — our lack of testosterone obviously made us less threatening but raised the possibility of emotional outbursts.

We were not physically threatening but neither did we succumb to emotional outbursts. We internalised our anger and suppressed it until the meetings were over. Thoughts, however, did run through our heads whilst we sat talking calmly and rationally about the murder of our brother. To drive our message home and to get to the truth, I imagined taking the three of them hostage. That would wipe the smug and insincere smiles off their faces! The thought of holding a gun to Adams's head in some perverse way satisfied me immensely. Paula could stand guard at the door, and Bridgeen and Claire could stand watch over Kelly and McAuley. The truth would be forced from Adams and maybe we wouldn't even send for Jock. I never got as far as contemplating a satisfactory outcome to this scenario. I never got beyond the hostage situation. Of course, this image was more to do with power than violence. For a few seconds, I claimed the power Adams and his cohort possessed but was denied to us. The gun was symbolic of the power held not only by Adams but also by those who had murdered Robert.

This was fantasy, however; the only weapon we had was truth and words to fire it. Adams exchanged warm pleasantries with Bridgeen and Claire. I could feel a draught coming from him toward me. This didn't bother me at all but what did was the patronising attitude towards Paula, chastising her continuous praise of the police. Kelly also accused her of referring to Sinn Féin/IRA. She denied this — anyway, it hardly mattered what she said; we were not getting anywhere, were we? Their preoccupation with trivia was displayed with an arrogance and lack of compassion. We were not their equals, or so they perceived. It was clear from their demeanour and approach that we were viewed simply as 'upstarts' who didn't deserve answers and to whom Adams certainly didn't think he should answer. For our part, we didn't see in front of us men of integrity or principle, just three men refusing to help to bring Robert's murderers to justice — three men who had the power to do so but wouldn't. The gang in Market Street had the protection of the political and military organisations these three men represented; we had no one; and Robert had only us.

We had come along in the hope of squeezing something out of

Adams, and for once we had an agenda so that we wouldn't forget to mention anything. We had a tendency to do this; important issues would regularly be omitted at meetings because of our failure to note things down. On this occasion, most issues were raised although far from resolved. Paula told them that she and Bridgeen were moving from the Short Strand because the intimidation was getting worse. Both Davisons' relatives had physically attacked her sons and the recent attack on Bridgeen's home was the last straw for her. Adams said that if there was anything they could to do to help, they would. I didn't doubt this. Out of sight, out of mind.

When we raised the point of McCormick and Davison being on the republican wing, they simply denied that one existed. McAuley explained that the republican wing differed considerably from what it had been years ago. The prison authorities placed prisoners on the wing; the IRA didn't. I argued that this was hardly the point: in the public mind, placement on the republican wing sent a strong message that Davison and McCormick were still in the bosom of the IRA. People interpreted information at face value. I asked if anyone charged with murder could be placed on the republican wing even if they didn't belong to the movement — after all, the IRA had denied that Davison was a member. Round in circles we went: the witnesses, the murderers and so on. We explained about the witness who was afraid to come forward and asked if his safety could be guaranteed. Adams said that he could assure the witness that he wouldn't be in any danger from the IRA, but he couldn't guarantee the actions of the people involved — a total cop-out given that the people involved were still under the control of the IRA. He insisted that the IRA had asked people to come forward but they were refusing.

'They are walking up and down the Mountpottinger Road without a care in the world,' I pointed out. 'There is no sign of the isolation and ostracism that you talked about happening.'

'Self-preservation,' said Kelly. 'They are forcing themselves on the community out of self-preservation.'

'I don't accept that.'

'These people are cowards; there is no way they are defying the IRA.'

'People will do anything to survive,' said McAuley.

I leaned across the table to him. 'These people are nothing but cowards,' I said. 'We shouldn't forget that. It doesn't take courage for nine men to follow one man down a street and beat and stab him.'

They gestured in acknowledgment of this and I continued, 'Maybe I am giving the IRA too much credit. But I do not accept that people like the Brennans are defying the IRA Army Council. I don't believe that the IRA told them to go in and they said no and then flaunt themselves in the Short Strand despite disobeying orders.'

Again they tried to persuade us that 'self-preservation' was the reason for their bravado. Adams also claimed that the community tolerated the murderers.

'What happened would never be tolerated in West Belfast,' he claimed. 'The Short Strand is a strange wee place.'

We agreed with that but to try to pass the responsibility on to the community was low. Apart from cowardice and fear, the only reason why people in the Short Strand tolerated the murder of its residents by the IRA was that the IRA told them to. Simple.

Adams then looked to McCauley on his right, and then left to Kelly, before leaning forward towards us conspiratorially and saying, 'I have a theory. I haven't even told these two about this.' And he gestured towards Kelly and McAuley.

His tone implied something new, maybe even truth. I got momentarily excited at the prospect that eventually we were getting through. Was Adams going to reveal something that would suggest or, God forbid, prove that Sinn Féin was in any way genuine? We leaned closer expectantly.

'I think that Devine was the target that night,' he said. Everyone, including Kelly and McAuley, waited. 'Devine has a history with McCormick's brother, Applegate.'

'Applegoat,' murmured Kelly.

Adams didn't seem to hear him and went on, 'This Applegate—'

'Applegoat,' Paula said a bit louder than Kelly.

We laughed softly as did Kelly and McAuley, not only at Adams's understandable mistake but also at the absurdity of the name. Adams was alone in his bemusement. He stopped speaking long enough to glance sharply at Kelly, and he immediately adopted his serious demeanour. Adams continued with his theory. Devine's presence in the bar that night had ignited the altercation, his history with Applegoat had created bad feeling between him and McCormick, and the attack that night was against him. Robert had got caught in the middle of the madness. Devine, along with Gowdy and McKay, were the key witnesses who should be concentrated on. He finished and we sat looking at him impassively. Even Kelly looked a little dejected, a questioning look on his face. It was tempting to ask Adams, 'Where have you been for the past few months?'

Was it possible that Adams hadn't known any of this? It appeared so and, if that were the case, it wasn't good enough. In hindsight, he was more likely feigning naivety or had simply spent a few minutes focusing on details. Anyway, none of it altered the facts. Sinn Féin and the IRA were responsible for Robert's murder and the cover-up, which Adams refused to acknowledge at all because it was the cause for the continued wall of silence. We were to find out only months after this meeting that Gowdy had been taken away on the night of Magennis's for a number of hours and Devine was taken away blindfolded no fewer than three times in the months following Robert's murder. Devine and Gowdy had told the police 'what they were prepared to tell' and McKay had refused to speak with them, yet Adams was suggesting that the focus should be put on them. It was plain that the IRA had already focused on them. Would anyone in Ireland believe that Adams knew nothing of this? His treatment of us was abominable: we had been fobbed off and treated with nothing but contempt.

The only outcome of this meeting was Adams's acknowledgment that it wasn't simply a 'bar brawl'. He said that following Robert and Brendan down Market Street when it was clear that they were leaving 'was unforgivable' and claimed that the 'leadership were bullshitted'. Neither did he contest two important facts: that Jock was present during the attack and that a gun had been sent for, although a question still hung over whether or not it had arrived on the scene. The gang was under the authority of an IRA commander and the release of a gun had to be sanctioned by the IRA. These details confirmed the involvement of the IRA as an organisation, not just individuals. This didn't move anything on, however. The meeting was cosmetic and it was the last one we had with Sinn Féin. This was in July, after Terry Davison had been charged with Robert's murder and Jim McCormick with the attempted murder of Brendan Devine. Over the next few months and following year, political progress would reinforce the Provisionals' protection of the murderers, and the hammer blows against the wall of silence softened, eventually petering out, leaving only us to deliver the blows.

The IRA declared in July that it would decommission its weapons. This huge step predictably created great excitement amongst the Irish and British establishments. We were less excited. It seemed to us that the IRA was more prepared to hand in guns than 'killers'. Our call for justice was in danger of being buried by the IRA's concession of one of the Provisionals' major bargaining chips. The graffiti pronouncement, 'Not an ounce, not a bullet', scrawled on the walls of the Falls Road and the Strand, was quickly scrubbed out. Now the IRA was giving more than an ounce; it was handing over the lot.

Many people had commented that the IRA 'would never hand over Robert's murderers'; the same had been said about decommissioning. In fact, there was a lot 'the IRA wouldn't do' but had done. Its stance on the protection of Robert's murderers was not immovable or definitive. The ability of the IRA to move would materialise only if the will existed to make it do so. Decommissioning was weakening that will and, as the day drew closer for 'actual decommissioning' to take place, the airwaves buzzed with the excitement of its political repercussions and potential.

Chapter 8 ⌒

| THE AWARDS

Our visit to Washington had internationalised our campaign and by the end of March journalists were coming from as far away as Australia to interview us. The general consensus was that we had taken on the IRA and were brave and courageous women. We also hailed from a community that had traditionally protected the IRA, and this increased our appeal. We were bemused by the descriptions of us as 'brave' and 'courageous' women: 'angry' and 'indignant' was how we felt. Those looking in from the outside, however, saw something else and decided that we should be recognised for our fight for justice in the face of adversity. When the first awards were offered as early as March, we rejected them immediately and firmly. Awards were the last thing we had expected and some of us scoffed at the idea and argued that it would give credence to accusations that we were seeking the limelight. We were angry that people seemed to be focusing on us rather than on Robert's murder and the cover-up. I decided that accepting awards would be wrong because it would readjust the focus, and we had to keep that firmly on Sinn Féin and the IRA. We politely refused the Lord Mayor of Dublin's invitation and the *Sunday Independent*'s 'People of the Month' award. Satisfied that we had made the right choice, we forgot about the issue and carried on with our plans.

As the weeks rumbled on, we began to realise that the focus of the pressure being applied to Sinn Féin was shifting and that coming clean over Robert's murder was no longer central. Sinn Féin triumphed at the polls in May and Adams's call to the IRA to decommission cooled the heat from the political fall-out of Robert's murder. It was clear that, despite our two months' hard campaigning from Washington to Europe, Sinn Féin and the IRA hadn't been shifted one inch in their determination to protect the murderers. We had received two threats and the murderers were walking carefree about the area. The death knell was tolling for our public campaign.

It was thought that the awards would be one way of keeping our profile up. We revisited our position and discussed the pros and cons of accepting them. Gemma remained hostile to any suggestion of accepting awards but I believed that we could avert the danger of the campaign becoming about 'us', if we used the acceptance speeches as a way of refocusing minds. Paula and I argued that the awards would enable us to keep the media profile up. Gemma, the most hostile to the media intrusion, was not convinced. The begrudgers' accusations were raised, as was the 'it's a waste of time' train of thought. Paula and I were of the opinion, however, that we had no choice; none of it was pleasant but it had to be done. The other option was to stay quiet and go away. Falling out of the public eye would also mean falling out of the public mind — the old idea of 'out of sight, out of mind' was exactly what Sinn Féin wanted. We argued strongly that criticism was just another way of trying to shut us up. It was impossible to campaign without attracting criticism, impossible to please everyone or stay on everyone's side. Ultimately we had to do what we felt was right and not be dictated to by begrudgers and opponents. Our biggest critics were the murderers' biggest advocates. Were we going to be swayed by these people? If not, we were just going to have to develop very thick skins.

Claire and Bridgeen said that they would go along with whatever was decided; Donna, although sympathetic to Gemma's arguments, decided that accepting the awards could do no harm, even if it did no good. Apart from anything else, it seemed rude to refuse the awards. Dublin City Council had passed a resolution in support of our campaign, and the award ceremony at the Mansion House was in recognition of the support of the people of Dublin. The *Sunday Independent* award had been voted for by the public; to refuse to acknowledge this support didn't feel right. The 'pro-award' opinion carried the day and the Lord Mayor of Dublin, Michael Conaghan, and the *Sunday Independent* were contacted. Once we had decided to accept one award, we had committed ourselves to accepting others.

The Taoiseach was present at the *Sunday Independent* awards. He had won the Person of the Year Award for something or other, and he was also presenting us with the Person of the Month Award (February,

I think). During his introduction spiel, he told the audience that he had 'been everywhere with these girls'. We looked at each other with raised eyebrows. Later, we talked light-heartedly about Bertie's claim, some of us branding him a 'lyin' git' and suggesting that we should have challenged him on his public claim. Although a white lie, and seemingly unimportant, it did illustrate the disingenuousness of political leaders in relation to our campaign. We had met with Bertie Ahern only once officially since Robert's murder and, on reflection, like the British, he had taken a back-seat approach to our campaign but unlike the British paid homage to it in public. The US administration and Senators were more on hand to offer help and advice and were much more prepared to criticise Sinn Féin. Bertie's claim that he had 'been everywhere with these girls' was far from the truth.

THE MANSION HOUSE

The Lord Mayor of Dublin pulled out all the stops when it came to receiving us. He had arranged a Garda escort through Dublin and I must admit it was one of the most embarrassing experiences the others and I have ever had. Michael Conaghan was genuinely concerned about the threats against us from the IRA and was determined that we were not going to be assassinated on his patch. The taxi-man, however, thoroughly enjoyed chasing the gardaí through Dublin, crashing traffic lights, weaving in and out of traffic like something possessed, and dodging unsuspecting pedestrians. He told us he had dreamt of doing such a thing! We, on the other hand, were mortified, and sat in the car purple with embarrassment. We slunk down in our seats and hid our faces. We could see people turning to each other and saying, 'I wonder who it is?'

'Jesus Christ, this is awful,' I moaned. 'I don't believe this is happening.'

'This is madness,' someone else groaned in discomfort.

We were relieved when the journey came to an end, but were further embarrassed at the crowd the Garda escort had attracted. In a calm and measured fashion, we ran into the Mansion House to escape the enquiring eyes of the public. Of all the awards ceremonies we attended, the places we had been and the people we had met, our time at the Mansion House was one of the two most pleasant experiences we had during the whole campaign. The other was at the Humbert Summer

School in Co. Mayo, particularly sitting outside Bessie's Bar overlooking the sea where General Jean-Joseph Humbert landed in 1792, and drinking Magners with the locals who were adamant that the IRA would know all about it if we came to any harm! The Mansion House ceremony was a prestigious affair but in no way pompous or pretentious. It was a privilege to be honoured there, but more importantly the value of Robert's life was recognised by the people of Dublin. The IRA and Sinn Féin, in contrast, claimed that it was in the name of the Irish that they couldn't deliver justice.

In September, the Irish people spoke again of their support for us. We received the Irish People of the Year award at the ESB and Rehab People of the Year Awards, alongside celebrities such as Terry Wogan and Bob Geldof, but more importantly alongside ordinary people. A group of teenage friends received an award on behalf of Palmerstown Community School for its campaign against the deportation of a Nigerian pupil, Olukunle Elukanlo. The campaign had succeeded, and Olukunle proudly presented his friends with the award, a testimony to their friendship. Our faith in human nature had been severely damaged and so it was touching to see such friendship and commitment amongst friends. It also reminded us how let down Robert had been by his friends.

The first couple of awards ceremonies were relatively low-key affairs — a dinner, a few speeches and photographs; nothing too stressful or grand — but the award in Germany took it up a level. For some reason, the Germans had shown a keen interest in our campaign from the beginning. German journalists and camera crews had spent hours interviewing and filming us for news and documentaries for the German audience. As a result of this, we were contacted in April and informed that we had been awarded the Die Quadriga for our campaigning work. We had never heard of this before and were taken aback when we read the philosophy behind the award and were more surprised that we were being accorded such accolades.

die quadriga is [awarded] every year on 3rd October in Berlin in the Komische Opera to four personalities [from] political, economic, social and cultural life, who [through their commitment] point the way to the future for enlightenment, regeneration and [a] pioneering spirit. The [source of the name] die quadriga [is] the legendary ensemble at the Brandenburg Gate [which encapsulates] the virtues of harmony, friendship, valour and state wisdom for the welfare of the whole. [...] The collective dream of welfare and freedom, individual willingness to turn things around for the better and the political will to collectively overcome the challenges were and are the message of the years 1989/1990. die quadriga is devoted to all those as a result of whose courage walls have fallen and borders have been crossed.

Personalities from politics, business, culture and society, who feel committed through vision, courage and responsibility, are honoured with die quadriga. (www.diequadriga.com)

It was frightening and daunting to be held in such high esteem; at times it felt like a burden in itself. Although grateful for the accolades, we were nervous, not because we didn't believe in the principles of Die Quadriga but because we didn't necessarily believe in our ability to deliver on them. In the eyes of Werkstatt Deutschland and others, of course, we already had, simply by challenging the IRA and refusing to be silenced.

We travelled to Germany in October to receive the award, and although we were aware that the other award-winners included international statesmen such as Chancellor Helmut Kohl and the Aga Khan IV, we didn't expect the formality of the occasion. The award ceremony was as daunting as the philosophy behind it. Other dignitaries in attendance included Mikhail Gorbachev, who was presenting Helmut Kohl with his award, and Sir Tim Berners-Lee (the inventor of the internet). The Mansion House was like the Mad Hatter's Tea Party compared to the Die Quadriga: no sleeping in corridors as the cello player and pianist had done at the Lord Mayor's awards ceremony! We stayed in a five-star hotel in Berlin — pure luxury that the prices reflected; fortunately most costs were covered by the organisation. The two-day event included an evening reception, planting of cherry trees and lunch at the Schloß Sanssouci, and the award ceremony at the Komische Oper.

To add to the stress, Paula fell ill with a bug on the first evening and Gemma on the second. Paula couldn't attend the first evening reception or the event at the castle, whilst Gemma had to leave the latter hurriedly to join Paula in her sick bed. It was a nightmare which was made worse by the fact that we hadn't bargained on the number of formal receptions and events and did not have enough clothes with us. Claire and I stuck out like sore thumbs at the lunch at Sanssouci castle. As the day wore on, the formality and stress began to take their toll and, to make matters worse, half an hour before the awards ceremony, we realised that we didn't have a speech prepared, and there was no way we could have improvised. Paula had been nominated to deliver the speech and Gemma had been assigned to write it, but as she had fallen ill, I was left to write out a speech on the back of a piece of cardboard half an hour before we were due to leave. If we could have been transported out of there, we would have gone. The formality of the occasion and the dignitaries made us nervous and uncomfortable. We felt more at home in Bessie's Bar than in this hotel.

Completely stressed, we decided to have a last cigarette before heading downstairs to the waiting cars. The rest of the awards party — Gorbachev *et al.* — had, according to a disgruntled and indignant head organiser, been waiting for ten minutes. The organiser wasn't pleased and shouted to Paula as she left the hotel, 'You have kept Mr Gorbachev waiting seven minutes!' He then looked at his watch and corrected himself: 'Ten Minutes. RUN, RUN!!' he commanded. Paula glared at him and, angry at his ranting, refused to hurry. She coolly walked down the path into the car. We'd have to stop smoking to stay out of trouble!

The ceremony was a lavish affair and it was obvious that we were the odd ones out. It wasn't hard to detect the dignitaries' entourages who pushed a path through the crowd for the Aga Khan and Gorbachev; Donna was elbowed out of the way by one of the bodyguards. Her face told the story. Eventually we got seated and composed ourselves, praying for a quick ceremony and exit. The most enjoyable part of the evening was listening to Helmut Kohl tell the story of the fall of the Berlin Wall and how the trust between himself and Gorbachev had brought it about. The actress, Dr Maria Furtwängler, was presenting the award to us, and before we went up on stage she gave a brief explanation of our campaign. During this, she told the audience that the IRA and its leader Gerry Adams had offered to shoot the 'murderers'. We exchanged amused glances: the Germans, well known for their bluntness, obviously equated Adams and P. O'Neill as one and the same!

It was our turn to go up on stage, and I felt sorry for Paula having to address such an audience. Gorbachev and Kohl sat in the front seats, with earphones for translation. Paula took to the podium and delivered the speech in a nervous but controlled tone. She said afterwards that both Kohl and Gorbachev nodded in recognition at the bits of the speech I had highlighted for emphasis. This was good to hear. As long as we held our own in such company, we did Robert proud. Backstage, Gorbachev put us at our ease by approaching and asking for a photograph to be taken with us. We apologised for having kept him late earlier, and he joked that he understood that it was a woman's prerogative!

We had no sooner returned from Germany than we had to repack our suitcases and head off to London for another awards ceremony. The acceptance of this award had caused difficulties. It was the Pride of Britain award, sponsored by the *Daily Mirror*. The newspaper itself had given good coverage of our campaign, and the award was in support of us, but I felt that the title 'Pride of Britain' could cause us difficulties. We were oversensitive to the 'anti-republican' mud thrown at us, and at this time still hoped that pressure from within the republican community would force Sinn Féin and the IRA to deliver justice. Paula had already accepted the award but when I was told of the title, I decided that our acceptance of it had the potential to damage our campaign. I wrote to the organisers, thanking them for the award but explaining that regretfully we would have to decline. Such decisions illustrated the very complex position we had been placed in: we felt that we couldn't accept the support of the British people because of the name of the award. When one of the spokespeople for the *Mirror* contacted me to try to change my mind, I felt ungrateful and silly. When he asked what the problem was, I said simply, 'Frankly we're not British and it's called the Pride of Britain. Now Gerry [not Adams!] you know as well as I do that the Shinners have been trying to undermine us by claiming that we are anti-republican. Accepting awards titled the Pride of Britain is only giving them ammunition.'

'It's Pride of Britain and Northern Ireland,' he said in the hope of changing my mind.

'Well, why doesn't it say that, then?' I asked.

'It will say that on screen. It has to because of the political sensitivity.'

The celebrity aspect to the awards also caused us concern. Our critics would pounce on images of us cavorting with celebrities. A dislike of the celebrity culture also compounded my instinctive desire not to attend the ceremony. After a lengthy discussion around the merits of the award and how much damage, if any, accepting it could do, I decided to confirm our attendance. The fact that the British Prime Minister, Tony Blair, was presenting us with the award, and the former President of the US, Bill Clinton, had recorded a video message, changed my mind, and calmed my unease. Ultimately, however, we were reconciled to accepting the award by the fact that the British people had voted for it, and it was their support we wanted to acknowledge and appreciate.

Paula, Claire, Bridgeen and I travelled to London to collect the award. During the evening, Tony Blair requested a brief private meeting with us and, when he and his Chief-of-Staff, Jonathan Powell, met us, we discussed Sinn Féin's role in the cover-up of Robert's murder. It was during this meeting that Blair made a remark that would encapsulate his government's complacent approach to IRA murder. After we had provided a brief overview of the details of Robert's murder and the cover-up, and the refusal of Sinn Féin to compel its members to co-operate with the police investigation, he asked, 'Could you not approach the women in Sinn Féin? Maybe they would be more open to applying pressure from within.'

'Absolutely no point,' I replied, vexed at the suggestion. 'The women are nothing but "Gerry's babes"!' The faces of Michelle Gildernew, Bairbre de Brún and Caitriona Ruane swam in front of me. *Why would we want to approach those people?* I thought to myself, anger beginning to bubble up.

The phrase 'Gerry's babes' caused Blair's eyes to widen and his face to twitch. He shifted in the chair and glanced questioningly at Powell. I immediately realised my mistake. I hadn't used the term as an affront to him but simply to conceptualise Gerry's power over the party and the people in it.

'They'll do whatever Gerry tells them to do,' I said, trying to clarify my point. 'Whatever Gerry says, goes. There is little point in talking to anyone else.'

Blair listened sympathetically to our call on him to bring pressure on Sinn Féin but he promised nothing other than to raise the matter with Sinn Féin. We would wait and see. An official meeting would soon be arranged and we could press him further.

Blair's weak suggestion regarding the women in Sinn Féin was, on reflection, a disgrace and consistent with the 'internal housekeeping' policy that had been adopted by his government in relation to the IRA ceasefire. At this time, however, we did not realise this and so didn't focus on British complicity with Sinn Féin.

In November, Claire and I flew to London to receive an award at an event titled Women of the Year Lunch. I had been in contact with the organisation for over a month but knew little about it apart from the fact that it celebrated the achievements of women in various fields. The President of the organisation was Joan Armatrading, a singer and feminist. Safe enough territory, I thought. The awards ceremony was taking place at the London Guildhall, and Claire and I hurried there, arriving only a few minutes before the press conference with the award-winners was to begin. We were warmly welcomed by the organisers and directed into a small room for a quick coffee and chat before the press conference took place.

I sat down and Claire occupied a chair facing me; the chairwoman sat next to Claire and we started chatting about the award. I asked who else was being presented with awards and the chairwoman explained that the nurse who had inspired the setting up of Live Aid by Bob Geldof would be receiving one. She told us that Bob had seen her on a news bulletin some twenty years before, feeding starving children in Africa, and the image had led to Band Aid and the famous 'Do They Know It's Christmas?' record, which in turn had led to Live Aid. Tina Turner was also being recognised, she continued, but before she could explain for what (apart from the obvious), a press officer interrupted and told her that the media were waiting. She appeared a little put out by this and said that she needed a few minutes to run through the details with us. Thank God she asserted her authority on this occasion! Turning back to us, she said nonchalantly, 'Where were we? Yes, Baroness Thatcher is being awarded a lifetime achievement award.'

My jaw dropped and I looked at her dumbstruck. The expression of sheer disbelief on my face told her that something was wrong.

'Is there a problem?' she asked worriedly.

I couldn't speak and just sat staring through her for at least a minute. I couldn't believe it! Of all the people to be present — Margaret Thatcher. Claire murmured, 'Oh, shit', and looked across at me appealingly. The press corps was outside, the press officers were pushing for us to go out and get our pictures taken along with the other award-winners, and we were in a blind panic.

'Is that a problem?' the chairwoman repeated, urgency in her voice now. I eventually found my voice and said, 'Yes, this is a problem. This could destroy us.'

I jumped up from the chair and excused myself from the room; I needed time to think. Time was something we didn't have, however. The press was getting restless and the organisers were keen to get on with the show. My head swam with outcomes to the various scenarios and possibilities. A picture of us with Margaret Thatcher would be priceless to Sinn Féin. Livingstone had described us as 'unionism on tour' because we had gone to the US. A picture with Thatcher would be a godsend to the likes of him.

It had been during the premiership of Margaret Thatcher that ten men had died on hunger strike. She was the most hated British figure in Ireland since Cromwell, and her attempt to criminalise the IRA was constantly invoked by Sinn Féin when it was under pressure. In fact, during the early months of our campaign, Sinn Féin's mantra had been, 'Republicans will not be criminalised.' The provisional leadership had portrayed our campaign as an attempt to do just that, and standing with Thatcher could do nothing but give credence to their propaganda.

I had never been in such an awkward situation in my life before. Joan Armatrading was sent for, and together we discussed the possibilities. What if we didn't stand on the same platform? And didn't have photographs together? Could one of us accept, or accept in absence? Could we say that we were unable to attend? And on it went. Panic was in the air and we were faced by a serious dilemma. We hadn't intended to cause such a fuss or mess but we had to focus on what was important. If we accepted the award, purely through fear of offending the organisers, that would be a cowardly move. But we felt as if we were throwing their goodwill in their faces. It was a terrible position.

Finally Claire and I decided that there was nothing we could do but leave the ceremony. We felt dreadful. The organisers were completely understanding and forgiving. I told Joan that I blamed myself also: I hadn't checked who else was receiving awards. Frankly it hadn't entered my head to do so — I could never have imagined such a scenario cropping up. The title 'Women of the Year' didn't hint at any danger. I was assured that even if I had asked, I wouldn't have been told, as the organising committee had decided, for the first time, to keep the award recipients secret from each other. 'They'll not do that again,' I thought. After I had explained to Joan the connection of Thatcher to Ireland and our campaign, she was sympathetic, and it was agreed that we would put out a statement explaining our position.

We went into a small room and went over the wording of the statement. As we were chatting, we discovered that the Women of the Year was celebrating its fiftieth year, hence the inclusion of Margaret Thatcher. I asked one of the organisers why Thatcher had been chosen to receive the 'lifetime achievement award'.

'For becoming the first woman Prime Minister,' she replied. 'We thought that was an achievement that should be recognised.'

'Hmm,' I responded.

After the statement had been drawn up, Claire and I slipped out the back of the Guildhall and away from the press. We put the whole thing down to experience.

Of course, the press at home had got hold of the story. We downplayed the incident but there were some eager to criticise us for our rejection of Thatcher. Bernard Ingram, one-time press officer of Thatcher, called us hypocrites. *Well, he would say that, wouldn't he?* we thought. We were told by a journalist that she had rung around the unionist politicians to gauge a response but none except David Ervine was available to comment. According to Ervine, our 'mask had slipped'. We were bemused and angry at his analysis. On the other hand, Lord Tebbit, a man whose wife had lost both legs in the Brighton bomb, said that he fully understood why we didn't share the platform with Lady Thatcher. He went on to say that Thatcher herself would have understood why we couldn't have shared a platform with her, given the nature of our campaign.

Tebbit rightly asserted that the Provos would have used it as a way of isolating us further from our community. Ervine's analysis was as far off the mark as Livingstone's. Ironically both held us in disdain but it didn't take a genius to work out why. Both had good reason to try to keep people like us quiet. The late David Ervine was the political representative of the UVF; how many Protestant families were in our situation? Ervine's treatment of campaigners from within his own community, particularly Raymond McCord, mirrored Sinn Féin's treatment of us. It wasn't our masks that had slipped. The real point was that the likes of Ervine and Livingstone talked of 'justice' in obscure terms or applied it to specific cases where the responsibility for delivering did not belong with their group. Tebbit's comments killed the controversy and put an end to the story. Ervine had looked amateurish, lacking in compassion, and opportunistic.

The episode illustrated the isolated position we were in — attacked from all sides and scrutinised constantly. Did Robert's brutal murder slip from these people's minds? we wondered. Did they forget why we were campaigning? Rarely were the murderers mentioned in the critics' venom and, if they were, it was out of obligation. The murderers were condemned in passing but little focus was put on their actions, and very little emphasis was placed on the violation of Robert's human right to life or the essential importance of justice. The critic — be it Sinn Féin, newspaper columnists or letter writers — would always note the worthiness of our campaign and proclaim their support for justice and then follow up with a 'however' or 'but', and a much longer piece would ensue on the wrongs of our campaign. It never failed to surprise us how every move we made was used against us. But this was the world we were thrust into after Robert's murder. It was a very sick and complex world, and one in which the concepts of freedom, justice and equality were seriously misunderstood and misused. Ironically, the so-called 'peace process' had made it dangerous to campaign for justice. A peace that restricted freedom just didn't seem right to me.

By the end of 2005, we had received up to ten awards for our attempt to bring Robert's murderers to justice. It was a great honour to be granted such recognition and support and a privilege to accept these awards that were offered by well-intentioned and principled people. Although wary at first of accepting awards and fearful that the focus would be taken away from Robert's murder and placed on us, we felt that the decision to accept had been the right one. We found ourselves in some predicaments — some funny, others stressful — but ultimately the awards enabled us to keep Robert's murder in the public eye and Sinn Féin culpability under the spotlight. Passing into 2006, the attention of award-givers had shifted to other worthy causes, and rightly so. Our campaign was far from over, however, and although the world's spotlight was off us, we continued with our campaign.

Chapter 9 ∾

| THE MEDIA

Essentially we are an introverted family, shy of cameras and hostile to intrusion. There are no family photo albums or video movies, only a scattering of photographs throughout the immediate and extended family. The photographs taken of us as children depict an uncertain bunch, staring warily at the camera; some of us smile whilst others are morose; none of us looks comfortable. We hated having our photographs taken. We were all the same and had been since we were young; even our parents disliked the click of cameras and the insistence of 'Say cheese'. It was a trait everyone in the family shared, although Robert had become more amenable to having his picture taken since the birth of his sons, pride in them overriding his distaste for the camera. Gerard hadn't been too bad and he always smiled confidently into the camera, but he never sought it out. The rest of us avoided it like the plague.

Robert's murder turned our lives into one big picture show. We had more photographs taken in those first weeks than in a lifetime. We had to pose for the cameras at a time when we felt that the bottom of our world had fallen out. Photographers would ask us to smile, look this way or that so that they could capture their interpretation of the accompanying story and us. The photographs never told the true story and were only a snapshot of that moment but being visible was important and so we had to put aside our natural aversion to the camera and comply, to a degree, with the photographers' instructions. We drew the line at nursing children or making tea, a request that always made me irritable.

Those who accused us of 'glory hunting' and 'seeking attention' couldn't have been more wrong. The newspaper coverage made us uncomfortable; none of us liked gracing the pages of newspapers and magazines. It wasn't just that the pictures made us look fat, old or — on a rare occasion — good; it was the exposure that caused us the most unease. The whole experience was an assault on our way of life. Stripped of our anonymity, we had to cope with the trauma of Robert's murder in the full glare of the world's media. It was almost inhumane. Numb with grief and anger, we were exposed to the harsh and cruel world of public scrutiny, but our anger and indignation acted as our shield. Without the media, we would have got nowhere and that was the simple truth. This was the only vehicle we had to tell our story and it empowered us. The media restored the balance between 'them' — the Provos — and 'us'; 'they' didn't have all the power and could be stripped of it through exposure. It had been the media who had exposed Sinn Féin's involvement in the cover-up and alerted us to the political back-up Robert's murderers could expect. Alex Maskey and Joe O'Donnell's comments on television had ignited our suspicions that first day, and from then on in we had listened and watched the unfolding of the cover-up carefully. If Maskey and O'Donnell could use the media to hide the truth, we could use the media to expose it.

Virgins to the world of the media, we did not carry the same inhibitions and suspicions as seasoned campaigners. We spoke unguardedly and recited every little thing we knew about Robert's murder and who was involved. We spoke freely and angrily of the 'scumbags' who had murdered him and the people from the area who had helped to clean it up. We told them of the people who had washed the blood off the clothing of the murderers and of the women who had facilitated the cover-up of our brother's murder. We spoke of those who refused to speak to the police and lambasted those who hid behind the republican mantra to facilitate murder. We cursed the IRA men who were visiting witnesses, and community activists who were instructing locals not to talk about the murder. We told of how posters appealing for people to go to the police with information were being covered up and of how the old cliché, 'whatever you say, say nothing', was being enforced by the IRA. We told every piece of minutiae to the listening journalists and tried to explain the dynamics of the Short Strand and how even the subtlest hint or look of disapproval from an IRA man could silence tongues.

One woman told us how a school official in the local primary school had laminated Robert's murder poster and put in on the pin board. While collecting his children from school, a renowned and senior IRA man asked her who had put the poster up. It was clear from his tone of voice that he did not approve. The woman told how she felt uneasy and was afraid to admit that she had put it up. A seemingly small incident, it spoke volumes about how the IRA and Sinn Féin controlled and contained such areas. Such tactics disgusted us and the media gave us an opportunity to release our frustration and hit back with words. A blanket of silence enveloped the Short Strand, tucked in by the IRA and Sinn Féin. Fear of the IRA seeped from the church to the local playgrounds. It was everywhere, poisoning the morality of the people. Those it couldn't poison, it frightened. The media afforded us an opportunity to smash the cliché, 'whatever you say, say nothing', and so, whatever we knew, we spoke of.

We gave the names and, where possible, addresses of those involved and were not afraid to name members of the Third 'Hallion' Battalion. Our enthusiasm to speak the truth was partly the cause of the media's enthralment with our story. The Northern Bank robbery a month before Robert's murder, coupled with the difficulties in the 'peace process', gave it an added potency. How far we would have got if this hadn't been the case, we will never know. Unlike many others, we were in a rare position: the murder of 'ordinary' men like Robert mattered, for now anyway.

Doors and ears were opened to us and it would have been 'morally unjust' for us not to have used them. The concept that everyone had a 'moral duty' to fight for justice was voiced to me by Anthony McIntyre in a discussion during which I was moaning about the unfairness of being questioned on the failure of many other victims to get justice. I had been asked what I would say to 'the many people in Northern Ireland who haven't got justice and ask, "Why should your brother get justice?"' I had stumbled over the question, saying something about everyone deserving justice and the fact that one person not getting justice should not prevent others from doing so. The issue of the other victims of Northern Ireland's Troubles was always raised in an offensive and confrontational manner, 'You're not the only ones' a prelude to criticism.

Attempting to portray us as selfish, conceited, media- and establishment-pampered charlatans was defensive and a deflection from the truth. The 'victims issue', as it has come to be called in Northern Ireland, is of a very complex, difficult, divisive and fragmented nature. Throw into the mix the 'whataboutery' of Northern Ireland politics and it is not difficult to understand why we were easy targets for the more banal sections of society. I had mulled over this question in my head but couldn't clarify my thoughts on it. We had to take care to remain focused on Robert, and branching out into other sensitive areas would have brought us into the shark-infested political waters, but still the question of other victims would be raised with us. The accusation that we were mere 'political puppets' also impinged on this question and, with just a couple of words, Anthony had managed to clarify a very important aspect to our campaign. We had a 'moral duty' to fight for justice for our brother; we had an opportunity to do so and to fail in either aspect would have been 'morally unjust'.

Warnings about the fickleness and unscrupulous nature of the media came in equal measure to the warnings about politicians. If the politicians were 'sharks', the media were 'piranhas', stripping a story to its bone. 'They don't care about Robert; it's just a story to them,' was one of the many warnings we received over the months. Well-intentioned people mostly imparted this advice but other people had ulterior motives for their warnings. The dangers of over-exposure, public apathy or on occasion sensationalism constantly buzzed in our ears. 'Are you not afraid people will get fed up listening about your campaign?' one journalist asked whilst we were in Wexford for the Labour Party Conference.

'The people of Ireland cannot afford to get tired of listening to calls for justice,' I replied, a quiet anger beginning to bubble inside. I resisted the temptation to retort in a manner more befitting the nature of the question, *Any more fed up than with reality tv?* Ultimately the media would soon move on and Robert would be yesterday's news. We had to make an impact whilst we could. Making enemies of the press would do no good, but at times it was difficult to remain temperate in the face of provocative questions.

Other sections of the press, particularly the section sympathetic to Sinn Féin, simultaneously criticised our campaign whilst supporting our call for justice. Our cause, they said, was just; but our campaign was wrong and those who supported it were hypocrites, they decreed, citing some past misdemeanour or act in their personal lives as the basis of the hypocrisy. No one was exempt from their scathing comments, including old friends such as Senator Ted Kennedy. His refusal to meet with Adams brought the 'poison' pen of Danny Morrison on him. Morrison wrote a disparaging piece in relation to Kennedy that reached Kennedy's staff. A friend in Washington reported to me that it angered the Kennedy camp so much that the Bush administration told them, 'Just say the word and we'll ban them.'

Belonging to the wrong side was also reason enough to be scribbled off the approved list of those it was 'OK' for us to seek help from. We understood the motives behind the criticism from obvious Sinn Féin sympathisers, but we were less patient with journalists who masqueraded as objective observers. Others criticised our campaign on the grounds that it was overshadowing other, and presumably more important, campaigns for justice, which was a fallacy and disingenuous. To claim that one type of justice is more important than another is a false premise. As Martin Luther King famously said, 'Injustice anywhere is a threat to justice everywhere.' Surely anyone in Northern Ireland getting justice was good for everyone? Justice wasn't or shouldn't have been seen as a competition. The use of such false arguments to undermine our call for justice infuriated us. The sight of 'know-it-alls' sitting on panels spouting such nonsense was galling. Such criticisms stank of a lack of understanding of the principle and ideal of justice itself, and of republicanism, or else it was jut plain duplicity. Such criticism goaded us rather than silenced us.

Throughout those first hectic months, we were not in control of our lives and seemed to be at the beck and call of the media constantly. If we were not running to interviews, we were going to meetings with the police, politicians and legal advisers or else attending awards ceremonies. The media were insatiable. By early March, we had given over 800 interviews, and by June this had become thousands. It was demanding and exhausting work, and at times it felt like a full-time job. We didn't have the luxury of a press officer and we had to adopt a multitude of skills overnight. The navigation of the media's many agendas, audiences and angles all had to be considered, even before the journalist arrived. Essentially, journalists were in charge of the story and we filled in the gaps. They dictated the central message to emerge and presented their image of us to the reader. The journalist's

interpretation of our campaign was the substance of the piece. We were
neatly moulded and intertwined into the fabric of the bigger mosaic. At
times, we cursed the journalists whose articles reflected very little of
what we had said, despite a two-hour interview; worse were the
journalists who quoted us completely out of context. Eventualities of
this kind were just some of the hazards we had to deal with, but fear of
the media would have paralysed our campaign to the delight only of
the Provos. We just had to run the risks and hope for the best.

Some elements of the media were easier to deal with than others.
Newspapers were not too bad. Journalists would show up at a pre-
arranged time, record the interview on a Dictaphone and leave. Radio
would do this also, or record on the phone, or run the interview live by
phone. Little time was taken up by this, although at the beginning we had
to travel to studios for live shows which could be a nuisance. The two
areas of the media that took up the most time were magazines and TV.
They could take hours and it was worse when they wanted us all together.
Paula and I mainly dealt with the media, not through choice but because
we were available and did most of the talking. At times, we found
ourselves acting as project co-ordinators for journalists who would ring
up asking for an interview with all six. Even though we would explain
that getting all six would be impossible, the journalists would persist in
the request and, for some obscure reason, we would feel obliged to
comply. Of course, this was a practical nightmare, particularly when
dealing with those of us who were reluctant and at times hostile to the
media. On reflection, it was also an added unfair burden on Paula's and
my shoulders, but our total inexperience of dealing with the media
meant that they were able to take advantage at times.

For six months, not a day went by without a journalist visiting
Paula's or meeting us in coffee shops. Living with journalists became a
way of life, and some would hang around long after they had bagged
their interview. Most journalists were very courteous and considerate
of our situation and were aware of their intrusion into our lives. Some,
however, took ridiculous advantage of Paula's hospitality. A southern
newspaper had sent up one of its journalists to do a Sunday piece. She
arrived in the morning and was still there late into the evening. The
house had been busy as usual and we had passed her on numerous
occasions, nodding congenially. 'Have you done that interview with her
yet?' I would ask Paula from time to time.

'No, not yet, but she doesn't seem to want one.'

As the hours passed and still the journalist made no attempt to pin any of us down, but just stood about drinking tea, listening and chatting to the occupants of the house, Paula decided to push her on the interview. She told the journalist that she would have to do it quickly as it was getting late and Paula was getting tired and the rest of us were leaving. Amazingly the journalist asked Paula if she could stay in her home for a couple of days to get a 'feel' for who we were and what it was like being us at this time. Paula was dumbstruck. Her home had been like an open house for months but this was stretching it. She refused the request but, unbelievably, the journalist had the brass neck to push the issue. Her editor had wanted her to try to get Paula's agreement, as it would be good for the story. Her persistence didn't pay off, and Paula shooed her out the door. For the next couple of days, however, the same journalist arrived in the morning and hung around for most of the day. The descriptions 'sharks' and 'vultures' were certainly apt for this journalist. This was a rare experience, however, and, despite the odd journalist who overstayed their welcome, most were professional and considerate.

It was not unusual for four or five interviews to be going on at the same time in Paula's house. Journalists were pencilled in to the big purple book and, sometimes, double bookings were made. The phone would ring and someone would shout out, 'Quiet, it's Radio 4 (or RTÉ or Radio Five, and so on).' Children would be told to 'shush' and chased upstairs whilst the interview took place. Journalists came and went all day. On one occasion, I had to fly to London for a fifteen-minute slot on the *Jonathan Dimbleby* show — the whole way to London alone, for a fifteen-minute slot. Martin McGuinness was on the same programme but his interview was via satellite from Derry — why couldn't I have done that? It was obvious, however, that the programme-makers preferred interviews face-to-face but McGuinness had probably refused to go the whole way to London for one interview. We, on the other hand, didn't have the luxury of refusal — or maybe we did; we simply didn't know. We had no one to advise us on the media or anything else, so we said 'yes' to nearly everything. We didn't feel confident enough to ask the show to pay for a travelling companion.

Almost overnight, we were transformed from people who broke out in sweats and rashes at the thought of public speaking, to people who appeared on news programmes and addressed political audiences and dignitaries such as Mikhail Gorbachev and Helmut Kohl. When we arrived at studios, if it was not a face-to-face interview, we were instructed to put on earphones and focus our eyes on the white page taped to the front of a blank camera a few yards away. We couldn't see the interviewer but they could see us — an uncomfortable exchange but in this way we spoke to veteran interviewers such as Sir David Frost, Jon Snow and Jeremy Vine. We never thought of asking what questions would be asked and sat waiting anxiously for the voice to reverberate in our ears, signalling the beginning of the interview. There were always recriminations afterwards about what we had or hadn't said, or had said the wrong way.

Spotlight (a local reputable investigative programme) caused chaos one day. The producers were keen to do a programme on our campaign, and the film team was in Paula's, gathering bits and pieces of material. We were due to meet with Gerry Kelly at Paula's on this day also. Paula completed her interview just minutes before Kelly arrived. The *Spotlight* team was understandably keen to film him either arriving or leaving. In fact, the makers had wanted to film the meeting. They were told 'no' on all counts. Kelly was unaware of the presence of the *Spotlight* team and we didn't want it to appear as if we had ambushed him. The team accepted the refusal and set about tidying up its gear, while we sat down with Kelly. It wasn't until the meeting was over that Paula realised that she was still wearing the microphone. She panicked, and paranoia set in: had the *Spotlight* team left this microphone on deliberately? Had every word spoken at the meeting been secretly transmitted to a *Spotlight* sound recorder? A camera was spotted on the floor in the living room. Had it been running throughout the meeting? The team fell under suspicion and madness set in. A small drama unfolded in the living room, and answers were demanded. The *Spotlight* team assured everyone that the microphone had been turned off and the camera had recorded only people's feet. Unsatisfied with this answer, someone called for a pen, and the producer was told that he would have to sign his name to a declaration of censorship. Nothing caught on camera or tape would be transmitted, and the producer's signature would guarantee that. A pen was called for again. Did the producer not know that our lives were at risk? This was serious business, in case he hadn't noticed. A pen was screamed for again. People were rushing to and fro from the kitchen, looking for a pen, but were too confused and nervous to focus long enough to find one. The worst scenarios were being contemplated. Secretly filming Kelly could only bring dire consequences upon us. Appearing to behave underhandedly wouldn't do us any favours. An air of panic filled the room, and the *Spotlight* team's protestations of innocence fell on deaf ears. Finally the pen arrived — a pink Barbie one with a fluffy top! — and was thrust towards the producer who was ordered to write out the declaration and sign it. He did so unhesitatingly, but we can only guess at the thoughts that must have been going through his head. With the panic over, the *Spotlight* team quickly made their exit and the house settled down again. Paula and the others sighed over the narrow escape. This episode, although farcical, was symptomatic of the real sense of vulnerability and fear that was just below the surface for us; our trust in people had been seriously undermined since 30 January. In the event, the *Spotlight* team produced a very professional documentary on the events surrounding Robert's murder.

The *Spotlight* madness was overshadowed by the Jake incident. Jake, Paula's mongrel dog, is half terrier and half anybody's guess. As Paula and Gemma sat with some of the children in Paula's living room one day, the noise of barking and growling drifted in from the back of the house and alerted them to an oncoming emergency. They perched at the window, straining to determine the cause of the noise. Within seconds, Jake came tearing up Paula's back yard, pursued by up to five bigger dogs. Everyone ran at the same time for the back door to let him in. He came rushing through the door, whimpering and shaking, and clearly the worse for wear. The other dogs were shooed away with loud shouts and objects thrown at them.

Jake's injuries were substantial and it was clear that he had been subjected to a ferocious attack. He was calmed down and Gemma bandaged his paw and nursed him until he settled. She was particularly upset by the attack: as a dog lover, she had a natural affinity with Jake. A few hours passed and the incident was forgotten. That was, until a journalist rang Paula asking for a comment. The journalist was ringing to confirm a few details before completing her article for the next day. She asked Paula if the Provos had brought the dogs in a white van. Paula was dumbfounded. 'Who brought what dogs?' she asked.

The journalist explained that Gemma had told her that she believed the attack on Jake had been orchestrated by the Provos! Paula strenuously refuted this nonsense. When I arrived, she was sitting still dumbfounded at Gemma's interpretation of the attack on the dog. I couldn't help but laugh at the absurdity of it. We could only imagine the headlines: 'McCartneys Gone Barking Mad'. Others improvised an interview with Jake:

'And did these dogs say anything to you, Mr Jake?'

'Yes, one shouted Up the Ra as it ran away!'

We mused over what had possessed Gemma to say such an absurd thing; paranoia and nerves must surely have taken over. 'And they must have sprayed him with something to attract the dogs,' she had decided. As amusing as it was, such a story appearing in a newspaper would have undermined our credibility. Paula rang the journalist back and gained a promise not to run with the story. We thanked our lucky stars that she had phoned Paula to check a few details.

The journalists visiting Paula's home came from far and wide. They ranged from students doing bits and pieces for their local television station to huge names in the media industry. CNN sent over one of its main presenters to interview us. Australia sent Andrew Denton, presenter of *60 Minutes*, who travelled to Northern Ireland for the sole purpose of doing a show on us. German and Swiss TV did in-depth pieces that took up quite a lot of our time. There was no doubt that the media were enraptured with our story, for a while anyway. We took every opportunity to highlight Robert's murder even if the impact of an article in Germany was questionable. The only media we tried to avoid were the 'women's magazines'. We tried our best to keep our campaign within the confines of serious news, and a piece in the Real Life section of 'trashy' magazines could safely be described as 'pointless', if not demeaning. This didn't stop these magazines from pursuing our story, however. We couldn't prevent them from reporting our story, but we refused to give them an interview. On one occasion, I asked one journalist working for such a magazine to refrain from writing about us out of respect.

Meanwhile, *Marie Claire* magazine had persuaded me to agree to an interview, assuring me that the story would not focus on our gender. During discussions with the journalist, he told me that the magazine would like a photograph of all six of us. I told him that he would have to take what he got. He then asked if I could tell the others to 'dress up a little' on the day of the photo shoot.

'What do you mean, dress up?' I asked warily.

'You know, sort of dress a little smart, like six strong professional women taking on the IRA.'

'We are not six professional women takin' on the IRA,' I replied. 'And I am not asking anybody to dress up as anything. Look, I thought we had agreed that this interview was not going to be about the "woman" thing?'

'It's not,' he assured me. 'I just wanted to make sure the camera captured your strength.'

'Yeah, sure,' I said. 'The photographer will have to do with whatever he gets on the day. I can't promise six of us will even be there.'

On the day, four of us arrived at Paula's, making a total of five. Not bad. As had become the norm, we had been busy all day, some with work, some with both work and interviews and others with children. We waited for the photographer to show up, and were impatient to get it over with. We hated the photo-shoots. The door rapped and in traipsed two young girls with boxes. Some of us were in the living room and others in the kitchen when they arrived.

'Who are they?' I asked.

'Someone said they're the hair and make-up people.'

'The what?'

'Hair and make-up.'

'What do you mean, hair and make-up?' My face screwed up. 'Why are they here?'

'It's for the photo-shoot? They want to do our hair and make-up.'

Donna and I looked at each other in amazement.

'Are they trying to be funny?' she asked. 'Jesus Christ, this is unbelievable. Hair and make-up!'

'What is he playin' at?' I said. 'I told him, what you see is what you get. He had wanted us to dress up in suits and I told him no. Either he takes us like this or not at all.'

'This is us', said Donna, pointing to her jeans and Parka coat, similar to what we were all wearing with some degree of variation. 'This is the campaign.'

'Jesus, could you even be bothered with gettin' make-up done?' I said, sighing and sinking exhausted into the chair.

'We may tell them that they have wasted their time.'

'Where's Bridgeen?'

'She's upstairs washing her hair.'

'Why?'

'They said they'd do her first so she's away to wash her hair.'

'Get her down here. Nobody is washing hairs an' all the rest of it. We'll be here for hours.'

Bridgeen was called downstairs and the girls thanked but their services refused. They were understanding and didn't mind at all. The boxes they had carried in contained some 'smellies' that they had brought us as gifts, and they left them with us. We did the photo-shoot, which took over an hour, as we stood like idiots with the photographer positioning us this way and that. When the pictures were published, my friend commented that we looked like the mafia, between the poses and the Parka coats! It could have been worse, given that the journalist had wanted suits, hair and make-up.

Being moulded to suit the audiences of journalists was the least dangerous aspect of cavorting with the media. Whatever we said could be used to discredit us with our allies or bolster the criticism of our opponents. Our refusal to condemn one particular party offended another, and we were criticised for meeting with President Bush for a variety of reasons. For some people, the United States *per se* was the enemy; for others it was Bush's foreign policy. We were criticised for seeking the President's support; we were criticised for meeting with Sinn Féin; we were criticised for speaking to the SDLP; we were criticised for speaking to republicans not affiliated with Sinn Féin; we were criticised for not standing with Margaret Thatcher; we were criticised for speaking to the British; and of course we were criticised for speaking to the media. No matter what we did, we were criticised by someone.

If we had responded to these criticisms, we would have been dragged into a political abyss. To succumb to such criticisms would have circumscribed us but we did have to be careful about what we said and about whom. There was no such thing as freedom of speech. This was one of the most frustrating things about being in the public eye. When comments, letters or articles were written that misrepresented, criticised or simply condemned us, the natural instinct was to respond, but arguing with such people over the airwaves or through the letter pages of newspapers was ultimately a waste of time. We had to absorb the criticism and remain focused on the issue. By doing this, we were able to avoid any major pitfalls, but our inexperience did come back to bite us from time to time.

It was easy to forget that journalists were just doing a job, and were interested in our story only from a purely professional perspective. Some would hang around Paula's house for hours, drinking tea and chatting about everyday things, and so naturally a naive element of trust would spring up between them and us. Consequently, talking loosely to journalists without inserting the infamous 'off the record' prelude led us into dangerous waters. The journalists who arrived at Paula's did so haphazardly and there was no structure to the interviews. At times, two or three journalists would sit together, scribbling the answers to questions from one or the other of us. On occasion, the line between interview and general chat would become blurred, and defences would go down. This lack of clarity and inexperience resulted in an uncomfortable experience for us all, but one which gave us insight into our very precarious and weak position. We could fall out of favour at any time and thus pressure would be off Sinn Féin and the IRA. Robert's murderers could walk free because of our loose tongues and outspokenness. Obviously it wasn't as straightforward as this, but we carried the weight of this responsibility.

On one occasion, an interviewer and I had conversed at length about the campaign. She had asked if I minded her recording the interview, which I didn't. After nearly two hours, the conversation developed into more of a chat than an interview and, during a conversation about US foreign policy, I made a disparaging but tongue-in-cheek remark about President Bush. The journalist published my remark and it was immediately picked up on by the press sympathetic to Sinn Féin. The article had been sent to some of Bush's personnel in an attempt to undermine their support for us. The journalist had meant no malice by publishing my remarks but I hadn't intended for those remarks to be public. However, obviously I had failed to say the magic words, 'off the record'. The attempt to put a dent in our US support failed, and we conjectured that either Sinn Féin or its supporters were behind the dirty trick. Maybe they thought that we had sent over Danny Morrison's article on Ted Kennedy. Someone had been hoping to lose Sinn Féin favour with Kennedy, but it wasn't us — that tactic was too Shinnerish in nature and hinted at a disgruntled ex-member. Either way, someone decided to reciprocate. This gave us a sharp lesson in the subtleties and complexities of alliances. It also gave us yet another insight into how low the Provos would go to discredit those they perceived as a threat.

At times, Sinn Féin had unsuspecting co-conspirators, in the guise of journalists. When we were in the States, some journalists decided to do a diary-type interview. They would ask us to give a run-down of our day, and then they would write it up in a format suitable to their own style of writing or, on occasion, to suit the palate of their readers. These diaries are just one illustration of how sexism is still alive and well in Britain and Ireland today. It is difficult to imagine men being asked to engage in the same level of journalistic trivia. Although most of these were nauseating but harmless, one in particular was so patronising and sexist in its nature that I had to ask the journalist to rewrite it.

I had spoken to a journalist on the second day of our Washington visit, and had told him of our coming engagements. It was a very informal chat over the phone, but when he wrote up his piece, another voice came through — that of an Essex girl! He faxed me a copy of his intended piece before publication and I was gobsmacked by the language used. It was obvious that my voice had been transformed down the phone line to fit the image created for his audience. It certainly wasn't me speaking. According to him, I put on 'my lippie' and 'got dolled up for the ball'. 'Lippie', 'dolled up' — I repeated the phrases to the others who were as gobsmacked as I was but who saw the funny side. Gemma read out the piece to the rest and they laughed at the description of my day according to the diary. It made me sound like a complete 'half-wit'; an image of dancing around handbags rose to mind when reading it. I rang the journalist, furious. I hadn't said any of the things written in the diary. Yes, I had told him that I would be attending the Ireland Fund dinner and it was evening dress but I was not 'getting dolled up'. He apologised and agreed to rewrite it. I said that I would prefer it if he just scrubbed the whole thing, but he was committed and couldn't. An hour or so later, a more accurate diary account was faxed through, and although I was not completely happy with it, it was a huge improvement on the last.

The episode was seemingly insignificant in terms of what was going on but I was determined that our sex would not render us of entertainment or curiosity value only. The warped nature of Northern Ireland politics was to blame for Robert's murder and the cover-up, yet the warped nature of sexism threatened to undermine our message. We couldn't allow that to happen.

Chapter 10 ⌒

CHARGES AND IRA DECOMMISSIONING

News of the arrests of Terry Davison and Jim McCormick travelled quickly round the family. The excited and nervous voices of relatives and friends tied up the phone line all that day. The arrests stirred a mixture of emotions. Happiness was not one of them. A feeling of nervousness and anticipation was mixed with a vague sense of relief. We were afraid to hope that this was the beginning of the end, and bore in mind that arrests did not necessarily lead to charges: in the first few weeks after Robert's murder, up to ten people had been arrested and released without charge, and the same could happen again. The police, however, appeared more confident this time round and there was much more publicity surrounding the arrests. McCormick's arrest in Birmingham was reported on the national news. A neighbour — ironically called Mr Ireland — described how he had been brought out handcuffed and in his underwear. Terry Davison's arrest was a low-key affair; he was taken from his home in Upper Stanfield Place in the Markets very early in the morning.

It was the first week in June, and for four solid months the Provos had remained resolute in their determination to protect Robert's murderers. We knew that the police had been working hard on the case but had been given no reason to expect charges soon, and so, when the news came through about the arrests, we held our breath for charges to follow. The police were allowed to hold the two men for forty-eight hours before either charging or releasing them. We waited anxiously to find out which it would be. Eventually, on 3 June, the phone call we had anticipated since 31 January came through. Terry Davison, aged 49 and uncle of Jock Davison, was charged with Robert's murder; Jim 'Dim' McCormick, aged 36, was charged with the attempted murder of Brendan Devine.

On 4 June, Paula, Gemma, Claire and Donna attended court to listen to the charges being put to Davison and to look him in the eye. They watched him closely as he stood in the dock. Standing so close to the man who police believed was responsible for plunging a knife into our brother's chest, clawing mercilessly at his face and inflicting other horrific injuries, was surreal. This man who had chosen to end Robert's life stood in human form but they could not relate to him as a human being. As expected, Davison pleaded 'not guilty', as did McCormick, and they were held on remand.

We were not triumphant at the bringing of charges. Apart from anything else, we knew that there was still a long way to go. Davison and McCormick were not the only two responsible for the events on the night of 30 January. At least nine people had participated in the attack on Robert, and many more had helped to get rid of vital evidence and had intimidated witnesses. Political representatives, particularly Maskey and O'Donnell, had attempted to provide political cover, declaring that a crisis in the peace process would result if the police didn't back off from harassing republicans. The charges against Davison and McCormick were small progress, taking all of this into consideration. The charges, however, had a significant impact on our ability to continue campaigning. The *sub judice* law meant that we had to be extremely careful about what we said to the media, and the latter were also wary of reporting on anything to do with the campaign.

June and July passed relatively quietly. The gradual distancing of friends was complete. Our isolation from the Short Strand community was successful in that we didn't feel we belonged to it any more. We couldn't go to the local club, church or shops without risking a confrontation. The murderers' support base may have been small but it was strong, and, over the years, the Provos had gained control over the important positions in the community: youth work, development work, CRJ (Community Restorative Justice, justice schemes based on the premise of bringing victim and perpetrator together so that the former could get redress and the latter learn from his/her crime. In nationalist areas, such as the Short Strand, they are widely regarded as another arm of Sinn Féin), and so on. They used these positions to enforce their own agenda on the people, and very few spoke out against it. Our campaign had divided the community between those who regarded Robert's murder as a 'crime' and 'wrong' and those who attempted to excuse it — mostly Provo supporters who tried to explain away his murder by putting it in the context of a conflict during which many people had lost loved ones. Deborah Devenney articulated this view, claiming that a '...large section of the community [is] angered by how high profile it [the McCartney case] has become, as the people here have lost people and never received justice or the same media attention' (Quoted by Ciara McGuigan, *Andersontown News*, 18 April 2005).

It was true that many people had lost loved ones during the Troubles — indeed, quite a few at the hands of the IRA — but Devenney was being disingenuous. Robert's murder had nothing to do with the conflict, and his murder by Provos didn't alter this fact. Devenney's reference to other victims was a depraved attempt to nurture resentment within the community against us. Her motives were clear: to protect the Provisionals.

Such attempts were successful to a degree. We watched as Robert's murderers went about their everyday lives unaffected by their actions. Confident in the protection afforded them by an immoral politics that for many years had ignored the murder of innocent Catholics and Protestants by paramilitary groups, they continued to strut about the Short Strand. Their untouchable status was not imaginary or indeed bravado. Maskey had proven this by his complaints to the British and Irish governments about the police searches in the Markets. These people had the weight of the peace process on their side. The IRA held the power to kick-start this process, and once it decided to do so, the republicans would again regain the 'political' high ground, but not the 'moral high ground' that Danny Morrison spoke of after the IRA's commitment to decommission. The 'political' and 'moral' are exclusive of each other in Northern Ireland politics.

WILL THE IRA DECOMMISSION?
The political pundits, observers and press waited with bated breath for the IRA's response to Adams's call to embrace 'exclusively democratic

means', and we continued to meet at Paula's home daily to talk about the latest developments or lack of them. News continued to filter through about the day-to-day lives of the suspects. News of their marriages, holidays and celebrations were reported back to us, and their apparent unconcern about what they had done compounded our hurt. Bridgeen had the daily heartache of answering Conlaed and Brandon's questions about their daddy. Was he in heaven? Did he have his car with him? Did he have his mobile phone? Why didn't he ring? Could he see them? Could he get a McDonald's in heaven? They recalled Robert's huge stature: 'Daddy was a giant, wasn't he, Mummy?' and so on. Since Robert's murder, Conlaed had become withdrawn, and sat crying alone. In light of this, and faced with having to pass her partner's murderers and their supporters every day, Bridgeen decided to take him out of school. Looking at Conlaed and Brandon was the hardest thing of all: we knew what they had been robbed of, what had been stolen from Robert. Yet the murderers' lives remained untouched by the murder. They continued to have children and to make plans for the future. It was difficult to understand how these people, on the one hand, could take a life so easily, yet on the other, could indulge themselves in it.

The political landscape was obsessed by the prospect of IRA decommissioning and the possibilities it could open up. We were obsessed by it also, but because of the doors it could close. Decommissioning was fraught with difficulties and complexities. Although the Good Friday Agreement stipulated that the political parties should use their influence to bring it about, there was a huge disparity in the interpretation of this. For unionists, it meant IRA decommissioning, and they held Sinn Féin responsible for delivering this, as they regarded Sinn Féin and the IRA as one and the same. They disregarded the former's protestations that it could only liaise with the IRA on behalf of the political establishment. To persuade the IRA to decommission, it had to be able to prove that politics worked, and as long as the institutions remained in storage, it could not do this. The bulk of Provisionals believed that decommissioning was a non-starter, despite the Good Friday stipulations.

Decommissioning was of huge symbolic significance to republicans and unionists, and in December 2004 the prospect of such seemed as far away as ever as the positions of both camps hardened. Many of the former regarded the notion of an army handing over its guns as ridiculous and preposterous — tangible evidence of defeat, so they argued. The unionists, specifically Dr Ian Paisley, exacerbated resistance by demanding photographic evidence of decommissioning in his 'sackcloth and ashes' speech. His demand for republican humiliation strengthened the IRA's hand within its own community and 'not an ounce not a bullet' was scrawled on the walls. The moderates argued that although decommissioning had to happen, it would happen only as part of a process. They argued that the guns had been silent for so long, or so they kept telling us — since the ceasefire in 1996, in fact — that it didn't matter if the IRA held on to them, as they were not using them. The IRA could always replenish; decommissioning was only symbolic, and so on. But this was Ireland and symbolism is important. The IRA's refusal to hand over its guns was regarded as valid in light of Paisley's demands. There was a strong resolve within the Provisionals to hold on to the weapons until concrete concessions had been achieved. But all this changed on 31 January 2005 and, in true Orwellian style, 'not an ounce, not a bullet' was quickly replaced by 'every last ounce of Semtex and every last bullet' on 28 July, when, unsurprisingly, the IRA issued a statement accepting Adams's challenge:

The leadership of Óglaigh na hÉireann has formally ordered an end to the armed campaign. This will take effect from 4pm this afternoon. All IRA units have been ordered to dump arms. All Volunteers have been instructed to assist the development of purely political and democratic programmes through exclusively peaceful means. Volunteers must not engage in any other activities whatsoever. The IRA leadership has also authorised our representative to engage with the IICD [Independent International Commission on Decommissioning] to complete the process to verifiably put its arms beyond use in a way which will further enhance public confidence and to conclude this as quickly as possible. We have invited two independent witnesses, from the Protestant and Catholic churches, to testify to this. The Army Council took these decisions following an unprecedented internal discussion and consultation process with IRA units and Volunteers. We appreciate the honest and forthright way in which the consultation process was carried out and the depth and content of the submissions. We are proud of the comradely way in which this truly historic discussion was conducted. The outcome of our consultations shows very strong support among IRA Volunteers for the Sinn Féin peace strategy. There is also widespread concern about the failure of the two governments and the unionists to fully engage in the peace process. This has created real difficulties. The overwhelming majority of people in Ireland fully support this process. They and friends of Irish unity throughout the world want to see the full implementation of the Good Friday Agreement. Notwithstanding these difficulties our decisions have been taken to advance our republican and democratic objectives, including our goal of a united Ireland. We believe there is now an alternative way to achieve this and to end British rule in our country. It is the responsibility of all Volunteers to show leadership, determination and courage. We are very mindful of the sacrifices of our patriot dead, those who went to jail, Volunteers, their families and the wider republican base. We reiterate our view that the armed struggle was entirely legitimate. We are conscious that many people suffered in the conflict. There is a compelling imperative on all sides to build a just and lasting peace. The issue of the defence of nationalist and republican communities has been raised with us. There is a responsibility on society to ensure that there is no re-occurrence of the pogroms of 1969 and the early 1970s. There is also a universal responsibility to tackle sectarianism in all its forms. The IRA is fully committed to the goals of Irish unity and independence and to building the Republic outlined in the 1916 Proclamation. We call for maximum unity and effort by Irish republicans everywhere. We are confident that by working together Irish republicans can achieve our objectives. Every Volunteer is aware of the import of the decisions we have taken and all Óglaigh are compelled to fully comply with these orders. There is now an unprecedented opportunity to utilise the considerable energy and goodwill which there is for the peace process. This comprehensive series of unparalleled initiatives is our contribution to this and to the continued endeavours to bring about independence and unity for the people of Ireland.

What had been cited as one of the main obstacles to the peace process was now no longer; it had been a huge hurdle to get over and, as was expected, was met with delight by the British and Irish governments. The British Prime Minister, Tony Blair, articulated how important the IRA's decision to decommission was to the British establishment and, when he described it as a step of 'unparalleled magnitude', he confirmed that it was enough for the British to kick-start the process:

> Today may be the day that peace replaced war, that politics replaced terror, on the island of Ireland. It is what we have striven for and worked for throughout the eight years since the Good Friday Agreement. It creates the circumstances in which the institutions can be revived.

The Irish were in full agreement with the British, and Bertie Ahern's response was almost a carbon copy of Blair's:

> Today's developments can herald a new era for all of the people on the island of Ireland. The end of the IRA as a paramilitary organisation is the outcome the governments have been working towards since the cessation of military activities in 1994. If the IRA's words are borne out by verified actions, it will be a momentous and historic development. Our focus now is on completing the implementation of the Good Friday Agreement, which has brought such immense benefits to this country.

The Americans responded with a much more measured and insightful approach. President George Bush reasoned that:

> This IRA statement must now be followed by actions demonstrating the republican movement's unequivocal commitment to the rule of law and to the renunciation of all paramilitary and criminal activities. We understand that many, especially victims and their families, will be sceptical. They will want to be certain that this terrorism and criminality are indeed things of the past.

Mitchell Reiss, President Bush's Special Envoy to Northern Ireland and a man whom we respected very much, observed:

We will soon see whether these words will be turned into deeds. Everybody would like to move as quickly as possible but let's move ahead clearly and do it in a way which gives reassurance. I am hopeful there will be a major act of decommissioning, an end to all the arms that the IRA has, in the next few weeks if not sooner.

Other political and church leaders reminded the public that other issues also had to be resolved, particularly the IRA's involvement in crime, and Sinn Féin's commitment to the rule of law. We were bemused by all the fuss, as it seemed to us that the IRA was more prepared to hand over its arsenal of guns than its murderers. Realistically, however, the IRA and Sinn Féin knew that they had exhausted the 'ballot box and armalite' strategy, and the game was up. Weighing up its options, the IRA concluded that decommissioning was the weakest of its bargaining chips, and it could afford to cash it in.

On 26 September 2005, the IRA's arsenal of weapons was declared officially decommissioned. The IRA had handed its guns over to the British in a process verified by Fr Alec Reid and former Methodist minister Harold Good. The integrity and independence of the two witnesses was stressed again and again. Fr Reid's work in trying, through persuasion, to bring an end to the IRA's campaign of violence was cited as evidence of his credentials. We were less impressed with the claim of Fr Reid's independence given his intervention on behalf of the IRA when Jeff Commander had been attacked just a few weeks prior to decommissioning.

Predictably the final act of decommissioning was greeted with delight by Tony Blair, who saw the road ahead clear for progress in the peace process. We listened and watched as the pressure was lifted from Sinn Féin and it began to recuperate. The sight and sounds of cooing over Sinn Féin sickened and angered us and we decided that we had to do something.

I arranged another trip to Washington in November, and Paula and I revisited the Senators and Congressmen we had met back in March. Our message was simple: decommissioning was positive but did not alter the reality of IRA criminality and the political cover being given to criminals. Senator Ted Kennedy and Senator Hillary Clinton once again met with us and reiterated their support. Senator Clinton was particularly outspoken about republicans' unwillingness to support law and order when they were 'culpable'. It was clear to us that Sinn Féin had regained some ground in the US: Congressman Peter King didn't meet with us the second time, and Congressman Jim Walsh asked if 'the British' were helping us. Anger bubbled inside me and I suppressed the desire to tell him what a fool I thought he was for buying Sinn Féin's line. We were not only witnessing politics at work but were victims of it. It was nauseating and frustrating.

Despite the enthusiasm of the British and Irish governments over decommissioning, the allegations of the criminality of the Provisionals would not go away. When the press contacted us about the IRA's statement, we asked what would happen if the IRA volunteers did engage in criminal activities — would they still be protected? We were disinterested in decommissioning — Robert had been killed with a knife, not a gun, and the IRA's iron and brutal fist had not been lifted. Ahern and Blair may have been unconcerned with this, but ordinary people were not. The political game in Northern Ireland had claimed thousands of lives, and the politicians were still playing the game. How could the IRA or Sinn Féin claim to be embracing exclusively democratic means when they harboured murderers?

Thankfully, however, the IRA decommissioning did not buy the political return that it might have done had it been carried out years previously. Criminality had become the bugbear of Sinn Féin's opponents and the DUP's excuse for refusing to share power. Adherence to the rule of law became a prominent issue, although Sinn Féin had hoped that it could hold off on signing up to the police until Stormont was up and running; the leaders envisaged that endorsement of the PSNI would be a process they would engage in whilst in ministerial positions (a reasonable view given that this is exactly what had happened since July 1998 when the institutions were set up). Sinn Féin as a democratic political party had sat in government despite the fact that it didn't endorse the law of the land, the only political party in western democracy to do so. Once again, it was a case of: 'It's Sinn Féin; what do you expect?'

INTERNAL HOUSEKEEPING
Rule of law was the hook upon which the setting up of the institutions hung. It was clear to us that Robert's murder was a clear indication of the Provos' disdain for the rule of law, and only by co-operating fully

with the investigation into his murder could Sinn Féin prove that it did not endorse murderers. We saw another opportunity to apply pressure and decided that it was now time to approach the British government for help. It had been a conscious decision of ours to seek help from the Irish government first and to postpone meeting with the British until we had built up a credible support base that could not be described as anti-republican. From the beginning of our campaign, the Provos had attempted to paint us as 'anti-republican' and 'political puppets', and seeking help from the British would have given credence to this rubbish. Our preoccupation with fending off 'anti-republican' accusations, together with a naive hope that the repulsion of the republican and nationalist community at Robert's murder would be enough to goad the IRA and Sinn Féin into delivering justice, meant that we were less concerned or focused on the British government's role. It was only with hindsight that we began to realise that it had been as unenthusiastic about our campaign as Sinn Féin.

The British government's core strategy of appeasement of Sinn Féin and its 'immoral' concessions to it and the IRA had been complicit in nurturing the environment in which Jock Davison and the IRA believed themselves immune to accountability. The British had adopted an ambivalent attitude towards IRA criminality, including the murder and mutilation of Catholics since 1998. The concept behind this policy was articulated by a senior civil servant as early as 1999 in response to the murder of Charles Bennett. When questioned as to whether or not the IRA had broken its ceasefire by murdering Charles Bennett, the Northern Ireland Office (NIO) responded:

> The Secretary of State [Mo Mowlam] has to decide whether an incident [the murder of Charles Bennett] is an internal housekeeping matter to the terrorist organisations or an attack on the entire community, ie the Omagh bomb, before making a determination of their ceasefire. (August 1999)

Charles 'Chucky' Bennett had been taken from his home and interrogated for several days before being shot. Press reports from the time state that RUC sources confirmed that Bennett was passing on information to the RUC about republican activities. This confirmation would have confirmed in the community's mind the validity of the

IRA's claims. This claim was rubbished by an Ombudsman's report in 2007, which concluded that Charles Bennett was not an informer. The 'internal housekeeping matter' referred to by the civil servant was the murder of people like Robert and many others. Over twenty Catholics had been killed in circumstances that the government categorised as 'internal housekeeping'. What the British government did, in reality, was to absolve itself of the responsibility of any democratic government, which is to protect its citizens. The British government in essence accorded the IRA the right to exist and rule over the nationalist populace.

This approach was articulated by Tony Blair when he ineptly suggested to us that we approach the 'Sinn Féin women' in the hope that they could pressurise their male leaders into behaving morally. Apart from the sexist undertones of this suggestion, it was clear that Blair very much viewed Robert's murder as 'internal housekeeping'. The onus was on Sinn Féin to sort it out or not. The only concern of the British government was how to get Stormont up and running again. A political chess game was in play and Robert was just a pawn. If justice had to be conceded to politics, so be it. Blair and his government, however, were out of step with the concerns of the people on the ground.

Despite the efforts of the media and politicians to play up the importance of decommissioning, the act was met with a tired response by the public. It had lost its allure and, although it removed a major obstacle from the path of the peace train, IRA criminality and the refusal of Sinn Féin to support the rule of law had replaced it. Fortunately for us, IRA decommissioning did not elevate Sinn Féin out of reach of criticism and pressure, and the Northern Bank robbery and Robert's murder had changed the political landscape. Sinn Féin's consistent and vehement denials of IRA involvement in criminality rang hollow. The party argued that such accusations were designed to undermine its political mandate. Gerry Adams declared sardonically in 2004 that 'republicans and criminality' could not be put in the same sentence. Sinn Féin's warnings about criminalising the 'republicans' always evoked emotive memories of the Hunger Strikers, and the party always managed to rally the nationalist people, lukewarmly if not enthusiastically, behind it. Evidence of this was that despite the widely held belief that the IRA was responsible for the Northern Bank robbery of December 2004, during which £26 million was stolen, many were still very critical of the fact that the blame was being laid at the Provisionals' door without cast-iron proof. Some sections of the nationalist community, despite accepting that the IRA had carried out the robbery, condemned the police's assertion of IRA culpability as politically motivated. Adams sounded convincing and, once again, the old mantra of nationalist victimhood and 'securocrat' mischief was regurgitated to insulate criminals from justice.

Up until this point, Adams and Sinn Féin had been able to manage the damage being done by the IRA's criminality; with a slithery tongue, Adams and Co. had been able to persuade many allies that pressurising Sinn Féin would only exacerbate the difficulties within the peace process. This strategy had served the Provisionals up until 30 January when a group of up to twenty Sinn Féin and IRA members decided to drop into Magennis's bar for a drink, after returning from marching in Derry in solidarity with the families and supporters of the Bloody Sunday victims. The unsuspecting patrons out to enjoy a Sunday drink and a bit of 'craic' couldn't have foreseen the turn of events triggered by the presence in the bar of Brendan Devine.

The existing bad blood between Devine and the Provos permeates the air, finally exploding into a full-blooded attack. Devine's throat is cut. Davison's hand is injured. The sight of Davison's blood infuriates him and his followers. Robert McCartney and Devine leave the bar and head for safety away from the salivating Provos. As they make their way down a dark and secluded street at the side of the bar, accompanied by Terry McKay and Ed Gowdy, the Provos regroup back at the bar and quickly draw up a plan of revenge. Armed with sewer rods and knives, the gang of Provos follows Devine and the others up the street. McKay quickly gets off side and Bobby Fitzsimmons takes Gowdy off side. The remaining gang members pursue Robert and Brendan down the street, beating them as they go. Robert is heard trying to reason with the gang, many of whom he knows. Trying to buy Devine time, he pleads with them, 'Nobody deserves this!' but his pleas fall on deaf ears. Determined to get to Devine who is a few paces ahead, they beat Robert to the ground. Some leave the pack and catch up with Brendan. Within minutes, if not seconds, knives are pulled out and the most senseless and cruel act of the night is carried out. A knife is plunged into Robert and twice into Brendan. They are left to die on the street, but not before the gang members attempt to remove their clothing, to avoid detection. Within half an hour, the IRA has forensically cleaned the scene and decided to give its murderous members cover.

For many involved in Robert's murder that night, the adrenaline of the events may have been exhilarating; for others it may have been frightening; for some it may have all been in a day's work. For us it was the beginning of a nightmare and a long campaign to bring Robert's killers to justice. For the IRA, it was the end.

APPENDIX I: FULL IRA STATEMENTS ON THE MURDER OF ROBERT McCARTNEY

STATEMENT 1: 25 FEBRUARY 2005

Following our investigation the IRA leadership, along with the leadership of the Belfast Command, initiated disciplinary proceedings through Court Martial.

This was in accordance with IRA Standing Orders. These proceedings were directed only against IRA volunteers.

The outcome of the Courts Martial include the dismissal of three volunteers, two of whom were high ranking volunteers.

One of these volunteers had already gone to a solicitor immediately after the incident to make a statement of his actions on that night.

The other two were advised in the strongest terms possible to come forward and to take responsibility for their actions, as the McCartney family have asked.

In our statement of February 15th, we made it absolutely clear that no one should hinder or impede the McCartney family in their search for truth and justice and that anyone who could help them in that search should do so.

A dispute broke out between a senior republican and a group of people that included Robert McCartney and Brendan Devine.

After an initial heated verbal exchange between the senior republican and Robert McCartney at that point another man and the senior republican were involved in a further heated exchange.

Blows were exchanged and a major melee erupted in the bar.

Neither that man nor the senior republican had weapons of any description in their possession though both were struck with bottles thrown by others.

Robert McCartney played no part in the melee.

Both Brendan Devine and the senior republican received serious stab wounds inside the bar.

A crowd spilled out onto the street. Verbal abuse and threats were being shouted by many of those present.

Some of those at the scene, including some republicans, tried to calm the situation.

The senior republican's wounds were tended by people at the scene and he was quickly taken to hospital.

In the meantime Brendan Devine, Robert McCartney and another man ended up in Market Street.

It is the view of our investigation that these men were leaving the scene.

They were followed into Market Street where Robert McCartney and Brendan Devine were attacked and stabbed.

Both men were stabbed by the same man. Robert McCartney died a short time later in hospital.

No materials under the control of or belonging to the IRA were produced or used at any time during this savage attack.

A member of the bar staff was threatened by an individual who then took the CCTV tape away and destroyed it.

Those at the scene are responsible for the clean-up or destruction of evidence at the scene.

There should be no misunderstanding of our position in that regard.

Any intimidation or threats in the name of the IRA or otherwise to any person who wishes to help the McCartney family will not be tolerated.

The internal disciplinary steps taken by the IRA are a matter for the IRA.

They are not intended to be, nor should they be, seen as a substitute for the requests of the McCartney family.

IRA volunteers fully understand that they are bound by rules and regulations and a Code of Conduct.

There will be no tolerance of anyone who steps outside of these rules, regulations or code.

Anyone who brings the IRA into disrepute will be held accountable.

STATEMENT 2: 8 MARCH 2005

Representatives of Óglaigh na hÉireann met with Bridgeen Hagans, the partner of Robert McCartney, and with his sisters before our statement of 25 February was issued.

The meeting lasted five and a half hours. During this time the IRA representatives gave the McCartney family a detailed account of our investigation.

Our investigation found that after the initial melee in Magennis's bar a crowd spilled out onto the street and Robert McCartney, Brendan Devine and two other men were pursued into Market Street.

Four men were involved in the attacks in Market Street on the evening of 30 January.

A fifth person was at the scene. He took no part in the attacks and was responsible for moving to safety one of the two people accompanying Robert McCartney and Brendan Devine.

One man was responsible for providing the knife that was used in the stabbing of Robert McCartney and Brendan Devine in Market Street.

He got the knife from the kitchen of Magennis's bar.

Another man stabbed Robert McCartney and Brendan Devine.

A third man kicked and beat Robert McCartney after he had been stabbed in Market Street.

A fourth man hit a friend of Robert McCartney and Brendan Devine across the face with a steel bar in Market Street.

The man who provided the knife also retrieved it from the scene and destroyed it.

The same man also took the CCTV tape from the bar, after threatening a member of staff and later destroyed it. He also burned clothes after the attack.

Reports in the media have alleged that up to twelve IRA volunteers were involved in the events in Market Street.

Our investigation found that this is not so. Of the four directly involved in the attacks in Market Street, two were IRA volunteers. The other two were not.

The IRA knows the identity of all these men.

The build-up to the attack and stabbings was also outlined to the family and subsequently set out publicly in the IRA's statement of 25 February.

The IRA representatives detailed the outcome of the internal disciplinary proceedings thus far and stated in clear terms that the IRA was prepared to shoot the people directly involved in the killing of Robert McCartney.

The McCartney family raised their concerns with the IRA representatives.

These included: Firstly the family made it clear they did not want physical action taken against those involved.

They stated that they wanted those individuals to give a full account of their actions in court.

Secondly, they raised concerns about the intimidation of witnesses.

The IRA's position on this was set out in unambiguous and categoric terms on February 15 and February 25.

Before and after this meeting with the family the IRA gave direct assurances on their safety to three named individuals who the family believe were the targets of intimidation.

Since we met the family, at that time, the good offices of an independent third party have been employed to reinforce these assurances with two of the three men.

To this point the third party has not been able to contact the other man.

We have urged any witnesses who can assist in any way to come forward. That remains our position.

The only interest the IRA has in this case is to see truth and justice achieved.

Since we issued our statement on February 25 there has been much political and media comment on what we had to say.

Predictably our opponents and enemies who have their own agendas have used this brutal killing to attack republicans and to advance their own narrow political interests.

The public will make their own judgement on this.

We sought and held a second meeting with the McCartney family in the presence of an independent observer.

In the course of this we reiterated our position in respect of witnesses, including our view that all witnesses should come forward. We also revisited details of the incident.

We disclosed the following to the family: The conclusion of the IRA's investigations are based on voluntary admissions by those involved.

The names of those involved in the attacks and stabbings of Robert McCartney, Brendan Devine and the assault on another man in Market Street were given to the family.

This included the names of the two men responsible for providing the knife, using the knife, destroying the knife, destroying the CCTV tape and burning clothes.

In addition we informed the family that: We have ordered anyone who was present on the night to go forward and to give a full account of their actions. That includes those who have already been subject to the IRA's internal disciplinary proceedings.

We are continuing to press all of those involved in the events around the killing of Robert McCartney to come forward. The IRA is setting out all of the above at length because it is important that those issues of truth and justice are successfully resolved.

We are doing our best to work with the family and to respect their wishes

STATEMENT 3: 23 MARCH 2005

On this, the 89th anniversary of the Easter Rising of 1916, we remember the men and women of every generation who have given their lives in the struggle for Irish freedom.

The leadership of Óglaigh na hÉireann extends solidarity to the families of our comrades who have fallen during this phase of the struggle. We remember those comrades with honour and pride.

We send solidarity to our volunteers and to our friends and supporters at home and abroad.

We think of our imprisoned comrades and their families at this time also.

Over ten years ago, the leadership of the IRA declared a complete cessation of military operations. We did so to enhance the development of the Irish peace process.

From then until now we have, on a number of occasions, demonstrated our continuing support for this process. At times of significant crisis or political impasse, we have taken initiatives to move the situation forward.

Our approach has been premised on the belief that the achievement of a just and lasting peace requires constant forward momentum in the peace process.

For the past two years, the peace process has been locked in stalemate and has slipped backwards into deepening crisis.

During that period, specifically in October 2003 and in December 2004, we agreed to significant initiatives as part of an agreement to break the logjam. On each occasion, other parties reneged on their commitments.

An unprecedented opportunity to transform the situation on the island of Ireland was thrown away by rejectionist unionism, aided and abetted by the two governments.

The DUP attempted to turn the initiative of December 2004 into a humiliation of the IRA.

The concerted efforts of both governments since then to undermine the integrity of our cause, by seeking to criminalise the republican struggle, is clear evidence that our opponents remain fixated with the objective of defeating republicans rather than developing the peace process.

The sustained campaign directed against the republican people over recent months is nothing new. We have seen and heard it all before. Those who opted to follow the Thatcher path will not succeed.

Our patriot dead are not criminals. We are not criminals. Republican men and women suffered deprivation and torture to defeat attempts to criminalise our struggle.

Ten of our comrades endured the agony of hunger strike and died defeating the criminalisation strategy.

We will not betray their courage by tolerating criminality within our own ranks. We will not allow our opponents to further their own petty self-interests by levelling false allegations against Óglaigh na hÉireann.

The IRA has spelt out its position in relation to the killing of Robert McCartney.

It was wrong, it was murder, it was a crime. But it was not carried out by the IRA, nor was it carried out on behalf of the IRA.

The IRA moved quickly to deal with those involved. We have tried to assist in whatever way we can.

Unfortunately, it would appear that no matter what we do it will never be enough for some.

Those in the political and media establishments who have been so quick to jump on the bandwagon have again laid bare their own hypocrisy.

This causes justifiable resentment among republicans. But it must not cloud the issue. Óglaigh na hÉireann expects the highest standards of conduct from our volunteers.

Struggle requires sacrifice and discipline. It promises hardship and suffering. Our fallen comrades rose to those challenges and met them head on.

The discipline and commitment of our volunteers and the wider republican base have been the backbone of our struggle. In these testing times, that steadfastness and determination are needed more and more.

We salute you and urge you to remain strong and united.

The crisis in the peace process and the reinvigorated attempts to criminalise us have not diminished in any way our determination to pursue and achieve our republican objectives.

Irish unity and independence provides the best context for the people of this island to live together in harmony. The primary responsibility now rests with the two governments.

They must demonstrate their commitment to a lasting peace. Pandering to the demands of those who are opposed to change is not the way forward.

APPENDIX II: PROPOSAL FOR RESOLUTION ADOPTED BY THE EUROPEAN PARLIAMENT

PROPOSAL FOR A JOINT RESOLUTION
in accordance with article 103 (3) of the Rules of Procedure

by Hans-Gert Poettering, Avril Doyle, Simon Coveney, Jim Higgins, Mairead McGuiness, Gay Mitchell, James Nicholson in the name of the EPP-ED Group
by Martin Schulz, Proinsias De Rossa, Gary Titley in the name of the PES Group
by Graham Watson, Marian Harkin in the name of the ALDE Group
by Brian Crowley, Eoin Ryan, Liam Aylward in the name of the UEN Group
by Jean Lambert, Raul Romeva Rueda in the name of the Greens/EFA Group

European Parliament resolution condemning violence and criminality by the self-styled 'Irish Republican Army' (IRA) in Northern Ireland, in particular the murder of Robert McCartney.

The European Parliament

A. Whereas on January 30, 2005, a citizen of Belfast, Robert McCartney, was brutally murdered by members of the self-styled 'Irish Republican Army' (IRA), who attempted to cover-up the crime and ordered all witnesses to be silent about the involvement of IRA members;

B. Whereas the sisters of Robert McCartney, Catherine McCartney, Paula Arnold, Gemma McMahon, Claire McCartney, and Donna Mary McCartney, and his partner, Bridgeen Karen Hagans, refused to accept the code of silence and have bravely and persistently challenged the IRA by demanding justice for the murder of Robert McCartney;

C. Whereas in the region of seventy witnesses are believed to have been present in the area of Magennis' Bar immediately before and after the fight that led to the death of Robert McCartney;

D. Whereas when outcry over the murder increased, the IRA and Sinn Féin, the political wing of the IRA, suspended or expelled some members;

E. Whereas the leadership of Sinn Féin has called for justice, but has not called on those responsible for the murder or any of those who witnessed the murder to cooperate fully and directly with the Police Service of Northern Ireland;

F. Whereas on March 8, 2005, the IRA issued an outrageous statement in which it said it 'was willing to shoot the killers of Robert McCartney';

G. Whereas those involved in the ongoing efforts to secure justice for Robert McCartney have been subject to a recent whispering campaign seeking to intimidate and to undermine the credibility of their case;

H. Whereas valuable work has been done by the EU Peace Fund in Northern Ireland and the Border counties;

I. Whereas peace and violence cannot coexist in Northern Ireland;

1. Condemns violence and criminality by the self-styled 'Irish Republican Army' (IRA) in Northern Ireland, in particular the murder of Robert McCartney;

2. Stresses in the strongest possible terms that the sisters and partner of Robert McCartney deserve the fullest support in their pursuit of justice;

3. Calls on the leadership of Sinn Féin to insist that those responsible for the murder and witnesses to the murder cooperate directly with the Police Service of Northern Ireland and be free from the threat of reprisals from the IRA;

4. Deplores the insidious whispering campaign aimed at intimidating and discrediting the sisters and fiancée of Robert McCartney in their fight for justice

5. Calls on the Council and Commission to provide all appropriate assistance to law enforcement authorities in Northern Ireland to see that the murderers of Robert McCartney are brought to justice.

6. Proposes that, if the Police Service of Northern Ireland is unable to bring a prosecution in relation to the murder of Robert McCartney, the European Union grant a financial contribution, in conformity with the Financial Regulation, toward the cost of legal fees incurred by the McCartney family in their quest for justice, by way of civil proceedings;

7. Asks in this connection that the Commission should make such a contribution from the budget line in the general budget of the EU intended for aid for the victims of terrorism;

8. Instructs its President to forward this resolution to the Council, the Commission and the governments and parliaments of the Member States and candidate countries, and the Council of Europe.

INDEX